Springer Series in Information Sciences 8

Editor: King-sun Fu

Springer Series in Information Sciences

Editors: King-sun Fu   Thomas S. Huang   Manfred R. Schroeder

Teuvo Kohonen

Self-Organization and Associative Memory

With 93 Figures

Springer-Verlag
Berlin Heidelberg New York Tokyo 1984

Professor Teuvo Kohonen

Department of Technical Physics, Helsinki University of Technology
SF-02150 Espoo 15, Finland

Series Editors:

Professor King-sun Fu

School of Electrical Engineering, Purdue University,
West Lafayette, IN 47907, USA

Professor Thomas S. Huang

Department of Electrical Engineering and Coordinated Science Laboratory,
University of Illinois, Urbana, IL 61801, USA

Professor Dr. Manfred R. Schroeder

Drittes Physikalisches Institut, Universität Göttingen, Bürgerstraße 42–44,
D-3400 Göttingen, Fed. Rep. of Germany

ISBN 3-540-12165-X Springer-Verlag Berlin Heidelberg New York Tokyo
ISBN 0-387-12165-X Springer-Verlag New York Heidelberg Berlin Tokyo

Library of Congress Cataloging in Publication Data. Kohonen, Teuvo. Self-organization and associative memory. (Springer series in information sciences ; 8). Bibliography: p. Includes index. 1. Self-organizing systems. 2. Memory. 3. Associative storage. I. Title. II. Series: Springer series in information sciences ; v. 8. Q325.K64   1983   001.53'9   83-16919

Typesetting: K & V Fotosatz, Beerfelden
Offset printing: Beltz Offsetdruck, 6944 Hemsbach/Bergstr. Bookbinding: J. Schäffer OHG, 6718 Grünstadt
2153/3130-543210

Preface

A couple of years ago the Publisher and I agreed upon a revision of *Associative Memory — A System-Theoretical Approach* (Springer Series in Communication and Cybernetics, CC 17). It turned out that this field had grown rather rapidly. On the other hand, there were some classical publications which had motivated newer works and which, accordingly, should have been reviewed in the context of present knowledge. It was therefore felt that CC 17 should completely be reorganized to embed both classical and newer results in the same formalism.

The most significant contribution of this work with respect to the earlier book, however, is that while CC 17 concentrated on the principles by which a distributed associative memory is implementable, the present book also tries to describe how an adaptive physical system is able to automatically form reduced representations of input information, or to "encode" it before storing it. Both of these aspects are, of course, essential to the complete explanation of *memory*.

Although the scope is now much wider than earlier, it was felt unnecessary to alter some rather independent parts of the old edition. Sections 2.1, 6.1 – 7, 7.1, 2, and 8.1 can be recognized as similar to the corresponding sections of CC 17, except for some editing and reorganization. On the other hand, about 2/3 of the present contents are completely new.

The book now concentrates on principles and mechanisms of memory and learning by which certain elementary "intelligent" functions are formed adaptively, without externally given control information, by the effect of received signals solely. A significant restriction to the present discussion is set by the stipulated property that the systems underlying these principles must be *physical*; accordingly, the basic components cannot implement arbitrary arithmetic algorithms although this would be very easy to define even by the simplest computer programs. The signal transformations must be as simple as possible, and the changes in the system variables and parameters must be continuous, smooth functions of time. This clearly distinguishes the present ideas from the conventional Artificial Intelligence approaches which are totally dependent on the use of digital computers and their high-level programming languages.

It is frequently believed that it is impossible to implement higher information processes without components the characteristics of which are very nonlinear. It may thereby be thought that all decision processes must be based on inherently nonlinear operations. If, however, the system properties are time-variable, then this requirement can be alleviated. In fact, even a linear system with time-variable parameter values already behaves in a nonlinear way. Another remark is that although nonlinearities are needed in some places for decision operations, it is not mandatory that every component and elementary processing operation be nonlinear; there are many functions, especially those performing statistical averaging of signals, which best can be realized by linear circuits. We shall revert to this argumentation in Chapter 4. Finally it may be remarked that if nonlinearities are needed, they may best be included in more or less fixed preprocessing circuits, especially on the sensory level.

The early phases of Artificial Intelligence research around 1960 were characterized by an enthusiastic attempt to implement learning functions, i.e., a kind of elementary intelligence, using networks built of simple adaptive components. In spite of initial optimistic expectations, progress was never particularly rapid which led to an almost opposite reaction; until quite recent years, very few researchers believed in the future of such principles. My personal view is that the first modelling approaches to learning machines were basically sound; however, at least a couple of important properties were missing from the models. One of them is a genuine memory function, especially associative memory which can reconstruct complete representations such as images and signal patterns from their fragments or other cues; and the second flaw of the early models was that the importance of the spatial order of the processing units was never fully realized. It seems, however, that in the biological brains a significant amount of information representations is encoded in the spatial location of the processing elements. We shall later see in Chapter 5 that a meaningful spatial encoding can result in a simple self-organizing physical process which uses similar components as those applied in the early learning machines; the only new feature to be introduced is a characteristic local interaction between neighbouring elements.

Associative memory is a very delicate and complex concept which often has been attributed to the higher cognitive processes, especially those taking place in the human brain. A statement of this concept can be traced back to the empiricist philosophers of the 16th century who, again, inherited their views from Aristotle (384 – 322 B.C.). It is nowadays a big challenge to launch a discussion on associative memory since its characteristics and nature have been understood in widely different ways by different scientists. Perhaps the most high-browed one is the approach made in psycholinguistics where the aim is to relate conceptual items structurally to produce bases of knowledge. Another specialized view is held in computer engineering where, traditionally, associative memory is identified with certain searching methods named *content-addressing*. The only task has thereby been to locate a data set on the basis of a matching portion in a keyword. Between these extremal conceptions, there is a continuum of various associative memory paradigms.

The contents of this book may be seen as a progression, starting from a systematic analysis of the most natural basic units, and ending with the internal representations and associative memory. Thus the main purpose of this representation is to demonstrate the gradual evolution of intelligent functions in physical systems, and to reveal those conditions under which a passive memory medium switches over into an active system that is able to form meaningful compressed representations of its input data, i.e., abstractions and generalizations which are often believed to be the basic constituents of intelligence.

Some material presented in this book has resulted from collaboration with my colleagues Pekka Lehtiö and Erkki Oja, to whom I am very much obliged. Several pictures relating to computer simulations have been prepared by Kai Mäkisara. Thanks are also due to Eija Dower for typing the manuscript.

This work has been made under the auspices of the Academy of Finland.

Otaniemi, Finland   *T. Kohonen*
August 1983

Contents

1. Various Aspects of Memory

In order to control behaviour, the biological brains must be able to form *internal models* of the sensory environment and its history. Such a "miniature environment" to which all decisions are related is provided by *memory*. The recollections from memory occur as operands in thinking and problem-solving operations. In an exact scientific approach to these phenomena, a somewhat confusing aspect is that thinking and reminiscence are mental operations associated with the cognitive ability of living organisms. The fact that biological memory closely interacts with mental processes is an old notion:

> "Thus memory belongs to the faculty of the soul to which imagination belongs; all objects which are imaginable are essentially objects of memory; all those that necessarily involve images are objects of memory incidentally."　　　　　　　　　　　　　　　　　(Aristotle, 384 – 322 B.C.)

1.1 On the Purpose and Nature of Biological Memory

1.1.1 Some Fundamental Concepts

The principles of biological information systems have remained almost a mystery although plenty of evidence has been collected which assigns basic physical and chemical properties to them. System theory thus faces a challenge to reveal at least the fundamentals of these principles. Not only is this approach interesting from the point of view of providing concrete explanations to some mental effects, but such a theory has interest in its own right, possibly making it feasible to apply these principles to inorganic systems, too.

One particular difficulty in the physical modelling of memory arises from the fact that the human mind, as a result of a long intellectual evolution, is able to deal with *concepts* that appear to be distinct and unique items, almost like material objects. The degree of specificity connected with the concepts is so high that very complex abstract structures of knowledge have been formed into our thinking. This development has led to the creation of languages and especially of the written language which obeys its own strict rules. It has often been stipulated that any concrete models of memory processes ought to reflect similar complexity and perfection; therefore the modelling task does not seem very easy or tempting. We may already here refer to the results presented later in Chap. 5; it seems possible that representations even for abstract items may be formed in certain self-organizing processes.

The concept of memory can be understood in many different ways. It usually involves a *storage mechanism* which utilizes a storage *medium*, its operation may be called the *memory function* which cooperates with the other functions of the organism, and by virtue of these facilities memory is able to generate very complex phenomena, ranging from simple mental ideas to complex sequences of thinking. When talking of memory, one ought to specify what particular aspect of it is meant.

There has been much speculation about the separability of the memory function from the other operations of the brain: one of the extreme views holds all attempts to make a distinction between "memory", "thinking", "emotion", "will", etc. purely artificial. It is true that the mental processes make use of the brain as a whole, and it is not possible to separate the memory function *locally* from the processors as the case would be with the digital computers.

Physiologically it might be more accurate to describe the brain network as a set of *adaptive processors*, and memory is then involved in all variable parts of them. If this view were taken quite strictly, it would not be possible to describe the memory function until all the processing functions of the brain were discovered. Such a purism, however, would put a stop to memory research. In other branches of natural sciences like in physics, a more practical stand has been taken; it has been possible to explain the essence of many complex phenomena by considering *idealized paradigms*, and it is not difficult to imagine in which way the true phenomena are obtained as mixtures of these paradigms. This will be the approach made in this book, too. It is thereby also believed that if these principles were applied to artificial constructs, the function of memory might be demonstrated in a pure form.

There are some further properties in the animal (and human) memory which ought to be taken into account in any psychological discussion, but which, from an universal modelling point of view, may be less relevant. If one were to describe the *performance* of human memory, one could not avoid making a distinction between *short-term memory* (STM) and *long-term memory* (LTM). The former has a retention time of some minutes whereas the memory traces of LTM must be considered permanent. These two modes of memory have a widely different capacity, too. However, it is not quite clear whether the distinction between STM and LTM ensues from the memory mechanisms underlying them; a view of two memory units of different kind which pass information to each other seems rather naive. The phenomena associated with the STM and LTM might well be different states of the same system; nobody can yet give a definite answer to this. Let it be mentioned that the old notion about STM representing reverberatory signal patterns has never been verified. For this reason, the various "kinds" of memory do not occur in the present discussion until briefly in the final Chap. 8.

1.1.2 The Classical Laws of Association

In a small book entitled *On Memory and Reminiscence* [1.1], Aristotle stated a set of observations on human memory which were later compiled as the Classical Laws of Association. The conventional way for their expression is:

> Mental items (ideas, perceptions, sensations, or feelings) are connected in memory under the following conditions:
> 1) If they occur simultaneously ("spatial contact").
> 2) If they occur in close succession ("temporal contact").
> 3) If they are similar.
> 4) If they are contrary.

Obviously simultaneity or close succession of signals is necessary for their becoming mutually conditioned or encoded in any physical system, whereas in a process of recall, the evoked item (or part of it) might have, e.g., a high positive *correlation* (similarity) or a negative one (contrast) to that item which is used as the input *key* or *search argument*. Consequently, it seems that Laws 1 and 2 relate to writing, and 3 and 4 to reading. These laws, however, seem to neglect one further factor which is so natural that its presence has seldom been considered. This is the *background* or *context* in which primary perceptions occur, and this factor is, to a great extent, responsible for the high capacity and selectivity of a human memory. We shall discuss this effect in Sects. 1.3.2 and 3.

The following significant features in the operation of a human associative memory shall thus be noticed: (i) Information is in the first place searched from memory on the basis of some measure of *similarity* relating to the key pattern. (ii) Memory is able to store and recall representations as *structured sequences*. (iii) The recollections of information from memory in the most general sense are *dynamic processes,* similar to the behaviour of many time-continuous physical systems. In fact, Aristotle made several remarks on the recollections being a *synthesis* of memorized information, not necessarily identical to the original occurrences.

1.1.3 On Different Levels of Modelling

It is possible to divide the memory models into two main categories: *physical-system models* and *information-processing models*. In the category of *physical-system models* all those models are included that try to answer the following question: How is it possible, using a collection of relatively simple elements connected to one another, to implement the basic functions of associative memory? Although it is possible to implement memory mechanisms by many different physical systems, we are here mainly interested in principles according to which the systems are able to encode associations and subsequently to recall them selectively and independently.

The physical-system approach may be contrasted with *information-processing models* that conceive man (or any intelligent system) as an information-processor executing internal programs for testing, comparing, analyzing, manipulating, and storing information. In order for the human beings to be capable of this, one has to assume that the *mental processor* had some sort of associative-memory capacity.

A great number of studies have also been published on *associative data structures*. The aim of these has been to develop a representational format that permits the storage of the meaning of a word or a sentence, or more generally, the storage of organized knowledge. *Quillian* [1.2] has formulated the central thesis of his early work on *semantic networks* as follows: "What constitutes a reasonable view of how semantic information is organized within a person's memory?" This is a typical competence question. A more technological approach was, of course, later adopted in the development of data-base software tools. Semantic network models and models of mental processing may be seen as complementary: for instance, in order to explain linguistic abilities, one has to postulate both processing functions and data structures.

1.2 Questions Concerning the Fundamental Mechanisms of Memory

The traditional approaches to memory have in no way been concerned with the explanation of the *memory function* itself. Below we are trying to delineate what kind of questions a physicist or an engineer might ask if he were presented the task of studying memory, and suggest some answers which further will be justified in the rest of this book.

1.2.1 Where Do the Signals Relating to Memory Act Upon?

The signals to the brain come from sensory detectors, often via several processing stations. There are also proprioceptive detectors in the body which signal its internal state. The brain, especially the *cerebrum* which constitutes 6/7 of the central nervous system in humans, is a complex interconnected system in which the primary signal patterns are transformed spatially as well as in sequential processes. As a result, characteristic spatio-temporal patterns can be observed all over the brain network. It is not quite sure to which extent the patterns in each part of the brain leave memory traces, but there certainly exists no particular area which would be dedicated to memory. On the other hand, some lower parts like the *hippocampus* as well as certain portions of the *thalamus* have been demonstrated to play an important role in the control of consolidation of memory traces.

We shall not discuss the whole brain, or even memory as a single "black box". On the contrary, in a systematic approach it is necessary to start with the analysis of the neural tissue, without specification where it is taken from. This approach seems justified since anatomical studies have revealed that the local network structures, especially in the neocortex, are remarkably uniform from one area to another. The same cell types and roughly the same local connections are found, independently of the location from which a section is taken. We shall try to derive the properties of memory from *intrinsic properties of the neural medium*.

In view of the above argumentation, the input and output signals in the memory models can be regarded as local activity patterns; they may represent any (sensory) modality, and it is not even necessary to specify the meaning of individual signals. *The semantic value of the brain signals seems to correspond to a particular location of the tissue*, as we will see in Chaps. 5 and 8.

From the modelling point of view it is neither necessary to point out, how interpretation of the neural signals, or formation of the cognitive state, results from neural activity. In some neurophysiological theories, a practical, *"reductionistic"* stand is taken; the neural responses and the mental effects caused by them are assumed *identical*. In this view, the task of memory is extremely easy: it has only to reproduce the neural signals at the places where they earlier occurred. Even in more "spiritual" approaches, this view can be useful. In any case, physiological experiments have shown a very close correspondence between the various locations of the brain and the perceptive effects.

It may thus be clear that the nature of information processing in the brains and in the computers is completely different; in the latter, memory is a separate unit, and there is a continuous traffic of operands between it and the other parts.

1.2.2 What Kind of Encoding is Used for Neural Signals?

The second unavoidable question concerns the *representations* of information in memory: how are the sensory signals transformed, or as it is frequently said, "encoded" before they leave memory traces? For a long time there was a belief held that some kind of pulse code is associated with the neural signals. However, although many kinds of pulse patterns are found in the nervous systems, their rhythms are completely predictable from the properties of elementary trigger circuits, without any "intelligence" associated with the subsequent intervals. In other words, binary codes, such as those applied in the digital computer technology, can hardly occur in the central nervous system; the only significant expression of "information" seems to be involved with the density or frequency of the neural pulse trains. This, of course, is not yet sufficient to explain the internal representations.

On the other hand, in the brain networks there seems to be plenty of specificity associated with *spatial location* of a neural response. There exists a coarse specialization of the brain areas according to the various sensory modalities (visual, auditory, somatosensory, etc.), as well as different levels of operation (speech, planning of actions, etc.) (Fig. 1.1).

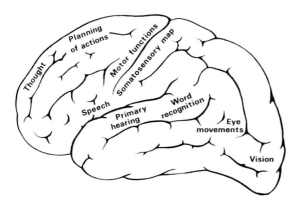

Fig. 1.1. Brain areas

Recordings performed all over the brain system have also indicated that most locations in the brain tissue are in correspondence with exciting conditions termed as "receptive fields". Such a receptive field can be a very concrete concept: for instance, in the visual cortex of the brain there exist cells which give a response when a certain type of light pattern falls on a certain portion of the retina. This configuration on the retina would then be called the *receptive field of the cell* in question. In the somatosensory cortex there are cells which have their receptive field somewhere on the skin (Fig. 1.2).

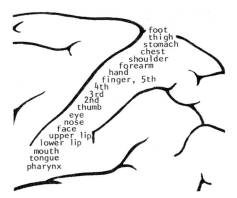

Fig. 1.2. The somatosensory map

However, the "receptive fields" could also be defined more generally; the brain contains cells which respond to a particular *feature* of the environment, e.g., to an area in the visual field, or to a range in an abstract feature space like that of acoustic frequencies (Fig. 1.3) or colours. Of course, a single cell alone may not possess such an encoding ability: the specificity of the response more probably results from computations made in a hierarchy of cells converging upon this place.

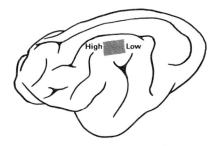

Fig. 1.3. The tonotopic map (of cat)

It thus seems that the neural tissue, especially in the highest parts of the central nervous system, is organized according to sensory features, and it is possible to discover various kinds of *ordered feature maps* in different brain areas. In Chap. 5 we shall give a description of processes in which such maps can be formed. It does not seem impossible that map-like spatial organizations can be found for more abstract concepts, too.

1.2.3 What are the Variable Memory Elements?

Even though we shall revert to this question later in Chap. 8, it will be possible to state briefly that according to the contemporary standpoint, the most significant changes in the signal transmission properties of the neural tissue are caused by changes in the connections between neural cells, named *synapses*, which have a rather complicated internal structure. The synapses, together with the neural fibres or *axons* which transmit signals, must be considered like miniature organs with characteristic electro-chemical processes taking place within them. The purpose of a synapse, however, is nothing more than to provide a proper signal coupling between neural cells. The strength of this coupling can be made variable by altering the chemical composition, size, or form of the synapse. For a stronger coupling, the axons can sometimes create multiple parallel synapses, and regression of an unnecessary synapse is a usual adaptive phenomenon, too. The changes in the efficacy of a synapse can be transient, with time constants ranging from some minutes to, say, 24 hours. It is also evident that the strengths of synaptic connections can be set permanently to certain values.

For the above reasons it seems reasonable to assume that the most important memory effects in neural networks are associated with the synaptic connections. For modelling purposes it is not even necessary to know or assume exactly what particular mechanisms underly these changes: the coupling strength can be taken as a mathematical "memory parameter". Some details of physiological phenomena at synapses are discussed in Chap. 8.

1.2.4 How are Neural Signals Addressed in Memory?

The next unavoidable question in an attempt to concretize the memory function concerns the *addressing* of data. This problem is not separable from that of the storage mechanism, as shown by the following thought experiment.

Even though a certain sensory experience would generate a characteristic spatial (or spatio-temporal) pattern of neural signals over some brain area, it would not be enough just to imprint this pattern as such to the place where it acted, or to simply sensitize the corresponding cells so that they react to this pattern later more easily. Although this kind of views of memory have sometimes been held, they must be regarded as immature ones. It is true that sensitization of cells to specific features is needed to create the *feature maps*, as demonstrated in Chap. 5, but we must also realize that the same feature can be present in an immense number of different occurrences. The representation of a single sensory experience consists of a *set of features*, and all elements in such a set should then be encoded by each other. Mutual conditioning of signals of this kind has frequently been called *associative learning*. Assume a set of neural cells, each one representing a certain feature value of observation. Associative learning then means that there is a *link* between every pair of cells, the strength of which is set to a value proportional to the *correlation* of the respective activity values of the cells. The memory traces would then correspond to *changes in these links,* not to changes in the cells themselves. A reader who is unfamiliar with neural networks might be embarrassed by the huge number of links thereby needed. He may neither be quite convinced about the ability of such a memory to keep the various "memorized" patterns separate, or to have a sufficient *selectivity* in recall. One of the purposes of this book is therefore to demonstrate that transformation functions of this kind are indeed capable of encoding a great number of separate representations without confusing them; if mixing of the patterns anyway takes place, it will serve meaningful purposes such as making generalizations over related patterns. We shall point out in Chap. 8 that the neural networks indeed have an immense number of interconnections when compared with the number of cells. Furthermore, it is possible to show that *every* pair of cells need not be interconnected; for a certain statistical accuracy it will suffice that the number of interconnections, if they are spread statistically in their environment, is much larger than the number of cells.

In order to illustrate the selectivity which is attainable in simple "auto-associative learning", we shall present the results of a computer simulation on such a model. It has to be made completely clear in the beginning that *this is not an attempt to model the visual system of animals*; optical images are only used because their quality can easily be esteemed visually. We are neither showing any other details here, such as the contrast enhancement of these pictures before they are stored, or the exact transformation functions which will be later explained in Chaps. 4, 6, and 8. In this simulation the dots, or their locations, correspond to neural cells, and the size of the dot is proportional to the activity value of that cell. There were 500 "memorized" pictures in this experiment (or a subset of 160 pictures in another experiment) and each picture left memory traces in the links between the dots; Fig. 1.4a presents examples of these pictures. Due to the mutual conditioning of cells, this kind of memory is then able to reconstruct or *recall* memorized pictures from incomplete cues or *key patterns:* if, for instance, the key patterns in Fig. 1.4b were applied, the memory system would reproduce the activity patterns shown in Figs. 1.4c or d, respectively. For details of this experiment, the reader should consult the original publication [1.3].

Comparison Between Localized and Distributed Memories. Most readers may be more familiar with digital computers, which hold data in subsequent addressed storage locations, than with the principles of the human brain. Therefore it will be necessary to make a clear distinction between the existing computer memories and the biological ones. (It may happen that the latter kind of memories will be applied in future technology, but this development has hardly yet begun.)

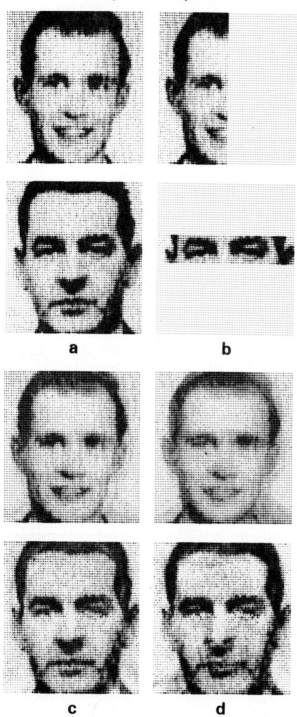

a   b

c   d

Fig. 1.4a – d.
Caption see opposite page

The most fundamental principle for computer memories utilizes *location addressing*. Consider Fig. 1.5 which shows an eight-location memory provided with *address decoders* and *read/write channels*. Each storage location can hold a string of bit values of fixed length (usually 8, 16, or 32 bits), named a *word*. These bit values are stored as states in a set of *bistable circuits* (flip-flops), and transfer of data to and from the storage locations is made with the aid of logic gates (not shown explicitly) which are connected to common bit lines.

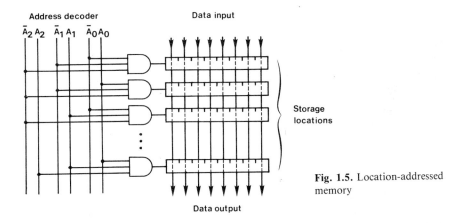

Fig. 1.5. Location-addressed memory

What is most central for this discussion is the operation of the address decoders: each one is a special logic circuit which gives an active response only for a particular *address code*, given in this example as a three-bit number, or a set of three binary-valued signals. Only one of the decoders can fit a particular code (like a key fits a lock) so that only one decoder will become active at a time and control the corresponding storage location for reading or writing.

There is another design in computer technology which is often mistakenly called "associative memory"; a more proper name for it is *content-addressable memory*. A very simple version of it is shown in Fig. 1.6.

The address decoder is replaced, in this circuit, by a *directory* circuit which is a special localized memory, with logic circuits at every storage location performing a *comparison operation*. The purpose of the comparison circuits [1.4] is to compare a particular *keyword*, applied at the inputs of the directory, in parallel with the contents of all locations, and an active response is obtained at the outputs of all locations where a match is found. Because of a possibility

Fig. 1.4a – d. Demonstration of associative recall from a linear system. (a) Samples of original images. (b) Key patterns. (c) Recollections from a memory with 160 stored images. (d) Recollections from a memory with 500 stored images

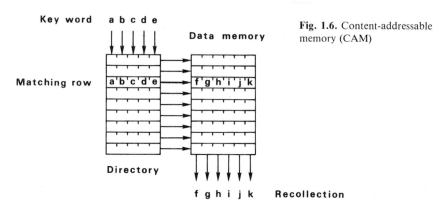

Fig. 1.6. Content-addressable memory (CAM)

for *multiple match*, this memory would actually need a more complicated circuitry to resolve between them [1.4]. For simplicity we shall omit the multiple-match problem and assume that the contents of all locations in the directory are different, whereby at most one active response (denoted by the boldfaced arrow in Fig. 1.6) can be obtained. This response then acts as a control signal for the *data memory* in which the auxiliary information associated with the keywords is held, and from which it can be read out. (There are also *autoassociative* memories in which the matching can be made by incomplete keywords, and the complete contents from the directory part can then be read out.)

The principles of computer memories can hardly be realized in biological organisms for the following reasons: i) All signals in computers are binary whereas the neural signals are usually trains of pulses with variable frequency. ii) Ideal bistable circuits which could act as reliable binary memory elements have not been found in the nervous systems.

To make the distinction between computer memories and "natural-like" memories still more obvious, we may consider Fig. 1.7 which delineates a piece of brain network as it is often simplified, leaving only so-called principal cells in it (Chap. 8).

Above we held the view that in some way or another, for instance, by a suitable adaptation of the input weights, different input signal values will cause different cells to become active. We may again regard the combination of input signals as a "key", and the cells as "locks". This analogy is very near to the operation of neural circuits in the brain. However, a similar analogy was also used to explain the decoder circuits of computer memories; so where is the principal difference? Couldn't we regard a cell with a specific response as equivalent to a storage location?

One should notice that in the neural cells *there is no storage for any records at this location*. What would then comprise the data to be stored? As

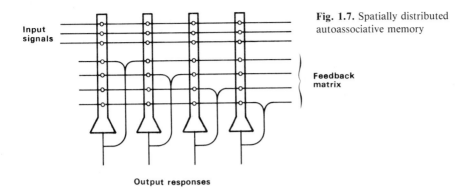

Fig. 1.7. Spatially distributed autoassociative memory

stated earlier, it is *the set of responses* which must be memorized as a whole, and these responses cannot be transferred to any separate memory; they must be memorized on the place where they were obtained. The "address" and the "data" are then one and the same thing.

Figure 1.7 delineates the addressing principle which has been termed *auto-associative network* in this book. If each of the units or cells would receive a set of signals, then it is to be expected that some cells (namely, those to which the input pattern fits) will give an active response. If the response pattern has to be memorized autoassociatively, it means that *each of the cells must be encoded by the responses of all the other cells in this group.* In the simplest way this is implemented using variable feedback: if a feedback connection is consolidated *when both the sending and the receiving cell of this feedback line are active simultaneously,* then a specific interconnecting network is formed, which will be able to reconstruct those parts of the memorized pattern which were not present in the key, as shown in Fig. 1.4. We shall perform a thorough quantitative analysis of this function in Chaps. 4 – 8; let it suffice to state here that *memory in this kind of networks is distributed spatially over the matrix of feedback connections.* Such a memory might then also be named "hololologic"; the name "holographic" is also usable as long as there is no danger of confusion with optical holography.

There may be a long way from the simple network principle to a complete system which is able to represent memories relating to all possible situations of life. There are many researchers who do not believe in the possibility of such an explanation. What they fail to realize, however, is the enormous capacity of the human brain tissue: there are in total at least 10^{12} neural cells in the brain, and it seems safe to say that, on the average, each cell receives and sends 10^3 to 10^4 variable interconnections to the other cells. We shall return to the specifications of biological memory in Chap. 8, after certain questions of theoretical nature have been settled. We shall then be able to see that the brain network, even if it were based on such simple functional principles, has the capacity of encoding and describing all the occurrences during the human life with sufficient accuracy.

In the next section we shall discuss some basic operations which are common to all implementations of memory, biological as well as artificial, distributed as well as localized. It should be realized that the same principles may also occur at any level of organization.

1.3 Elementary Operations Implemented by Associative Memory

1.3.1 Associative Recall

It was mentioned above, and it is a rather general notion among brain researchers, that information processing operations within the brain can be expressed in terms of *adaptive filter functions*. The general idea is that the brain is organized in a number of *"functional units"* (e.g., tightly cooperating groups of cells, whereby the composition of such a group may vary from task to task; it is possible to think that typical groups comprise 10^3 to 10^5 neurons). The groups also cooperate tightly with each other so that the brain actually ought to be discussed as an integrated system. However, in an attempt to analyze the fundamental information processing operations, we may discuss an isolated piece of the neural network, possibly corresponding to the above "group". This network will have well-defined *inputs* and *outputs* (Fig. 1.8).

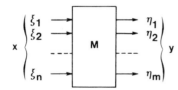

Fig. 1.8. Filter model for associative recall

The basic operation of such a "filter" is to transform an ordered set of concomitant input signal values, denoted $x = (\xi_1, \xi_2, \ldots, \xi_n)$, into another ordered set of output signals, denoted $y = (\eta_1, \eta_2, \ldots, \eta_m)$. In the basic network, all connections are assumed so short that signal delays need not be taken into account. If x and y are regarded as multidimensional *vectoral* variables (Chap. 2), then y is some vector function of x which further contains some *parameters*. These parameters determine the variable transmission properties of the network;

$$y = y(x, M),\tag{1.1}$$

where M is the set of parameters. The transformation (1.1) is assumed *adaptive* in the sense that the parameters are changed by the effect of the transmitted signals. This kind of changes are usually called *memory effects*.

Associative recall is a particular type of adaptive filter operation. We may distinguish between two types of it, namely, *heteroassociative* and *autoassociative* recall. We had an example of the latter in the demonstration shown in Fig. 1.4. These case of heteroassociative recall is more general. In Chap. 3 we shall discuss simple system models for its physical implementation; Chap. 6 deals with optimal heteroassociative mappings from a mathematical point of view.

If we have a set of different input vectors $X = \{x^{(1)}, x^{(2)}, \ldots, x^{(k)}\}$ and another set of output vectors $Y = \{y^{(1)}, y^{(2)}, \ldots, y^{(k)}\}$ then this system is said to implement a perfect heteroassociative recall if

$$x^{(1)} \to y^{(1)},$$
$$x^{(2)} \to y^{(2)},$$
$$\ldots$$
$$x^{(k)} \to y^{(k)}.\tag{1.2}$$

The responses have thereby been defined to have ideal *selectivity* with respect to X. In a way, the content-addressable memory had this property; and the optimal associative mappings of Chap. 7 have this property in a more general sense.

It is now possible to define a *perfect autoassociative recall* along the same lines. In this case the $x^{(p)}$ are not arbitrary but they are somehow derived from the $y^{(p)}$ to be recalled. For instance, if vectors $x^{(p)}$ and $y^{(p)}$ would have the same dimensionality (the same number of component signals), and $x^{(p)}$ is obtained from $y^{(p)}$ by setting a subset of its elements to zero, then we have the case demonstrated in Fig. 1.4.

For the purposes of subsequent discussion, we shall now tentatively use the following definition.

Definition 1.1. An ideal autoassociative memory is a system which holds copies of distinct input signal sets $x^{(p)}$, $p = 1, 2, \ldots, k$ in its internal state, and produces the copy of a particular set $x^{(r)} = (\xi_1^{(r)}, \xi_2^{(r)}, \ldots, \xi_n^{(r)})$, $r \in \{1, 2, \ldots, k\}$ to the outputs, whenever (in the recall mode) the inputs are excited by a set of signals $x = (\xi_1, \xi_2, \ldots, \xi_n)$ in which a specified subset of the values ξ_i matches with the corresponding subset of the $\xi_i^{(r)}$.

1.3.2 Production of Sequences from the Associative Memory

We shall now consider another important aspect in the theory of associative memory, namely, the mechanism by which *timed sequences* of representations can be memorized and reconstructed. This is often called the problem of *temporal associations* or *temporal recall*. We shall further emphasize that the sequences of recollections are usually *structured*, i.e., they may branch into alternative successive sequences depending on some kind of *background* or *context information* (Sect. 1.2.3); the sequences may also become cyclic.

The theory of automata (e.g., [1.5]) deals with machines which are intended for production of sequences of machine states. The fundamental machine, the *finite-state machine*, is an abstract system which has a finite set of internal states S, it accepts one element of a finite set of "input states" I (e.g., patterns of input signals), and it produces another element of a finite set of "output states" O (e.g., patterns of output signals) thereby undergoing a state transition. This transition is a function of the present input state as well as the internal state; the output is another function of the input state and internal state, respectively. The new internal state of the system and the output state are formally defined by a pair of mappings (f, g) such that if $s_i^{(t)}, s_i^{(t+1)} \in S$, $i_i^{(t)} \in I$, and $o_i^{(t)} \in O$, then

$$f: s_i^{(t+1)} = f(s_1^{(t)}, \ldots, s_m^{(t)}, i_1^{(t)}, \ldots, i_n^{(t)}),$$
$$g: o_i^{(t)} = g(s_1^{(t)}, \ldots, s_m^{(t)}, i_1^{(t)}, \ldots, i_n^{(t)}) . \tag{1.3}$$

If the system variables are signals in digital computing circuits, a sequentially operating system is obtained by feedback of output signals of a combinational circuit to its inputs as shown in Fig. 1.9. The effective output signals are obtained by another combinational circuit. Time delays usually exist in the internal signal paths or in the feedback; it is the amount of feedback delay which sets the time scale in the dynamic (sequential) process. One should realize that the internal state of the system is a *static* variable, and a dynamic (sequential) operation is implemented by the effect of *delayed feedback*.

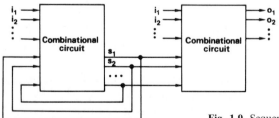

Fig. 1.9. Sequential circuit, basic form

Sequences are also implementable by autoassociative memories defined above. We shall approach the problem of temporal associations using a simple system model which also has the appearance of a finite-state machine (Fig. 1.10). The central block in it is some embodiment of autoassociative memory, with three types of input: external inputs K and C, and feedback input F. The system has an output port for recollection R. The feedback F is derived from R via a time delay; in the simplest case we may have $F(t) = R(t-1)$, in which t, an integer, is a discrete-time variable. The memory shall have two modes of operation, *writing* and *reading*, explained below.

There is a characteristic feature in the system of Fig. 1.10 which distinguishes it from other sequential circuits. The internal states are not arbitrary; on the contrary, as the central block represents a memory, its different internal states shall correspond to replicas of the pairs of patterns (K, C) received at the input. Furthermore, the feedback pattern F shall be associated with the input so that a set of *ordered triples*

$$\{(K(t), C(t), F(t))\}$$

is in fact stored in the memory during the *writing mode.*

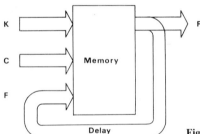

Fig. 1.10. Associative memory for structured sequences

The two external inputs K and C are assumed to have specialized roles in the sequential process, although the memory makes no difference between them. A sequence of inputs $\{K(t)\}$ is assumed to comprise the *central temporal pattern,* whereas C assumes the role of *background* or *context* and is usually stationary during a particular sequence. For different K-sequences, the prevailing background C shall be different; this makes it possible to distinguish between different sequences, although the same $K(t)$ patterns occur in them.

One further specification shall be made: for the encoding of a temporal process, it will be necessary to generate an output $R(t)$ and a feedback pattern $F(t)$ during the writing of each triple. [In some memory circuits it is possible to obtain a replica of the input during the writing process. In the simplest case we thus have $R(t) = K(t)$ during writing.]

Assume now that the sequence of external inputs $\{(K(1), C), (K(2), C), \ldots, (K(N), C)\}$ has been received and stored. When the first input $(K(1), C)$ arrives, the F input has no signals at it; an input with no signal shall be denoted by the symbol $\emptyset$ ("don't care"). (In some models $\emptyset$ can simply be the zero value of a set of signals, whereas there are content-addressable memories for which special codes are used for $\emptyset$.) Upon associative search, the value $\emptyset$ shall be neglected. According to the above consideration, the *effective input sequence* shall now be

$$S = \{(K(1), C, \emptyset), (K(2), C, K(1)), \ldots, (K(N), C, K(N-1))\},$$

which contains the set of triples stored as such.

The *associative recall* of a memorized sequence is now made in the *reading mode*, e.g., by the application of a *key input* $(K(1), C, \emptyset)$. For the recollection of the rest of the sequence, no further keys $K(k)$, $k = 2, 3, \ldots$ shall be necessary. (The reading could also be started in the middle of a sequence.) The memory is assumed to produce a recollection $K(1)$ at its output port; this pattern will be mediated to the F input by a unit time delay as $F(2) = K(1)$. Reading will now be continued automatically, but the $K(k)$ input, $k = 2, 3, \ldots$, thereafter attains an "empty" or $\emptyset$ value. The next input is $(\emptyset, C, K(1))$ which will match in its specified part with the second term in the sequence S. Consequently, it will produce the output $K(2)$, and a continued process will retrieve the rest of the sequence $K(3), K(4), \ldots, K(N)$.

Thus it has been shown that the associative memory is able to store a great number of independent sequences, each one being retrievable by its own key input, consisting of a (K, C) pattern.

Above we have avoided the mention of one further problem. It may occur that some input pattern, say, $(\emptyset, C, K(k))$ may match several triples stored in the memory, whereby it is not clear, what its successor state should be. This is the *multiple-match* situation. It should then be realized that the system of Fig. 1.10 is the simplest model containing feedback loops. If there are several feedback paths with different delays, then the model will be able to recall more complicated sequences; in fact, a machine with k different feedback paths is needed to recall correctly a sequence that contains several identical subsequences of length $(k-1)$.

Example 1.1. Human beings and animals learn facts about their environment and temporally related occurrences by association of rather restricted spatio-temporal relations in their memories; knowledge about more complex information structures comes from the automatic linking of such elementary observations, perhaps in many repetitions. The following example might bear some resemblance to natural memorization. The symbols $a, b, \ldots, A, B$ stand for spatial patterns of signals, and $\emptyset$ is an empty pattern ("don't care"). (It is assumed that empty patterns do not produce responses.) Assume that the following timed sequences of pairs $[K(t), C(t)]$ have been presented at the input during storage phases:

$\{(a, A), (b, A), (d, A)\}$;

$\{(b, A), (d, A), (e, A), (\emptyset, A), (\emptyset, \emptyset)\}$;

$\{(a, B), (c, B)\}$;

$\{(c, B), (d, B)\}$;

$\{(d, B), (f, B), (\emptyset, B), (\emptyset, \emptyset)\}$.

The alternative sequences obtainable during recall can now be represented by a structured graph of Fig. 1.11 where a circle represents an output pattern, an arrow points to the next output state, and the arrow is labeled by the due context pattern $C(t)$ (i.e., A or B, respectively).

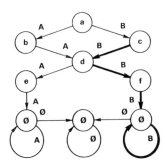

Fig. 1.11. A structured sequence

A temporal recollection can be triggered at any time later if the network is excited by one particular pattern that together with its context occurs in the graph; this will cause an output which in turn by means of the delayed feedback selectively evokes the next pattern in the sequence, and so on. For instance, if the pair (c, B) is applied at the input, then the sequence drawn in boldfaced arrows is recalled. Notice that
- this sequence was never stored in a complete form, and the learning of a continuous sequence from shorter memorized segments has thereby been demonstrated;
- the order in which the segments are presented during the storage phase can be arbitrary;

- the states a and d occur in two different subsequences where they have a different context;
- it is necessary to terminate the sequences by empty patterns; when the context pattern (A or B) has been switched off, the system enters the "empty" sequence (quiet state) where it waits for new key patterns.

More-Complicated Models. Apparently the single-feedback circuit is the most fundamental construct from which structured sequences can be obtained. Nonetheless it is possible to imagine more-complex systems, too. A memory unit may have several inputs and outputs for patterns, for instance, for several distinct items which can be memorized in a single process. A memory system may be built of many units, interconnected by channels with different delays, etc. The activity in one channel may comprise the context to another, etc. Obviously the discussion then becomes very complicated and even more so if the patterns occur asynchronously. It may be possible to imagine, although cumbersome to analyze, the behaviour of such systems.

1.3.3 On the Meaning of Background and Context

It is obvious from the previous example that in order to achieve a sufficient selectivity in associative memory, especially in temporal associations, an appreciable amount of *background information* (represented by the C signals in Fig. 1.10) must be provided. Background information may be received, e.g., from observation of the surroundings. The presence of background in human information processing is often taken to be so self-evident that it is usually omitted from consideration, even in otherwise well-planned psychological experiments. This may be understandable because in a particular environment and during the experimental session, the signals belonging to the background are usually steady. From the information-processing point of view, however, a steady background cannot be neglected; in the discussion of the information-processing capacity, and especially in the estimation of information content in the sensory signals, a constant background may have a significant contribution.

There is another essentially constant factor in most information-processing tasks which has a more delicate nature than simple background. It is the *context* in which the received information occurred. In linguistics, context is often defined by the whole subject area under discussion; on the other hand, in cognitive processes, those pieces of information contributing to the context may come from different levels of abstraction of the observation. For instance, a subject in the traffic may receive context information from the road signs, other vehicles, time of the day, "internal model" of the roads existing in the driver's memory, etc. The factors defining such a "context" are then temporarily stored in memory; the background is determined *internally*.

One further remark should be made. Especially in data-base technology, context has sometimes been defined as the local data structure in which a particular item occurred (Sect. 1.4.5). Apparently this is a rather restricted view.

1.4 More Abstract Aspects of Memory

1.4.1 The Problem of Infinite-State Memory

When dealing with natural information such as images or signals, one big problem is that any available memory capacity is sooner or later filled up. By advanced instrumentation it is easy to gather a great deal more information than can ever be represented in artificial, localized memory systems. This is the *problem of infinite-state memory*, as it is often referred to. This problem is familiar from systems theory, especially from the *theory of adaptive (optimal) filters*. The central principle in the latter is to represent a dynamical system or filtering operation by a finite set of parameters. These parameters are *recursively updated* by all the received signals, whereby they can be regarded as a kind of *memory* for all received information. We shall discuss in Chaps. 3 and 4 many constructs which operate according to this principle.

A characteristic of all devices discussed in this book is that the memory shall be able to *recall* the stored representations as faithfully as possible, with a selectivity depending on some *measure of similarity* thereby applied. It then seems that the available memory capacity could be utilized more efficiently if only significant details were represented accurately, and for those parts which are more common, average or stereotypic representations were used. It seems that the human memory, to a great extent, operates in this way; although a single occurrence can cause clear memory traces, recollections are often only stereotypic, affected by earlier experiences. Biological systems almost without exception tend to optimize their resources, and this principle must also be reflected in the utilization of memory. One general principle for the implementation of infinite-state memory is to assume that there exist continuous-valued state variables y_k in the memory which are able to average over respective inputs x_k. Consider, for simplicity, the occurrences of x_k as discrete items $x_k^{(i)}$. The state variable is then assumed to change as

$$y_k^{(i+1)} = f(y_k^{(i)}, x_k^{(i)}) , \tag{1.4}$$

where f can attain many possible forms; the simplest of them is a weighted sum of $y_k^{(i)}$ and $x_k^{(i)}$ whereby a moving arithmetic average is formed over the sequence of $\{x_k^{(i)}\}$. In more complex cases the recursion may involve scale transformations. When something is *recalled* from memory, then it may be thought that an external search argument x is compared with the set of representations of different items $\{y_k^{(t)}\}$ existing in memory at time t; the one for which some similarity measure $S(x, y_k^{(t)})$ is maximum, will be picked up and recalled. Notice that this process of memorization and recall is not only able to smooth over an arbitrary number of representations of an item but also to *synthesize* new information. For instance, the "averaged" representation $y_k^{(i)}$ may have resulted from realizations $x_k^{(i)}$ with inherently different contents.

1.4.2 Invariant Representations

Based on subjective experiences, it is often maintained that an associative memory or a recognitive scheme is not genuine, unless it has the ability of identifying an object from its transformed versions; for instance, a visual object ought to be identifiable regardless of its position or location, or the size of an image projected from it on the retina of the eye. In psychology, such a phenomenon is, in general, called *stimulus equivalence*; if different stimulus patterns represent the same object or have the same meaning, they are experienced similar.

Although the requirements of invariant representation are usually connected with the *recognition* process and not so much with *memorization*, we may nonetheless consider what possibilities there are for the representation of information which is invariant with respect to certain transformation groups of the primary signals.

Invariant Transformation Functions and Features. There are two common approaches to the problem of invariant representation: (i) The similarity criterion applied in associative recall is defined in terms of certain *transformation functions* instead of the original patterns; e.g., the modulus of the complex two-dimensional Fourier transform is invariant with respect to an arbitrary displacement (translation) of the original image in its plane, and the modulus of the two-dimensional Mellin transform is invariant with respect to an arbitrary affine (e.g., size) transformation. (ii) The original pattern is represented by a set of local patterns (*local features*) extracted from it, each one of the local features being encoded independently of its position, orientation, and size.

There are almost endless possibilities for the definition of *features* for patterns; notice that the transformation functions are also cases of them. It has amply been proved that invariance with respect to a single transformation group is easily achievable, whereas *simultaneous* invariance to translation, rotation, changes in size, etc., has not succeeded. It seems that the requirement of invariance thereby may have been understood as too categorical. It ought to be known that even the biological systems are not perfectly ideal in this respect; for instance, recognition of an object becomes much more difficult if the latter is rotated by more than 45 degrees. On the other hand, the invariance properties may be restricted to part of the observations; for instance, in the visual scene, several independent objects may simultaneously have this kind of invariance, which indicates that some integral transformation function of the whole scene cannot be the solution.

Interpolation and Extrapolation. It would perhaps be more expedient to ask whether there exist representations or recognition schemes which are able to *extrapolate* or *interpolate* patterned information with respect to a few reference patterns that represent the objects in different variations. This author is of the opinion that the linear mappings discussed in Chap. 6 have a remarkable interpolating and extrapolating ability if the patterns are rather "smooth" and several variations of them are used as reference patterns. This view has been validated in some voice identification experiments, in which several (say, five or more) slightly different versions for each pattern were used as a set of reference patterns. With optical images, the recognition scheme can similarly be made to interpolate and extrapolate with respect to reference patterns with random translational, rotational, and other variations.

Linguistic Approach. Because of difficulties in the implementation of invariant mappings, another line of research has often been taken. This approach starts with an assumption that the recognitive scheme actively takes part in the analysis of patterns. One method thereby applied tries to solve the recognition problem by *linguistic analysis*. This approach is probably based on a view that a natural (visual) recognition process is similar to a thought process, operating on elements which are related in a semantic way. The task begins with *identification of pattern primitives*, and their geometric or topological *relations* are then expressed without attention being paid to exact coordinates. Such a structure of relations often already has the wanted invariance properties. This approach has been used in modern pattern recognition technology [1.6]; however, it is not clear how it could be implemented in the neural realms.

Invariance Through Abstraction. Finally we would like to mention a possibility for the production of representations that are optimally invariant with respect to signal statistics. This concept will become more lucid in Chap. 5. Let it be mentioned here that certain self-organizing processes are able to form *maps* of the features present in the primary observations. These maps are then also able to *average* conditionally over irrelevant feature variables. It seems that such a process is the most natural way to compress information, thereby preserving the invariant features or structures.

1.4.3 Symbolic Representations

It has been a common view that the central nervous system processes information in symbolic form [1.7]. This was obviously postulated for the following reasons: (i) Symbols can be made *unique* whereby they facilitate long and complex operation sequences. (ii) Symbols can be associated with *concepts*, which in the simplest form are representations of *clusters* in more or less variable occurrences. (iii) As the concepts can be defined on different levels of abstraction, a more accurate *meaning* can be given to an occurrence at an increased economy of representation.

An extreme form of symbolism would be a "brain code", the existence of which, however, has never been verified experimentally. Now it has to be emphasized that a symbolic representation need not be identified with a code. It seems sufficient that any substitute pattern that is simpler and more invariant than the original occurrence can be associated with the latter; in this book some possibilities for the embodiment and processing of structured relations between such representations are delineated.

A trivial and also common way to define a concept is supervised association, or classical conditioning of a symbol with a pattern. However, a much more important and intriguing problem concerns mechanisms by which a symbolic representation could *automatically* be formed in an adaptive system. One possibility is formation of certain discrete states in the system corresponding to distinct statistical "eigenfeatures" of the input information (Sect. 4.4.1). Sometimes simpler representations are formed, for example, by amplitude discrimination of signals and dropping of weak segments from sequences (cf. formation of nicknames). Classification, especially false identification with earlier prototypes, is obviously one process which assigns illustrative names to new occurrences.

As to the remaining problem, formation of symbols referring to different levels of abstraction, it is useful to observe that those parts in representations which are most *general* are often also more *constant* and vice versa. This may allow differentiation between hierarchical levels on the basis of conditional probabilities of the subpatterns.

In view of the new results to be introduced in Chap. 5, it now seems that a fundamental process of automatic symbol-formation, or representation of items by analogies using other representations (that is, abstraction) ensues from the self-organizing ability of certain adaptive networks. Information is thereby represented as *spatial maps* over "memory fields" (cf. also Sect. 8.2). If the ability to form maps were ubiquitous in the brain, then one could easily explain its power to operate on *semantic* items: some areas of the brain could simply create and order specialized cells or cell groups in conformity with high-level features and their combinations.

1.4.4 Virtual Images

Another question which is frequently posed in the connection of biological memories concerns the *reconstruction* of recollections. It is apparent that we experience the mental images as if they had the same structure as the objects that they represent. If, on the other hand, the observations are decomposed into features, it then may seem necessary to have an inverse transformation by which the original appearance is reproduced. The requirement of inverse transformation, however, seems to be based on false reasoning; for one thing, even if this were possible, how would we then be able to analyze the reconstructed mental image? We would need another set of "sensory detectors", etc. Philosophically this would lead to the problem of "regression", and such a chain of successive mappings would have no end. For practical reasons it seems necessary to abandon the requirement of reconstruction.

It should be realized that whatever transformations there appear in the neural system which lead to an organized perception, *these transformations are probably identical during immediate sensory observation and reminiscence.* It has sometimes been said that the brain is "blind", i.e., within itself it has no sensory organs but has to operate on the incoming signals. On the other hand, the problem of cognition belongs to the faculty of philosophical problems, and can hardly be concretized. We have to assume that "the cognitive ability is there" although it is not necessary or possible to know whether it ensues from the properties of very large systems, or possibly from some "spiritual" factors. However, it seems possible to ignore this problem, if a practical stand is taken: *the mental state can be correlated with those signals which are obtained from a system containing memory.* The purpose of memory is then only to reproduce these output signals.

The above approach to the problem of recollections can nicely be dressed into the form of a principle which is termed *the principle of virtual images.*

Similar descriptions have been used in physics, especially in field theories of which we probably have very concrete experience: the images produced by all mirrors are virtual, and they are experienced as real. It is also possible to understand the virtual images produced by lens optics, holograms, etc. Why would it be hard to accept this principle if it were related to signal networks such as those formed by the neural fibers?

In most models of memory presented up to now, it has been stipulated that the memorized signals should be reconstructed during recall. Reconstructivity places severe demands on physical systems, e.g., neural networks. But we are going to show that the reconstruction of items can be made virtually.

In order to fully understand the principle of virtual images, we must take the nervous system as a whole that has different hierarchical levels. It is not necessary to know exactly how images are perceived by it; instead, it is assumed that some higher-level system or organizational function performs this, and *this system then operates on the signals obtained from a lower-level system that contains memory.* The memory traces have been formed by earlier input signals, but they are not directly observable. On the other hand, they cause perturbations in the input-output transfer relations of the network. *The higher system, acting like an analyzer, then assumes that the "memory" network is undisturbed but the perturbation is caused by additional virtual input signals that represent the recalled item* [1.8, 9].

Analytically, the principle of virtual images can be expressed in the following way whereby it lends itself to many different network models. It seems even possible to demonstrate various kinds of perceptory *illusions* with its help.

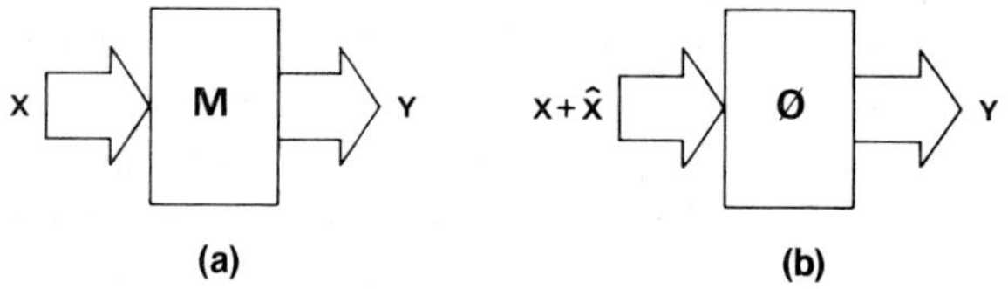

Fig. 1.12a, b. Illustration of the principle of virtual images

(a)   (b)

Consider the signal-transferring block shown in Fig. 1.12. In Fig. 1.12a, its state, denoted by M, contains memory traces. As the internal state is not directly observable, it would be natural to interpret the signals Y, as shown in Fig. 1.12b, as resulting from a transformation in an *empty* memory (with state $\emptyset$), and instead having an *effective input excitation* that contains the real input X as well as a "virtual image" $\hat{X}$. In this way, if Y stands for a set of output signals, one obtains, according to the previous considerations:

$$Y = F(X, M) = F(X + \hat{X}, \emptyset) \tag{1.5}$$

from which, given the law by which M is formed, $\hat{X}$ can be solved (accurately or approximately, e.g., in the sense of least squares).

We do not intend to carry out any more detailed analysis here; this general formulation, however, may be influential to many detailed studies.

1.4.5 The Logic of Stored Knowledge

Certain structured relations between data patterns were already reflected in the sequential recall processes, discussed in Sect. 1.3.2. In addition to these "temporal associations" certain *spatial* structures between representations are realized in the self-organizing processes of Chap. 5.

If we approach the problem of representation of knowledge from a more abstract point of view, it is also possible to consider the *meaning* expressed by such structures; for instance, we could try to find out how structures are able to represent the meaning of a word or a sentence, when the latter occur in the context of other representations.

One possibility for the definition of pure structures, especially for the representation and analysis of linguistic expressions, is to introduce *relations* which consist of ordered sets of items. It is possible to create rather complicated structures from elementary relations as will be seen below, and a widely held view is that knowledge in general might be representable by such relational graphs.

Relations. A linguistic relation between two expressions x and y is defined, for instance, by a statement of the type "the attribute R of object x is y". In this case x and R can be regarded as arguments of a *function* which attains the value y. Usually the domains of x and R consist of finite sets of discrete values (words or clauses) so that if the format of this statement is fixed, symbolically it is defined by an ordered triple (R, x, y). Variables in the ordered triple are often given the particular meanings A = "attribute", O = "object", and V = "value". An expression (A, O, V) is then read "the A of O is V". It may be obvious that there also exist more complex forms of linguistic statements which are defined by different kinds of relations, eventually involving more than three items.

Sometimes a notation $x \xrightarrow{R} y$ is used for the simplest type of relation which is then read "x is related to y by R".

Examples of relational triples are given below. Consider the following variables: $A \in$ {pronunciation, colour}, $0 \in$ {one, apple}, and $V \in$ {wən, red}. Then "one" is related to "wən" by the fact that "the pronunciation of one is wən", and an "apple" is related to "red" by the fact that "the colour of apple is red". Formally these statements can be represented as the triples (pronunciation, one, wən) and (colour, apple, red).

Relations are implementable in any physical memory as arrays of stored symbolic tokens corresponding to the variables. The role of A, O, and V is clear from the positions in the array. If there were an access to this memory on the basis of the pair (A, O), then the connected value V could be retrieved. The triples (A, O, V) can also be made accessible by programming methods on the basis of any of their elements. The searching operations thereby applied may become more clear from the following.

Structures of Relations. The formation of abstract structures of relations is illustrated next. The ordered triple notation (A, O, V) is used in the declaration of the relations. The notation $O \xrightarrow{A} V$, on the other hand, is useful for the representation of connections in abstract graphs that result. Consider the facts summarized in Table 1.1.

Table 1.1. Stored triples

Fact	Formal representation
Brother of Ann is Steve	(brother, Ann, Steve)
Father of Ann is Pete	(father, Ann, Pete)
Father of Pete is Sam	(father, Pete, Sam)
Sex of Ann is female	(sex, Ann, female)
Sex of Pete is male	(sex, Pete, male)
Residence of Pete is London	(residence, Pete, London)
Residence of Ann is London	(residence, Ann, London)

An abstract structure of cross-references, depicted in Fig. 1.13, then follows. Note that the invidual elements may occur in many declarations, although in the abstract graph they have been mentioned only once, in principle at least. Apparently the complexity of the graph depends on the number and type of facts (relations) declared.

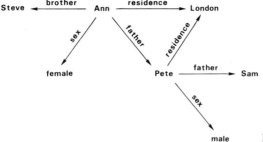

Fig. 1.13. A relational structure

It should be carefully noticed that *the structure of the graph has in no way really been represented in memory;* it is completely abstract or implicit, although its existence can be confirmed by tracing the cross-references. This may be regarded as a pragmatic property. Retrieval of knowledge from this graph needs a computational process exemplified below.

For the search of relevant information, the following strategy may be used. For instance, if all the stored triples shown in Table 1.1 were accessible by any of their elements, as the case is with autoassociative memories, then, to answer a question of the type "who is the father of Ann?" the following search could be executed: first, all triples with attribute "father" could be retrieved, and temporarily recorded, then the triples with occurrences of "Ann" could be found, and finally the intersection of these sets of triples could be computed, to find "Pete". Apparently, this is not a very natural process, although completely expedient for a computer. An attempt to devise a neural implementation for it will be given in Sect. 8.2.3.

On the Interpretation of Relations as Associations. Are the relations and associations one and the same thing? This question needs closer examination. Consider the following types of claims that occur in the literature: "An association is a two-termed relation, involving three symbols, one of which names the relation, the other two its arguments" [1.10]; "a relation consists of three components, an ordered pair of items and a link which specifies the type of association which relates items" [1.11]; and "an association is an ordered triple (A, O, V) of items ... called the components of the association" [1.12]. What has been said above is essentially that a relation $O \xrightarrow{A} V$ is thought to link the terms O and V, or that all components in a triple (A, O, V) are mutually linked. Apparently A cannot be understood as a simple link because it contains the representation for a label; a more expedient view might be that all elements $A, O,$ and V that have been stored together in this specific order are associated. But since items may be linked by the cross-references in an abstract way which also can be thought to form associations, the concept of association must be definable in a more general fashion, maybe using many more concomitant attributes.

2. Pattern Mathematics

When dealing with spatially or temporally related samples of signal values that represent "information", one needs a mathematical framework for the description of their quantitative interrelations. This is often provided by the vector formalism. The operations in vector spaces, on the other hand, can conveniently be manipulated by matrix algebra. These topics form the main contents of this section.

As a mathematical representation, this section is more referential than formally complete; it is intended to serve solely as a collection of notations and results used elsewhere in the book, for their better readability. It is to be remarked that especially in matrix algebra plenty of alternative notations are used. The nomenclature and symbols selected for this text are used by the majority of writers in these fields. For the application of the results it is urged that the reader familiarize himself with some central works on modern matrix algebra of which the excellent book of *Albert* [2.1] perhaps better than any other single text covers the formalism used here.

2.1 Mathematical Notations and Methods

2.1.1 Vector Space Concepts

Representation Vectors. Especially in the physical theory of information processes, spatially or temporally adjacent signal values are thought to form *patterns* which can be understood as ordered sets of real numbers. In pursuance of the methods developed in the theory of pattern recognition (cf. references in Chap. 7) such sets are described by *representation vectors* which are generalizations of the vectors of plane and space geometry. If there are n independently defined and somehow related real numerical values $\xi_1, \xi_2, \ldots, \xi_n$, they can be understood as coordinates in a space which has n dimensions. This space is denoted R^n and it is the set all possible n-tuples of real numbers each of which is from the interval $(-\infty, +\infty)$. (Note that a scalar is defined in the space $R^1 = R$.) Hereupon the scalars are denoted by lower-case Greek letters and vectors by lower-case Roman letters, unless otherwise stated. All indices and exponents, however, are denoted in Roman. A vector x is a point in R^n (expressed $x \in R^n$), the coordinates of which are $\xi_1, \xi_2, \ldots, \xi_n$. To visualize a vector (although this may be difficult in a multidimensional space) it may be imagined as a directed line from the origin to the point in question.

Consider a representation vector which is put to stand for optical patterns. These are usually composed of picture elements like a mosaic, and every picture element attains a scalar real value. The indexing of the elements can now be made in an arbitrary fashion. In Fig. 2.1, three different examples of indexing are shown.

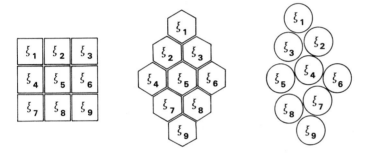

Fig. 2.1. Examples of pattern "vectors"

In all of them, the formal representation vector then attains the form $(\xi_1, \xi_2, \ldots, \xi_9)$. It should be noticed that this is a *linear array of numbers* in spite of the original images being two-dimensional.

Linear Vector Spaces. For analytical purposes, it will be necessary to define the concept of a vector space. A *linear vector space* $\mathcal{V}$ (over the reals) is generally defined as a set of elements, the vectors, in which the operations of vector addition $(+)$ and (scalar) multiplication $(\cdot)$ have been defined, and the following facts hold true: if $x, y, z \in \mathcal{V}$ are vectors and $\alpha, \beta \in R$ are scalars, then

A1) $x + y = y + x \in \mathcal{V}$ (commutativity)

A2) $\alpha \cdot (x + y) = \alpha \cdot x + \alpha \cdot y \in \mathcal{V}$ ⎫

A3) $(\alpha + \beta) \cdot x = \alpha \cdot x + \beta \cdot x$ ⎬   (distributivity)

A4) $(x+y)+z = x+(y+z)$ $\left.\begin{array}{c}\\\\\end{array}\right\}$ (associativity)

A5) $(\alpha \cdot \beta) \cdot x = \alpha \cdot (\beta \cdot x)$

A6)   There exists a zero vector 0 such that for every $x \in \mathscr{V}$, $x + 0 = x$.

A7)   For scalars 0 and 1, $0 \cdot x = 0$ and $1 \cdot x = x$.

An example of $\mathscr{V}$ would be R^n. The sum of two vectors is then defined as a vector with elements (coordinates, components) which are obtained by summing up the respective elements of the addends. The scalar multiplication is an operation in which all elements of a vector are multiplied by this scalar. (For simplicity of notation, the dot may be dropped.)

Inner Product. The concept of *inner product* refers to a two-argument, scalar-valued function which has been introduced to facilitate an analytic description of certain geometric operations. One very important case of inner product of vectors $x = (\xi_1, \ldots, \xi_n)$ and $y = (\eta_1, \ldots, \eta_n)$ is their *scalar product* defined as

$$(x, y) = \xi_1 \eta_1 + \xi_2 \eta_2 + \ldots + \xi_n \eta_n, \tag{2.1}$$

and unless otherwise stated, the inner product is assumed to have this functional form. It should be pointed out, however, that there are infinitely many choices for inner products, for instance, variants of (2.1) where the elements of the vectors are weighted differently, or enter the function (x, y) with different powers (Sect. 2.2.1).

In general, the inner product of two elements x and y in a set, by convention, must have the following properties. Assume that the addition of the elements, and multiplication of an element by a scalar have been defined. If the inner product function is now denoted by (x, y), there must hold

B1) $(x, y) = (y, x)$

B2) $(\alpha x, y) = \alpha(x, y)$

B3) $(x_1 + x_2, y) = (x_1, y) + (x_2, y)$

B4) $(x, x) \geqslant 0$ where equality holds if and only if x is the zero element.

Metric. In practice, all observable vectors must be represented in a space which has a *metric*. The latter is a property of any set of elements characterized by another function called *distance* $d(x, y)$ between all pairs of elements. For the choice of the distance function, the following conditions must hold:

C1) $d(x, y) \geqslant 0$ where equality holds if and only if $x = y$.

C2) $d(x, y) = d(y, x)$

C3) $d(x, y) \leqslant d(x, z) + d(z, y)$.

An example of distance is the *Euclidean distance* in a rectangular coordinate system, which is almost exclusively used in this book: for the vectors $x = (\xi_1, \ldots, \xi_n)$ and $y = (\eta_1, \ldots, \eta_n)$,

$$d(x, y) = \sqrt[+]{(\xi_1 - \eta_1)^2 + (\xi_2 - \eta_2)^2 + \ldots + (\xi_n - \eta_n)^2} \, . \tag{2.2}$$

Another example of distances is the *Hamming distance* which has been defined for binary vectors; a binary vector has elements which are either 0 or 1. The Hamming distance indicates in how many positions (elements) the two vectors are different. Apparently the rules C1 to C3 are valid for Hamming distances, too.

Norm. The magnitude of a vector can be defined in different ways. The name *norm* is used for it, and in general, the norm, in a set of elements for which scalar multiplication, addition, and the zero element have been defined, is a function $\|x\|$ of an element x for which the following rules must be valid:

D1) $\|x\| \geqslant 0$, and the equality holds if and only if $x = 0$.

D2) $\|\alpha x\| = |\alpha| \, \|x\|$ where $|\alpha|$ is the absolute value of α.

D3) $\|x_1 + x_2\| \leqslant \|x_1\| + \|x_2\|$.

The *Euclidean norm* can be defined by the scalar product:

$$\|x\| = \sqrt[+]{(x, x)} = \sqrt[+]{\xi_1^2 + \xi_2^2 + \ldots + \xi_n^2} \, . \tag{2.3}$$

Notice that the Euclidean distance $d(x, y)$ is equivalent to the Euclidean norm $\|x - y\|$. A space in which Euclidean distance and norm have been defined is called Euclidean space.

Angles and Orthogonality. Generalization of the usual concept of angle for higher-dimensional spaces is straightforward. The angle θ between two Euclidean vectors x and y is defined by

$$\cos \theta = \frac{(x, y)}{\|x\| \, \|y\|} \, . \tag{2.4}$$

Accordingly, the two vectors are said to be *orthogonal* and denoted $x \perp y$ when their inner product vanishes.

Linear Manifolds. The vectors x_1, x_2, ..., x_k are said to be *linearly independent* if their weighted sum, or the linear combination

$$\alpha_1 x_1 + \alpha_2 x_2 + \ldots + \alpha_k x_k \tag{2.5}$$

cannot become zero unless $\alpha_1 = \alpha_2 = \ldots = \alpha_k = 0$. Accordingly if the sum expression can be made zero for some choice of the α-coefficients all of which are not zero, the vectors are *linearly dependent*. Some of the vectors then can be expressed as linear combinations of the others. Examples of linear dependence can be visualized in the three-dimensional space R^3: three or more vectors are linearly dependent if they lie in a plane that passes through the origin, because then each vector can be expressed as a weighted sum of the others (as shown by the dashed-line constructions in Fig. 2.2).

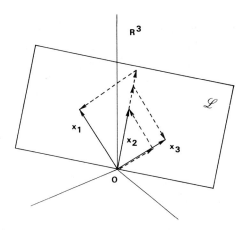

Fig. 2.2. Exemplification of linear dependence

Consider all possible linear combinations of the vectors x_1, x_2, ..., x_k where k is at most the dimensionality n; they are obtained when the α-coefficients take on all real values from $(-\infty, +\infty)$. The set of all linear combinations is called a *subspace* in R^n and denoted by $\mathcal{L}$. Examples of subspaces are planes and straight lines in R^3 which pass through the origin. In higher-dimensional spaces, very important linear subspaces are those *hyperplanes* which are defined as linear combinations of $n-1$ linearly independent vectors, and which divide R^n into two halfspaces. Now all linear subspaces, including R^n, are also named *linear manifolds,* and the set of vectors which define the manifold is said to *span* it. It is to be noted that the manifold spanned by the above vectors is k-dimensional if the vectors are linearly independent. In this case the vectors x_1, x_2, ..., x_k are called the *basis vectors of* $\mathcal{L}$.

Orthogonal Spaces. A vector x is said to be orthogonal to subspace $\mathscr{L}$ if it is orthogonal to every vector in it (abbreviated $x \perp \mathscr{L}$). Two subspaces $\mathscr{L}_1$ and $\mathscr{L}_2$ are said to be orthogonal to each other ($\mathscr{L}_1 \perp \mathscr{L}_2$) if every vector of $\mathscr{L}_1$ is orthogonal to every vector of $\mathscr{L}_2$. An example of orthogonal subspaces in R^3 are a coordinate axis and the plane of the two other axes of a rectangular coordinate system.

Orthogonal Projections. Below it will be pointed out that if $\mathscr{L}$ is a subspace of R^n, then an arbitrary vector $x \in R^n$ can be uniquely decomposed into the sum of two vectors of which one, $\hat{x}$, belongs to $\mathscr{L}$ and the other, $\tilde{x}$, is orthogonal to it.

Assume tentatively that there exist two decompositions

$$x = \hat{y} + \tilde{y} = \hat{z} + \tilde{z}, \tag{2.6}$$

where $\hat{y}$ and $\hat{z}$ belong to $\mathscr{L}$ and $\tilde{y} \perp \mathscr{L}$, $\tilde{z} \perp \mathscr{L}$. Now $\tilde{z} - \tilde{y} \perp \mathscr{L}$, but since $\tilde{z} - \tilde{y} = \hat{y} - \hat{z}$, then $\tilde{z} - \tilde{y} \in \mathscr{L}$. Consequently $\tilde{z} - \tilde{y}$ has thus been shown to be orthogonal to itself, or $(\tilde{z} - \tilde{y}, \tilde{z} - \tilde{y}) = 0$ which cannot hold in general unless $\tilde{z} = \tilde{y}$. This proves that the decomposition is unique.

The proof of the existence of the decomposition will be postponed until an orthogonal basis has been introduced. Let us tentatively assume that the decomposition exists,

$$x = \hat{x} + \tilde{x}, \quad \text{where} \quad \hat{x} \in \mathscr{L} \quad \text{and} \quad \tilde{x} \perp \mathscr{L}. \tag{2.7}$$

Hereupon $\hat{x}$ will be called the *orthogonal projection* of x on $\mathscr{L}$; it will also be useful to introduce the space $\mathscr{L}^{\perp}$ which is named the *orthogonal complement* of $\mathscr{L}$; it is the set of all vectors in R^n which are orthogonal to $\mathscr{L}$. Then $\tilde{x}$ is called the orthogonal projection of x on $\mathscr{L}^{\perp}$. The orthogonal projections are very fundamental to the theory of optimal associative mappings discussed in this book.

The Projection Theorem. One particular property of the orthogonal projections is important for the discussion of approximations: of all decompositions of the form $x = x' + x''$ where $x' \in \mathscr{L}$, the one into orthogonal projections has the property that $\|x''\|$ is minimum. This is called the *projection theorem*. To prove it, use is made of the definition $\|x'\|^2 = (x', x')$ and the facts that $\hat{x} - x' \in \mathscr{L}$, $x - \hat{x} = \tilde{x} \perp \mathscr{L}$, whereby $(\hat{x} - x', x - \hat{x}) = 0$. The following expansion then yields

$$\|x - x'\|^2 = (x - \hat{x} + \hat{x} - x', x - \hat{x} + \hat{x} - x') = \|x - \hat{x}\|^2 + \|\hat{x} - x'\|^2. \tag{2.8}$$

Because the squared norms are always positive or zero, there can be written

$$\|x - x'\|^2 \geq \|x - \hat{x}\|^2 \tag{2.9}$$

from which it is directly seen that $x'' = x - x'$ is minimum for $x' = \hat{x}$ whereby $x'' = \tilde{x}$.

Orthogonal projections in a three-dimensional space are visualized in Fig. 2.3.

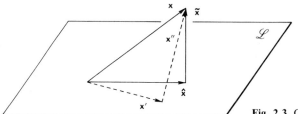

Fig. 2.3. Orthogonal projections in R^3

The Gram-Schmidt Orthogonalization Process. For the computation of the orthogonal projections, and to prove that an arbitrary vector can be decomposed as discussed above, a classical method named *Gram-Schmidt orthogonalization process* can be used. Its original purpose is to construct an *orthogonal vector basis* for any linear space R^k, i.e., to find a set of basis vectors which are mutually orthogonal and which span R^k.

To start with, consider the nonzero vectors $x_1, x_2, \ldots, x_p, p \geq k$ which span the space R^k. For a vector basis, one direction can be chosen freely whereby the first new basis vector is selected as $h_1 = x_1$. Unless x_2 has the same direction as x_1, it is easily found that the vector

$$h_2 = x_2 - \frac{(x_2, h_1)}{\|h_1\|^2} h_1 \tag{2.10}$$

is orthogonal to $h_1 = x_1$; the inner product (h_2, h_1) is zero. Therefore, h_2 can be chosen for the new basis vector. If, on the other hand, x_2 had the same direction as x_1, it would be represented by x_1, and can thus be ignored. Consider now the sequence of vectors $\{h_i\}$ where each new member is constructed according to the recursive rule

$$h_i = x_i - \sum_{j=1}^{i-1} \frac{(x_i, h_j)}{\|h_j\|^2} h_j, \tag{2.11}$$

where the sum over j shall include terms with nonzero h_j only. In this way a set of vectors h_i is obtained. To prove that all the h_i are mutually orthogonal, the method of complete induction can be used. Assume that this rule is correct up to $i-1$, i.e., the h_1, h_2, ..., h_{i-1} are mutually orthogonal, which means that for all $q < i$, and for nonzero h_j, h_q, $(h_j, h_q) = \|h_j\| \cdot \|h_q\| \cdot \delta_{jq}$ where δ_{jq} is the Kronecker symbol ($= 1$ for $j = q$, $= 0$ for $j \neq q$). By a substitution there follows

$$(h_i, h_q) = \begin{cases} (x_i, h_q) - (x_i, h_q) = 0 & \text{if} \quad h_q \neq 0 \\ (x_i, h_q) = 0 & \text{if} \quad h_q = 0 . \end{cases} \tag{2.12}$$

Therefore the rule is correct up to i, and thus generally.

From the way in which the h-vectors were constructed, there directly follows that the h_1, ..., h_i span exactly the same space as the x_1, ..., x_i do. When the process is carried out for the vectors x_1, x_2, ..., x_p among which there are known to exist k linearly independent vectors, the space R^k will be spanned exactly.

If a further vector $x \in R^n$ that may or may not belong to space R^k shall be decomposed into its orthogonal projections $\hat{x} \in R^k$ and $\tilde{x} \perp R^k$, the Gram-Schmidt process is simply continued one step further whereby $\tilde{x} = h_{p+1}$, $\hat{x} = x - h_{p+1}$.

Since the above process is always possible, and it was earlier shown that the decomposition is unique, the so-called *decomposition theorem* can now be stated: an arbitrary vector $x \in R^n$ can uniquely be decomposed into two vectors of which one is in a subspace $\mathscr{L}$ of R^n and the other is orthogonal to it.

Hyperspheres. Examples of vector sets which are not linear spaces are hyperspheres and their surfaces. These concepts are important in the discussion of projective mappings of pattern vectors. In the N-dimensional Euclidean space R^N, a hypersphere with radius ρ is the set of all points which lie within a distance ρ from the origin. The N-dimensional volume is a straightforward generalization of the three-dimensional one, being an integral of the volume elements $d\xi_1 d\xi_2 \ldots d\xi_N$, as expressed in a rectangular coordinate system.

Hyperspheres have been discussed in statistical mechanics. The volume of an N-dimensional sphere with radius ρ is (e.g., [2.2])

$$V_N = \frac{\pi^{N/2}}{(\frac{1}{2}N)!} \rho^N \quad \text{for even} \quad N,$$

$$V_N = \frac{2^N \pi^{(N-1)/2} (\frac{1}{2}N - \frac{1}{2})!}{N!} \rho^N \quad \text{for odd} \quad N, \tag{2.13}$$

or, in general, of the form $V_N(\rho) = \alpha_N \rho^N$ where α_N is a numerical constant. Equations (2.13) can also be expressed recursively,

$$V_{N+2}(\rho) = \frac{2\pi\rho^2}{N+2} V_N(\rho),$$ (2.14)

and two series of formulas (for N even and odd, respectively) can be computed starting with $V_2(\rho) = \pi\rho^2$ and $V_3(\rho) = 4\pi\rho^3/3$. The surface area of a hypersphere is obtained from $V_N(\rho)$ by differentiating it with respect to ρ.

Some of the lowest-order expressions for $V_N(\rho)$ and surface area have been represented in Table 2.1.

Table 2.1. Formulas for hyperspheres

Dimensionality N	Volume $V_N(\rho)$	Surface area $dV_N(\rho)/d\rho$
0	1 (point)	0
1	2ρ (line segment)	2 (two points)
2	$\pi\rho^2$	$2\pi\rho$
3	$4\pi\rho^3/3$	$4\pi\rho^2$
4	$\pi^2\rho^4/2$	$2\pi^2\rho^3$
5	$8\pi^2\rho^5/7$	$40\pi^2\rho^4/7$
6	$\pi^3\rho^6/6$	$\pi^3\rho^5$

Mass Projection of a Homogeneous Hypersphere. (The following discussion relies on a geometrical imagination of spaces which can be represented by illustrations only for R, R^2, and R^3, but may be difficult to visualize in a higher-dimensional case. Although the results are important for the discussion of associative mappings, their derivation may be skipped here without affecting the reading of the rest.)

One of the central features of the optimal associative mappings discussed below is that they orthogonally project representation vectors on subspaces of R^n, spanned by a set of *reference vectors*. If a representation vector happens to be of the form $x = x_i + v$ where x_i is one of the reference vectors which span a space $\mathscr{L}$ and v is a random vector from R^n, then apparently x_i is not changed in a projection operation, because it already lies in $\mathscr{L}$. On the other hand, since v is a general vector of R^n, it is probable that its projection is shorter. The central question is how much on the average the norm is reduced in the projection. This will be qualitatively shown for a simple distribution of v.

Consider a hypersphere with radius ρ in R^n that has a homogeneous mass distribution, i.e., in which the hypothetical number of vectors or points per differential n-dimensional volume element is constant within the sphere and zero outside. The projection of the sphere on subspace $\mathscr{L}$ is obtained, when every point is separately projected, and the density of the projections is computed. In order to keep track on the argumentation, it may be useful to consult the two examples of Fig. 2.4 that can be illustrated.

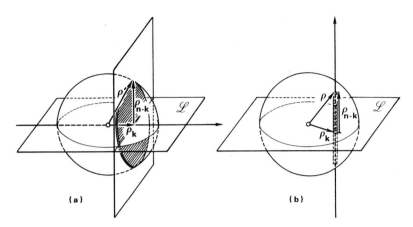

Fig. 2.4a, b. Projections of a sphere on subspaces of R^3

In Fig. 2.4a, a sphere is projected on a straight line; in Fig. 2.4b, the subspace onto which the projection is due is a plane. If the original space was n-dimensional and the subspace k-dimensional, then the set of all vectors which are orthogonal to $\mathscr{L}$ is an $(n-k)$-dimensional space named $\mathscr{L}^{\perp}$. Consider a point in $\mathscr{L}$ the distance of which from the origin is ρ_k, being less than or equal to the radius ρ. Consider further a differential volume element dV_k in $\mathscr{L}$ at this point (line element in Fig. 2.4a, surface element in Fig. 2.4b); the *projection density* $\mu(\rho_k)$ is now defined by the number of points in a slice of the original sphere which have their projection on dV_k. Since dV_k was assumed infinitesimal, apparently the following generalized Pythagorean formula is valid (it was in fact derived in (2.2)):

$$\rho^2 = \rho_k^2 + \rho_{n-k}^2 \tag{2.15}$$

with notations which may be obvious from Fig. 2.4. Now, although a strict mathematical proof is not given here, it may be obvious on account of spherical symmetry that the above slice of the original hypersphere is also a hypersphere, albeit of a lower dimension $n-k$. (It is a circular plate in Fig. 2.4a, and a line segment in Fig. 2.4b.) Consequently, the projection density on dV_k, denoted by $\mu(\rho_k)$, is obtained by using (2.13):

$$\mu(\rho_k) = \alpha_{n-k}(\rho^2 - \rho_k^2)^{(n-k)/2}. \tag{2.16}$$

The next task is to compute the root-mean-square (rms) distance of the points of the original hypersphere from the origin, and to compare it with the corresponding rms distance of the mass projection in $\mathscr{L}$. In averaging, it should be carefully noticed that all points in $\mathscr{L}$ which have the distance ρ_k from the origin must lie on a k-dimensional spherical shell with radius ρ_k. After these considerations, the rms distances in R^n and $\mathscr{L}$, denoted by σ_n and σ_k, respectively, can be computed:

$$\sigma_k^2 = \frac{\int\limits_0^\rho \rho_k^2 \mu(\rho_k) k \, \alpha_k \rho_k^{k-1} d\rho_k}{\int\limits_0^\rho \mu(\rho_k) k \, \alpha_k \rho_k^{k-1} d\rho_k},$$

$$\sigma_n^2 = \frac{\int\limits_0^\rho \rho^2 n \, \alpha_n \rho^{n-1} d\rho}{V_n(\rho)},$$

(2.17)

or, after substitution of $\zeta = \rho_k/\rho$ and some simplification,

$$\sigma_k^2 = \rho^2 \frac{\int\limits_0^1 \zeta^{k+1}(1-\zeta^2)^{(n-k)/2} d\zeta}{\int\limits_0^1 \zeta^{k-1}(1-\zeta^2)^{(n-k)/2} d\zeta},$$

$$\sigma_n^2 = \frac{n}{n+2} \rho^2.$$

(2.18)

The numerator and denominator in σ_k^2 can be expressed in terms of the *beta function* which is defined as

$$B(a, b) = 2\int\limits_0^1 \zeta^{2a-1}(1-\zeta^2)^{b-1} d\zeta,$$

(2.19)

whereby

$$\sigma_k^2 = \frac{B\left(\dfrac{k+2}{2}, \dfrac{n-k+2}{2}\right) \rho^2}{B\left(\dfrac{k}{2}, \dfrac{n-k+2}{2}\right)}.$$

(2.20)

By application of the following generally known formulae

$$B(a, b) = \frac{\Gamma(a)\,\Gamma(b)}{\Gamma(a+b)}, \quad \Gamma(a+1) = a\Gamma(a) \quad (a > 0), \tag{2.21}$$

where $\Gamma(\cdot)$ is the *gamma function*, there is obtained

$$\sigma_k^2 = \frac{k\rho^2}{n+2} \tag{2.22}$$

and finally

$$\sigma_k/\sigma_n = \sqrt{k/n}\,. \tag{2.23}$$

The result of this analysis has even more generality because it can be shown that it holds exactly for other spherically symmetrical mass distributions, too; for instance, for a spherical shell or for a multivariate symmetric Gaussian distribution. The validity for a distribution which is uniform in a hypercube centered around the origin (nonspherical case) has been demonstrated in [2.3]. Other nonspherical distributions give values for σ_k/σ_n which qualitatively comply with the $\sqrt{k/n}$-law.

2.1.2 Matrix Notations

Matrices, Their Sums, and Matrix Products. The concept of a matrix may be generally known. It might be necessary to point out that formally matrices are ordered sets of numbers or scalar variables indexed by a pair of indices. If index k runs through $(1, 2, \ldots, p)$, l through $(1, 2, \ldots, q)$, and m through $(1, 2, \ldots, r)$ the following ordered sets of elements α_{kl} and β_{lm} can be named matrices. The sum of two matrices (of the same dimensionality) is a matrix in which every element is a sum of the respective elements of the addends. The *matrix product* of sets $A = (\alpha_{kl})$ and $B = (\beta_{lm})$ is defined by

$$A \cdot B = C, \tag{2.24}$$

where C is a further ordered set (γ_{km}) with elements defined by

$$\gamma_{km} = \sum_{l=1}^{q} \alpha_{kl}\beta_{lm}. \tag{2.25}$$

The definition of the matrix product has been introduced for the description of linear transformations by operator products.

For brevity, the dot symbol in matrix products may be dropped. A matrix product is defined only for such pairs of indices in which an element like l

above is common. Multiplication by a scalar is defined as multiplication of all elements with it.

Matrix-Vector Products. A vector is an ordered set, and can be understood as a matrix with one-index elements. Consider the matrix $A = (\alpha_{kl})$, and four vectors $b = (\beta_k)$, $c = (\gamma_l)$, $d = (\delta_l)$, and $e = (\varepsilon_k)$, where k runs through $(1, 2, \ldots, p)$ and l through $(1, 2, \ldots, q)$. The following matrix-vector products are then defined:

$$c = b \cdot A \quad \text{where} \quad \gamma_l = \sum_{k=1}^{p} \beta_k \alpha_{kl},$$

$$e = A \cdot d \quad \text{where} \quad \varepsilon_k = \sum_{l=1}^{q} \alpha_{kl} \delta_l. \tag{2.26}$$

Notice again the compatibility of indices.

Linear Transformations. The main reason for the introduction of matrices is a possibility to denote and manipulate with linear transformation operations on vectors. The transformation of vector x into vector y is generally denoted by function $y = T(x)$. In order to call T a *linear transformation*, it is a necessary and sufficient condition that for $x_1, x_2 \in R^n$,

$$T(\alpha x_1 + \beta x_2) = \alpha T(x_1) + \beta T(x_2) . \tag{2.27}$$

The general linear transformation of vector $x = (\xi_1, \xi_2, \ldots, \xi_n)$ into vector $y = (\eta_1, \eta_2, \ldots, \eta_n)$ can be expressed in the element form as

$$\eta_i = \sum_{j=1}^{n} \alpha_{ij} \xi_j \tag{2.28}$$

with the α_{ij} parameters defining the transformation.

Equation (2.28) can be expressed symbolically as a matrix-vector product. If A is an ordered set of parameters (α_{ij}), there follows from the above definitions that

$$y = A \cdot x . \tag{2.29}$$

The above definition of the matrix-vector product makes it possible to describe successive transformations by transitive operators: if $y = A \cdot x$ and $z = B \cdot y$, then $z = B \cdot A \cdot x$.

Array Representation for Matrices. For better visualization, matrices can be represented as rectangular arrays of numbers. Below, only matrices consisting of real numbers are considered. The dimensionality of a matrix is expressed by the product of rows and columns; for instance an $m \times n$ matrix has m (horizontal) rows and n (vertical) columns. Matrices are denoted by capital Roman letters, and when they are written explicitly, brackets are used around the array.

The *transpose* of any matrix is obtained by rewriting all columns as rows, whereby a notation X^T is used for the transpose of X. For instance,

$$X = \begin{bmatrix} 1 & 5 \\ 2 & 1 \\ 3 & 3 \end{bmatrix}, \quad X^T = \begin{bmatrix} 1 & 2 & 3 \\ 5 & 1 & 3 \end{bmatrix}.$$

Row and Column Vectors. Since one-row and one-column matrices are linear arrays of numbers, they can be understood as vectors, called *row* and *column vectors,* respectively. Such vectors can be denoted by lower-case letters. In a matrix-vector product, the row vector always stands on the left, and the column vector on the right. For reasons which become more apparent below, representation patterns are normally understood as column vectors. For better clarity, column vectors are normally denoted by simple lower case letters like x, whereas row vectors are written in the transpose notation as x^T. Within the text, for typographic reasons, column vectors are usually written in the form $[\xi_1, \xi_2, \ldots, \xi_n]^T$ where the commas are used for clarity.

Symmetric, Diagonal, and Unit Matrices. A matrix is called symmetric if it is identical with its transpose, i.e., it is symmetric with respect to the main diagonal whereby it also must be square. A matrix is called diagonal if it has zeroes elsewhere except on the main diagonal. If all diagonal elements of a diagonal matrix are unities, the matrix is a *unit matrix,* denoted by I.

Indexing and Partitioning of the Matrices. The matrix elements, denoted by Greek letters, are identified by double indices for the rows and columns, respectively. Sometimes it will be necessary to compose a rectangular matrix from rows or columns which have a special meaning: for instance, in a so-called observation matrix X, representation vectors $x_1, x_2, \ldots, x_n$ may appear as columns and the matrix can then be written as $X = [x_1\, x_2 \ldots x_n]$.

Partitioning of the matrices can also be made more generally into rectangular submatrices. In the transposition of a partitioned matrix, the submatrices change their positions like the scalars in a normal matrix, and in addition they are transposed:

$$\begin{bmatrix} A & B \\ \hline C & D \end{bmatrix}^T = \begin{bmatrix} A^T & C^T \\ \hline B^T & D^T \end{bmatrix}.$$

For typographic reasons, the dashed lines are often dropped within the text and possibly replaced by a comma. For instance, an observation matrix can be written $X = [x_1, x_2, \ldots, x_n]$.

In the product of partitioned matrices, submatrices are operated according to the same rules as elements in matrix products. Submatrices then must have dimensionalities for which the matrix products are defined. For instance,

$$\begin{bmatrix} A & B \\ C & D \end{bmatrix} \begin{bmatrix} E \\ F \end{bmatrix} = \begin{bmatrix} AE + BF \\ CE + DF \end{bmatrix}.$$

Comment. It is possible to regard an $m \times n$ matrix as an element of the real space $R^{m \times n}$.

Some Formulas for Matrix Operations. In general, matrix products are not commutative, but they are associative and distributive. The following formulas can be proven when written in component form:

E1) $IA = AI = A$

E2) $(AB)C = A(BC)$

E3) $A(B+C) = AB + AC$

E4) $(A^T)^T = A$

E5) $(A+B)^T = A^T + B^T$

E6) $(AB)^T = B^T A^T$.

It should be noticed that in a product of two matrices the former one must always have as many columns as the latter one has rows, otherwise the summation over all indices is not defined.

Hadamard Products. There exists another type of matrix product which has a simpler multiplication rule, and which has applications in some nonlinear problems. The *Hadamard product* $C = (\gamma_{ij})$ of matrices $A = (\alpha_{ij})$ and $B = (\beta_{ij})$ is defined as

$$C = A \otimes B \quad \text{where} \quad \gamma_{ij} = \alpha_{ij} \beta_{ij}. \tag{2.30}$$

In other words, the respective matrix elements are mutually multiplied.

2.1.3 Further Properties of Matrices

The Range and the Null Space of a Matrix. The *range* of a matrix A is the set of vectors Ax for all values of x. This set is a linear manifold denoted $\mathcal{R}(A)$, and it is the subspace spanned by the columns of A. This can be shown by writing $A = [a_1, a_2, \ldots, a_k]$ and $x = [\xi_1, \xi_2, \ldots, \xi_k]^T$ and noticing by (2.26) that $Ax = \xi_1 a_1 + \xi_2 a_2 + \ldots + \xi_k a_k$ whereby Ax is found to be the general linear combination of the columns of A.

The *null space* of matrix A is the set of all vectors x for which $Ax = 0$. It has at least one element, namely, the zero vector. The null space is a linear manifold, too, denoted as $\mathcal{N}(A)$.

Rank of a Matrix. The rank of matrix A, abbreviated $r(A)$, is the dimensionality of the linear manifold $\mathcal{R}(A)$. Especially an $m \times n$ matrix A is said to be *of full rank* if $r(A) = \min(m, n)$. Without proof it is stated that for any matrix A,

$$r(A) = r(A^T) = r(A^TA) = r(AA^T). \tag{2.31}$$

In particular, $r(A) = r(A^TA)$ implies that if the columns of A are linearly independent, then A^TA is of full rank. In a similar way, $r(A^T) = r(AA^T)$ implies that if the rows of A are linearly independent, then AA^T is of full rank.

Singular Matrices. If A is a square matrix and if its null space consists of the zero vector only, then A is called *nonsingular*. A nonsingular matrix has an inverse (Sect. 2.1.4). Otherwise a square matrix A is *singular*. If $Ax = b$ is a vector equation which, when written for each element of b separately, can be regarded as a set of linear equations in the elements ξ_i of vector x, then the singularity of A means that in general a unique solution for this system of equations does not exist.

The determinant formed of the elements of a singular matrix is zero. All square matrices of the form ab^T are singular, which can be easily verified when writing out its determinant explicitly.

When dealing with matrix equations, extreme care should be taken when multiplying matrix expressions by matrices which may become singular. There is a possibility to end up with false solutions, in a similar way as when multiplying the sides of scalar equations by zeros.

Eigenvalues and Eigenvectors of Matrices. Consider a vector equation of the type

$$Ax = \lambda x, \tag{2.32}$$

where A is a square matrix of dimensionality $n \times n$; any solutions for x are called the *eigenvectors* of A. Notice that the "direction" of an eigenvector corresponding to the relative magnitudes of its elements is not changed in the multiplication by A.

Equation (2.32) is solved in the following way. Let the determinant formed of the elements of a square matrix M be denoted $|M|$. If $(A - \lambda I)x = 0$ must have solutions other than the trival one $x = 0$, the familiar condition known from systems of linear equations is that

$$|A - \lambda I| = 0 . \tag{2.33}$$

Apparently the determinant can be written in powers of λ, and (2.33) must be of the form

$$\lambda^n + \gamma_1 \lambda^{n-1} + \ldots + \gamma_n = 0 , \tag{2.34}$$

where the γ_i are parameters that depend on matrix A. This polynomial equation, also called the *characteristic equation* of A, has n roots $\lambda_1, \lambda_2, \ldots, \lambda_n$ some of which may be equal. These roots are the *eigenvalues* of A. Methods for the construction of eigenvectors can be found in numerous textbooks of linear algebra and will be skipped here. In this book an inverse problem, the construction of a matrix from a set of its eigenvectors is more central (Chap. 6). The *spectral radius* of matrix is defined as $\rho(A) = \max_i |\lambda_i(A)|$, where the $\lambda_i(A)$ are the eigenvalues of A.

Idempotent Matrices. A matrix is called *idempotent* if $P^2 = P$; from the iterative application of this condition it follows that for any positive integer n then holds $P^n = P$. Notice that $(I - P)^2 = I - P$ whereby $I - P$ is idempotent, too. The identity matrix I is idempotent trivially. Examples of idempotent matrices which are named *projection operators* will be discussed in Sect. 2.1.5.

Positive Definite and Positive Semidefinite Matrices. If A is a square matrix and for all nonzero $x \in R^n$ there holds that the scalar expression $x^T A x$ is positive, then by definition A is *positive definite*. If $x^T A x$ is positive or zero, then A is called *positive semidefinite*. The expression $x^T A x$ is named *quadratic form* in x.

Without proof it is stated [2.1] that any of the following conditions can be applied for the definition of a positive semidefinite (also named nonnegative definite) matrix, where the definition is restricted to symmetric matrices only.

F1) $A = HH^T$ for some matrix H.

F2)   There exists a symmetric matrix R such that $R^2 = A$, whereby $R = A^{1/2}$ is the square root of A.

F3) The eigenvalues of A are positive or zero.

F4) $x^T A x \geqslant 0$, as already stated.

If A is further nonsingular, it is positive definite.

Positive semidefinite matrices occur, for instance, in linear transformations. Consider the transformation $y = Mx$ which yields a vector; the inner product $(y, y) = y^T y$ must be nonnegative, whereby $x^T M^T M x$ is nonnegative, and $M^T M$ is a positive semidefinite matrix for any M.

Elementary Matrices. There exist matrices which have been used extensively in the solution of systems of linear equations and also occur in the projection operations discussed in this book. They are named *elementary matrices*, and in general, they are of the form $(I - u v^T)$ where u and v are column vectors of the same dimensionality.

In this book elementary matrices of the form $U = I - \alpha u u^T$, where $\alpha \in R$, $u \in R^n$, are applied. In the case that $\alpha = (u^T u)^{-1}$, U is idempotent and its null space, denoted as $\mathcal{N}(U) = \mathcal{L}(u)$, is the straight line spanned by u. The range of U is $\mathcal{R}(U) = \mathcal{L}^\perp(u)$.

Matrix Norms. The norm of a matrix can be defined in different ways, and apparently it must satisfy the general requirements imposed on the norm in any set. The *Euclidean matrix norm* is by definition the square root of the sum of squares of its elements.

The *trace* of a square matrix S, denoted $\mathrm{tr}(S)$, is defined as the sum of all diagonal elements. The Euclidean norm of any matrix A is then easily found, by writing out explicitly by elements, to be

$$\|A\|_E = \sqrt{\mathrm{tr}(A^T A)} \; .$$

Another definition of matrix norm which is different from the Euclidean norm can be derived from any definition of vector norm denoted by $\|\cdot\|$. Such a matrix norm is said to be consistent with the vector norm, and the definition reads

$$\|A\| = \max_{\|x\| = 1} \|Ax\|. \tag{2.35}$$

Notice that the Euclidean matrix norm is not consistent with the Euclidean vector norm.

2.1.4 Matrix Equations

Inverse of a Matrix. The usual definition of the inverse of a (square) matrix A, denoted by A^{-1}, is that $AA^{-1} = A^{-1}A = I$. In order that A^{-1} exist, A must be nonsingular.

Determination of the inverse of a matrix can be made in many different ways. In elementary matrix algebra it is frequently made by the determinant method. An alternative is the following: consider the solution of the matrix equation $AX = I$ where it is assumed that A is square and of full rank. If X and I are written in partitioned forms $X = [x_1, x_2, \ldots, x_n]$ and $I = [e_1, e_2, \ldots, e_n]$ then, according to the rules of matrix multiplication, the matrix equation is obviously equivalent to a set of vector equations

$$Ax_k = e_k \quad \text{for} \quad k = 1, 2, \ldots, n. \tag{2.36}$$

Take one of these equations and write it explicitly. For every fixed k this is a system of linear equations in n unknown scalar variables $\xi_{1k}, \xi_{2k}, \ldots, \xi_{nk}$:

$$\sum_{j=1}^{n} \alpha_{ij}\xi_{jk} = \varepsilon_{ik} \quad \text{for} \quad k = 1, 2, \ldots, n. \tag{2.37}$$

Each of these systems of equations has a unique solution if and only if the determinant of the coefficients α_{ij}, or $|A|$, is nonzero. The solution can be carried out, for instance, by the Gauss elimination method. In this way there is obtained a solution for every x_k separately which together constitute matrix X. This procedure, however, yields only the so-called *right inverse* of A. The *left inverse* is obtained by solving the matrix equation $XA = I$. The right and left inverses, however, will be found identical for a nonsingular matrix, and denoted by $X = A^{-1}$.

The Matrix Inversion Lemma. The following identity, usually called *matrix inversion lemma*, is frequently utilized in regression, estimation, and related problems. Assume that A and C are arbitrary matrices for which the inverses exist and B is a further matrix such that BCB^T has the same dimensionality as A. Then identically

$$(A + BCB^T)^{-1} = A^{-1} - A^{-1}B(B^TA^{-1}B + C^{-1})^{-1}B^TA^{-1}. \tag{2.38}$$

The proof follows after multiplication of the right-hand side by $A + BCB^T$ and regrouping of the terms [hint: $B(\ )^{-1} \equiv BCC^{-1}(\ )^{-1}$], whereby I results. Notice that usually C is of lower dimensionality than A whereby the computation of C^{-1} is lighter than that of A^{-1}.

The Pseudoinverse. Suppose that A and B are general rectangular matrices. Then, apparently, the above methods for the solution of matrix equations of the type $Ax = c$ or $x^TB = c^T$ do not apply even if it were assumed that solutions exist; moreover, the case must be considered that there do not exist any solutions. All such cases shall be discussed within the context of matrix equations of the form $AXB = C$. For their treatment, however, the concept of pseudoinverse, or the Moore-Penrose generalized inverse [2.4, 5] must first be introduced.

By definition, X is the *pseudoinverse* of matrix A (with real or complex elements) if all of the following conditions are valid:

G1) $AXA = A$

G2) $XAX = X$

G3) AX and XA are Hermitian matrices,

where a *Hermitian* matrix is defined as one having the property that it is identical with the complex conjugate of its transpose. The complex conjugate of a complex matrix has elements which are complex conjugates of the original elements. For a real matrix, the property of being Hermitian simply means that the matrix is *symmetric*.

It can be shown that *there exists a unique pseudoinverse for every matrix.* Although pseudoinverses are very fundamental to many parts of this book, the above existence theorem is skipped and the reader is asked to consult the original work of *Penrose* [2.4, 5], or some textbooks [2.1, 6–8]. It may here suffice to point out how pseudoinverses can be constructed, and to find out that the constructions fulfil the definition.

A Preliminary Example of Pseudoinverse; Vector Equation. Consider the vector equation

$$Ax = b, \tag{2.39}$$

where A is an $m \times n$ matrix, and x, b are column vectors, $x \in R^n$, $b \in R^m$. Suppose that $r(A) = m \leqslant n$. It can be proven by substitution in (2.39) that the following expression constitutes the solution:

$$x = A^T(AA^T)^{-1}b + (I - A^T(AA^T)^{-1}A)y, \tag{2.40}$$

where y is an arbitrary vector of the same dimensionality as x.

The condition $r(A) = m$ implies that AA^T which is an $m \times m$ matrix then has an inverse and x is immediately conceived as a solution; the fact that the solution is also general will become more obvious below.

The expression $A^T(AA^T)^{-1}$ will now be shown to comply with the definition of pseudoinverse. If it is tentatively denoted by X, then $AXA = A$ and $XAX = X$ are immediately found valid. Since $AX = I$, this expression is symmetric. To show that XA is symmetric, one further identity of usual matrix inverses is needed, namely, for any matrix A^{-1}, there holds $(A^{-1})^T = (A^T)^{-1}$. The simplest proof of this formula follows by noticing that $(A^{-1})^T$ is the solution of $XA^T = (AX^T)^T = I$. By the application of this identity to X^T it is found that $(XA)^T = A^TX^T = AX$, which completes the proof for that X is the pseudoinverse of A, of course provided that $r(A) = m$ as assumed.

In an analogous way it can be shown that if $r(A) = n \leqslant m$, then the expression $(A^TA)^{-1}A^T$ is the pseudoinverse of A. For the rank $r(A) = n < m$, however, the above vector equation (2.39) does not always have a solution.

Some Basic Formulas for Pseudoinverses. If α is a scalar, its pseudoinverse, denoted by α^+, is

$$\alpha^+ = \begin{cases} \alpha^{-1} & \text{if } \alpha \neq 0, \\ 0 & \text{if } \alpha = 0, \end{cases} \tag{2.41}$$

which can directly be verified by the definitions. From this simplest case one fundamental property of the pseudoinverse can be seen; the pseudoinverse, in general, is not a continuous function of the original matrix; in the scalar case, for instance, it makes an infinitely high jump when $\alpha \to 0$.

The pseudoinverse of a general vector a can be expressed in simple forms, too, as seen when substituting these forms into the definitions. Denoting the pseudoinverse by a^+,

$$a^+ = \begin{cases} a^T/a^Ta & \text{if } a \text{ is a nonzero vector}, \\ 0^T & \text{(zero vector) otherwise}. \end{cases} \tag{2.42}$$

For a general matrix A, either of the following formulas yields the correct expression for the pseudoinverse, denoted by A^+. Sometimes these formulas have been used for the definition of pseudoinverses [2.1]:

$$A^+ = \lim_{\delta \to 0} (A^TA + \delta^2 I)^{-1} A^T = \lim_{\delta \to 0} A^T(AA^T + \delta^2 I)^{-1}. \tag{2.43}$$

The proof will be omitted here. Notice that these expressions exist even if A^TA and AA^T do not have inverses. If the columns of A are linearly independent, then δ in the upper expression can immediately be put zero since $(A^TA)^{-1}$ then exists. If the rows of A are linearly independent, δ can be put zero in the lower expression.

A diagonal matrix can be denoted as $\operatorname{diag}(\alpha_1, \alpha_2, \ldots, \alpha_n)$ where the α-parameters are its diagonal elements. Since the product rules for diagonal matrices are simple, it can be seen from the definition of pseudoinverses that

$$[\operatorname{diag}(\alpha_1, \alpha_2, \ldots, \alpha_n)]^+ = \operatorname{diag}(\alpha_1^+, \alpha_2^+, \ldots, \alpha_n^+). \tag{2.44}$$

The Theorem of Greville. There exist several methods for the computation of the pseudoinverse of a general matrix [2.1, 6]. Some of them use library programs of large computer systems. One nice compromise between computational efficiency and programming simplicity is the recursive algorithm known as *Greville's theorem*. The idea is to partition the original matrix into columns and recruit them one at a time, thereby computing the pseudoinverse of the new submatrix from the already computed pseudoinverse of a smaller submatrix and the new column ([2.9]; cf. also [2.10, 11]).

If a matrix A, with k columns, is denoted by A_k and partitioned as $A_k = [A_{k-1} \mid a_k]$, with A_{k-1} a matrix having $k-1$ columns, then the theorem of Greville states:

$$A_k^+ = \left[\begin{array}{c} A_{k-1}^+(I - a_k p_k^T) \\ \hline p_k^T \end{array} \right], \quad \text{where}$$

$$p_k = \begin{cases} \dfrac{(I - A_{k-1}A_{k-1}^+)a_k}{\|(I - A_{k-1}A_{k-1}^+)a_k\|^2} & \text{if the numerator is } \neq 0, \\[4mm] \dfrac{(A_{k-1}^+)^T A_{k-1}^+ a_k}{1 + \|A_{k-1}^+ a_k\|^2} & \text{otherwise}. \end{cases} \tag{2.45}$$

The initial value A_1 is equal to the first column of A whereby $A_1^+ = a_1^T(a_1^T a_1)^{-1}$, provided that a_1 is a nonzero vector; if a_1 is a zero vector, then $A_1^+ = 0^T$.

The proof of this theorem is a bit elaborate and will be omitted. It may be carried out by a direct substitution in the definition of pseudoinverse.

Some Useful Identities. A few formulas for the manipulation with pseudoinverses are listed below. For complex matrices, these formulas are valid if the transpose is replaced by the complex conjugate of the transpose.

H1) $0^+ = 0^T$ (0 is a matrix full of zeroes)

H2) $(A^+)^+ = A$

H3) $(A^T)^+ = (A^+)^T$

H4) $(\alpha A)^+ = \alpha^{-1}A^+$ if $\alpha \neq 0$

H5) $A^+ = (A^T A)^+ A^T = A^T (AA^T)^+$

H6) $A^+ = A^{-1}$ if A is square and nonsingular

H7) $A^+ = (A^T A)^{-1} A^T$ if the columns of A are
linearly independent

H8) $A^+ = A^T (AA^T)^{-1}$ if the rows of A are linearly
independent

H9) $\mathscr{R}(A^+) = \mathscr{R}(A^T)$

H10) $r(A^+) = r(A) = r(A^T)$

H11) $A^T AA^+ = A^T$

H12) $(A^+)^T A^T A = A$

H13) $A^+ AA^T = A^T$

H14) $AA^T (A^+)^T = A$.

Solution of the Matrix Equation $AXB = C$. Consider the matrix equation given in the heading; A, B, and C may have any dimensionalities for which the matrix products are defined. It is first claimed that a necessary and sufficient condition for this equation to have solutions is that

$$AA^+ CB^+ B = C. \tag{2.46}$$

At first glimpse this seems a severe restriction. We shall see below, however (Sect. 2.1.5), that if the rows of any matrix A are linearly independent, then $AA^+ = I$; and if the columns of any matrix B are linearly independent, then $B^+ B = I$.

The validity of both of these conditions already guarantees the existence of solutions to $AXB = C$, and the condition stated in (2.46) is, in fact, still milder. To show that (2.46) is a necessary condition, suppose that X is a solution. Using the definition of pseudoinverse, it is then found that $C = AXB = AA^+ AXBB^+ B = AA^+ CB^+ B$; the existence of a solution thus implies (2.46). To show that (2.46) is a sufficient condition, there is found a particular solution, namely, $A^+ CB^+$, implicit in the condition itself.

The most important task, however, is to solve the equation. It is known from the theory of linear equations that the general solution is obtained if (i) one particular solution is found and (ii) the general solution of the corresponding homogeneous equation ($AXB = 0$) is then added to it. Now $A^+ CB^+$ was shown to be a particular solution; and by the identity $M = MM^+ M$ for any matrix M, all expressions of the form $Y - A^+ A YBB^+$ for an arbitrary Y of the same dimensionality as X are found to be solutions of the homogeneous equation. On the other hand, the identity

$X = X - A^+AXBB^+$ (for $AXB = 0$) implies that if X is any solution of the homogeneous equation, it is *of the form* $Y - A^+AYBB^+$. Consequently, the general solution of the original equation must then be of the form

$$X = A^+CB^+ + Y - A^+AYBB^+. \qquad (2.47)$$

The above result is due to *Penrose* [2.4].

The Minimum-Norm Solution of $AXB = C$. In the case that there are many solutions to the above equation, the one with minimum norm is of particular interest. Consider the following identity

$$\|A^+CB^+ + Y - A^+AYBB^+\|_E^2 = \|A^+CB^+\|_E^2 + \|Y - A^+AYBB^+\|_E^2. \qquad (2.48)$$

For the proof of (2.48), the following hint is given. Both sides are first written in explicit matrix form. Let us recall that the Euclidean matrix norm of any matrix A is $\sqrt{\mathrm{tr}(A^TA)}$. To show that the trace of the terms on the left-hand side in excess to those shown on the right is zero, the recently established Identities H11 and H12 are first applied where possible. Next, the generally valid identity $\mathrm{tr}(PQ) = \mathrm{tr}(QP)$ is utilized in order to facilitate the application of Identities H13 and H14. Since the norms are always positive semidefinite, it is then possible to write

$$\|A^+CB^+\|_E \leqslant \|A^+CB^+ + Y - A^+AYBB^+\|_E, \qquad (2.49)$$

the strict equality holding for $Y = 0$. Therefore, the minimum-norm solution of $AXB = C$ is $X = A^+CB^+$.

The Best Approximate Solution of a Matrix Equation. A solution to any task can be "best" only in the sense of a chosen criterion. If a matrix equation $F(X) = 0$, where F is a matrix-valued function, does not have solutions, substitution of a value $X = X_0$ yields the residual $F(X_0)$ for which the minimum may be sought. The minimum for a matrix can be expressed in terms of any norm. Two cases may now occur: (i) There is a unique value X_0 which yields the minimum, e.g., $\|F(X)\| \geqslant \|F(X_0)\|$ the strict inequality holding for $X \neq X_0$. Then X_0 is called the best approximate solution of $F(X) = 0$. (ii) There are many, perhaps infinitely many values of X_0 for which the equality in the above condition holds; they are all named approximate solutions. The *best approximate solution* X_0^* is then defined as the minimum-norm approximate solution; $\|X_0\| \geqslant \|X_0^*\|$.

The Best Approximate Solution of $XA = B$. In another work [2.5], *Penrose* pointed out that the best approximate solution of $AXB = C$ in the sense of Euclidean matrix norm for the case in which exact solutions do not exist is $X_0 = A^+CB^+$. For the purpose of this text, a derivation is carried out for the matrix equation $XA = B$ which occurs in the associative mappings (Chap. 6).

When the Euclidean norm of $XA - B$ is to be minimized, an equivalent task is to minimize $\operatorname{tr}(R)$ where $R = (XA - B)(XA - B)^T$. To solve this problem, the following trick is used: it can be verified, by the application of Identities H 13 and H 14 of Sect. 2.1.4 that R may be written in the form

$$R = (BA^+ - X)AA^T(BA^+ - X)^T + B(I - A^+A)B^T. \tag{2.50}$$

Now $(BA^+ - X)AA^T(BA^+ - X)^T$ is positive semidefinite on account of its form, and $\operatorname{tr}(BA^+ - X)AA^T(BA^+ - X)^T$ becomes zero for $X = BA^+$. This must then be its minimum. On the other hand, since R in this problem is always positive definite, then $B(I - A^+A)B^T$ is positive definite, and $X = BA^+$ has thereby been shown to minimize $\operatorname{tr}(R)$, or the Euclidean norm of the residual $XA - B$.

2.1.5 Projection Operators

It will be shown that the decomposition of an arbitrary vector $x \in R^n$ into its orthogonal projections $\hat{x} \in \mathscr{L} \subset R^n$ and $\tilde{x} \perp \mathscr{L}$ can be expressed in terms of linear transformations whereby there always exists a symmetric matrix P such that $\hat{x} = Px$, $\tilde{x} = (I - P)x$. Then P is called the orthogonal projection operator on $\mathscr{L}$, and $I - P$ the orthogonal projection operator on the space $\mathscr{L}^\perp$ that is the orthogonal complement of $\mathscr{L}$. Let us recall that $\mathscr{L}^\perp$ was defined as the set of all vectors in R^n which are orthogonal to $\mathscr{L}$.

Consider the matrix X with $x_1, x_2, \ldots, x_k$, $k < n$ its columns. The vectors $x_i \in R^n$, $i = 1, 2, \ldots, k$ shall span the space $\mathscr{L}$. The decomposition $x = \hat{x} + \tilde{x}$ is unique and $\tilde{x}$ may be determined by the condition that it must be orthogonal to all columns of X or,

$$\tilde{x}^T X = 0 \tag{2.51}$$

under the normalizing condition $(x, \tilde{x}) = (\tilde{x}, \tilde{x})$ which directly follows from the orthogonality of $\tilde{x}$ and $\hat{x}$. The Penrose solution of (2.51) for $\tilde{x}^T$ is

$$\tilde{x}^T = y^T(I - XX^+) \tag{2.52}$$

with y an arbitrary vector of the same dimensionality as $\tilde{x}$. Using the symmetry of XX^+ and the properties of pseudoinverse, the following derivation then follows:

$$x^\mathrm{T}\tilde{x} = x^\mathrm{T}(I - XX^+)y = \tilde{x}^\mathrm{T}\tilde{x} = y^\mathrm{T}(I - XX^+)^2 y = y^\mathrm{T}(I - XX^+)y. \quad (2.53)$$

Now $y = x$ is a possible choice whereby

$$\tilde{x} = (I - XX^+)x. \tag{2.54}$$

Because $\tilde{x}$ is unique, then $I - P = I - XX^+$, and $P = XX^+$.

The above orthogonal projection operators are found symmetric and idempotent. In general, a matrix is called *projection matrix* if it is idempotent (although it may not be symmetric).

If it is denoted $X^\mathrm{T} = Y$, then the rows of Y are the columns of X. The projection operator on the space spanned by the rows of Y is

$$I - XX^+ = I - Y^\mathrm{T}(Y^\mathrm{T})^+ = I - Y^\mathrm{T}(Y^+)^\mathrm{T} = (I - Y^+ Y)^\mathrm{T} = I - Y^+ Y,$$

where the last result follows from the symmetry of $Y^+ Y$. We are now in a position to state the following rule: XX^+ is the orthogonal projection operator on the space spanned by the columns of X, and $X^+ X$ the orthogonal projection operator on the space spanned by the rows of X. The matrices $I - XX^+$ and $I - X^+ X$ are the orthogonal projection operators on the spaces which are the orthogonal complements of the column space and the row space of X, respectively.

Computational Forms of Orthogonal Projection Operators. If it becomes necessary to express the projection operators in explicit forms, any pseudoinverse algorithm can be applied. A simple formula can be derived from Greville's theorem: if X_k is a matrix with $x_1, x_2, \ldots, x_k$ its columns, and it is partitioned as $[X_{k-1} \,|\, x_k]$, it then follows from (2.45) that

$$X_k X_k^+ = X_{k-1} X_{k-1}^+ (I - x_k p_k^\mathrm{T}) + x_k p_k^\mathrm{T}, \tag{2.55}$$

where p_k is the expression in (2.45) with the a-vectors replaced by the corresponding x-vectors. If now $(I - X_{k-1} X_{k-1}^+)x_k$ is a zero vector, the above formula yields $X_k X_k^+ = X_{k-1} X_{k-1}^+$; for a nonzero vector, the upper expression of p_k holds, whence for both cases it can be written

$$I - X_k X_k^+ = (I - X_{k-1} X_{k-1}^+) - \frac{(I - X_{k-1} X_{k-1}^+)x_k x_k^\mathrm{T}(I - X_{k-1} X_{k-1}^+)}{\|(I - X_{k-1} X_{k-1}^+)x_k\|^2}.$$

$$\tag{2.56}$$

It should be noticed that $I - X_{k-1} X_{k-1}^+$ is the orthogonal projection operator on the space that is orthogonal to the space spanned by the $x_1 \ldots x_{k-1}$;

$I - X_k X_k^+$ is the corresponding projection operator with $x_1 \ldots x_k$ the spanning vectors. Equation (2.56) can be put into a form

$$\phi_k = \phi_{k-1} - \frac{\tilde{x}_k \tilde{x}_k^T}{\|\tilde{x}_k\|^2}, \tag{2.57}$$

where

$$\tilde{x}_k = \phi_{k-1} x_k \tag{2.58}$$

and the recursion starts with $\phi_0 = I$. After k steps, the orthogonal projection operator on $\mathcal{R}(X_k)$ is $P = I - \phi_k$.

The above algorithm also results from the Gram-Schmidt orthogonalization formulae written as

$$\tilde{x}_1 = x_1$$

$$\tilde{x}_k = x_k - \sum_{j=1}^{k-1} \frac{\tilde{x}_j (\tilde{x}_j^T x_k)}{\|\tilde{x}_j\|^2} \quad k = 2, 3, \ldots, \tag{2.59}$$

where the sum is taken over those indices j that correspond to nonzero $\tilde{x}_j$. Equations (2.59) directly yield (2.57) and (2.58) when it is denoted

$$I - \sum_{j=1}^{k-1} \frac{\tilde{x}_j \tilde{x}_j^T}{\|\tilde{x}_j\|^2} = \phi_{k-1}, \tag{2.60}$$

and

$$\tilde{x}_k = \phi_{k-1} x_k. \tag{2.61}$$

A further formula is useful, too: if q_j, $j = 1, 2, \ldots, k$ are *orthonormal basis vectors* of $\mathcal{R}(X_k)$, i.e., they are orthogonal and of unit norm and span the space $\mathcal{R}(X_k)$, then

$$X_k X_k^+ = \sum_{j=1}^{k} q_j q_j^T, \tag{2.62}$$

which directly follows from (2.57).

Fourier Expansion. By writing

$$x = \hat{x} + \tilde{x} = \sum_{j=1}^{k} (q_j, x) q_j + \tilde{x}, \tag{2.63}$$

vector x has been expanded in terms of orthogonal "functions" q_j and a residual $\tilde{x}$ the norm of which is minimized. This is the general form of *Fourier expansion* for vector functions, and the (q_j, x) are named the Fourier components of x.

2.1.6 On Matrix Differential Calculus

It was demonstrated above that the existence of solutions to algebraic matrix equations may be more problematic than in the scalar case. In the similar way it may be expected that matrix differential equations behave differently from the scalar equations. This is due to several reasons: matrix products in general do not commute, matrices may become singular, and first of all, a matrix differential equation is a system of coupled equations of the matrix elements whereby stability conditions are more complicated. Extreme care should therefore be taken when dealing with matrix differential equations.

Derivatives of Matrices. If the matrix elements are functions of a scalar variable, for instance time, then the derivative of a matrix is obtained by taking the derivatives of the elements. For instance, for a matrix A,

$$A = \begin{bmatrix} a_{11} & a_{12} \\ a_{21} & a_{22} \end{bmatrix}, \quad dA/dt = \begin{bmatrix} da_{11}/dt & da_{12}/dt \\ da_{21}/dt & da_{22}/dt \end{bmatrix}. \tag{2.64}$$

Partial derivatives of a matrix are obtained by taking the partial derivatives of the elements.

In the differentiation of products of matrices and other matrix functions, the noncommutativity must be kept in mind. For instance,

$$d(AB)/dt = (dA/dt)B + A(dB/dt). \tag{2.65}$$

This restriction is important in the derivatives of the powers of matrices: e.g., if A is square,

$$dA^3/dt = d(A \cdot A \cdot A)/dt = (dA/dt)A^2 + A(dA/dt)A + A^2(dA/dt), \tag{2.66}$$

and in general the above form cannot be simplified because the terms are not combinable.

The formulas of derivatives of general integral powers are found if the following fact is considered: if A^{-1} exists whereby $AA^{-1} = I$, then it must hold

$$d(AA^{-1})/dt = (dA/dt)A^{-1} + A(dA^{-1}/dt) = 0 \quad \text{(the zero matrix)};$$
$$dA^{-1}/dt = -A^{-1}(dA/dt)A^{-1}. \tag{2.67}$$

In general it is obtained:

$$dA^n/dt = \sum_{i=0}^{n-1} A^i(dA/dt)A^{n-i-1} \quad \text{when} \quad n \geqslant 1,$$

$$dA^{-n}/dt = \sum_{i=1}^{n} -A^{-i}(dA/dt)A^{i-n-1} \quad \text{when} \quad n \geqslant 1, |A| \neq 0. \tag{2.68}$$

The *gradient* of a scalar is a vector. In matrix calculus, the gradient operator is a column vector of differential operators of the form

$$\nabla_x = [\partial/\partial\xi_1, \partial/\partial\xi_2, \ldots, \partial/\partial\xi_n]^T, \tag{2.69}$$

and differentiation of a scalar α is formally equivalent to a matrix product of vector ∇_x and α:

$$\nabla_x \alpha = [\partial\alpha/\partial\xi_1, \partial\alpha/\partial\xi_2, \ldots, \partial\alpha/\partial\xi_n]^T. \tag{2.70}$$

If a scalar-valued function is a function of vector x, then the differentiation rules are most easily found when writing by elements, e.g.,

$$\nabla_x(x^Tx) = [\partial/\partial\xi_1, \partial/\partial\xi_2, \ldots, \partial/\partial\xi_n]^T (\xi_1^2 + \xi_2^2 + \ldots + \xi_n^2) = 2x. \tag{2.71}$$

Since ∇_x is a vector, it is applicable to all row vectors of arbitrary dimensionality, whereby a matrix results. For instance, $\nabla_x x^T = I$. In some cases it is applicable to products of vectors or vectors and matrices if the expression has the same dimensionality as that of a scalar or row vector. The following examples can be proven when writing by elements: if a and b are functions of x, and p and q are constants,

$$\nabla_x[a^T(x)b(x)] = [\nabla_x a^T(x)]b(x) + [\nabla_x b^T(x)]a(x), \tag{2.72}$$

$$\nabla_x(p^Tx) = p, \tag{2.73}$$

$$\nabla_x(x^Tq) = q. \tag{2.74}$$

Consider a quadratic form $Q = a^T(x)\psi a(x)$ where ψ is symmetric. Then

$$\nabla_x Q = 2 [\nabla_x a^T(x)] \psi a(x), \tag{2.75}$$

which can be proven by writing $\psi = \psi^{1/2}\psi^{1/2}$, whereby $\psi^{1/2}$ is symmetric.

2.2 Distance Measures for Patterns

The Classical Laws of Association (Sect. 1.1.2) describe associative recall as an operation in which a stored item is recalled from memory on account of having a high degree of similarity to the key pattern. It is plausible that the human memory is able to apply various searching strategies relating to different levels of organization and abstraction of knowledge; the similarity criteria applied on the higher levels may seem more complicated than those which occur in the simplest circuits (e.g., perfect or partial match). The purpose of this section is to introduce various similarity measures that have been used in physical as well as more abstract models of memory and recognition.

2.2.1 Measures of Similarity and Distance in Vector Spaces

It may be clear that *distance* and *similarity* are reciprocal concepts. It is a matter of terminology if we call distance *dissimilarity*. Below we shall give concrete examples of both.

Correlation. The comparison of signals or patterns is often based on their *correlation* which is a trivial measure of similarity. Assume two ordered sets, or sequences of real-valued samples $x = (\xi_1, \xi_2, \ldots, \xi_n)$ and $y = (\eta_1, \eta_2, \ldots, \eta_n)$. Their *unnormalized correlation* is

$$C = \sum_{i=1}^{n} \xi_i \eta_i . \tag{2.76}$$

If x and y are understood as Euclidean (real) vectors, then C is their *scalar* or *inner product*.

In case one of the sequences may be *shifted* with respect to the other by an arbitrary amount, the comparison may better be based on a translationally invariant measure, the maximum correlation over a specified interval:

$$C_m = \max_k \sum_{i=1}^{n} \xi_i \eta_{i-k}, \quad k = -n, -n+1, \ldots, +n . \tag{2.77}$$

In this case the sequences $\{\xi_i\}$ and $\{\eta_i\}$ are usually defined outside the range $i = 1, \ldots, n$, too. Of course, shifted comparison can be applied with any of the methods discussed below.

It will be necessary to emphasize that correlation methods are most suitable for the detection of periodic signals which are contaminated by *Gaussian noise*; since the distributions of natural patterns may often not be Gaussian, other criteria of comparison, some of which are discussed below, must be considered, too.

Direction Cosines. If the relevant information in patterns or signals is contained only in the *relative magnitudes* of their components, then similarity can often be better measured in terms of *direction cosines* defined in the following way. If $x \in R^n$ and $y \in R^n$ are regarded as Euclidean vectors, then

$$\cos \theta = \frac{(x, y)}{\|x\| \|y\|} \tag{2.78}$$

is by definition the cosine of their mutual angle, with (x, y) the scalar product of x and y, and $\|x\|$ the Euclidean norm of x. Notice that if the norms of vectors are standardized to unity, then (2.76) complies with (2.78), or $\cos \theta = C$. Expression (2.78) complies with the usual definition of *correlation coefficient* in statistics, provided that we understand the vectors x and y as sequences of numbers $\{\xi_i\}$ and $\{\eta_i\}$, respectively.

Notice that the value $\cos \theta = 1$ is defined to represent *exact match*; vector y is then equal to x multiplied by a scalar, $y = \alpha x (\alpha \in R)$. On the other hand, if $\cos \theta = 0$ or $(x, y) = 0$, vectors x and y are said to be *orthogonal*.

Euclidean Distance. Another measure of similarity, actually that of *dissimilarity*, closely related to the previous ones, is based on the *Euclidean distance* of x and y defined as

$$\rho_E(x, y) = \|x - y\| = \sqrt{\sum_{i=1}^{n} (\xi_i - \eta_i)^2} \,. \tag{2.79}$$

Although seemingly natural for the detection of differences, $\rho_E(x, y)$ in reality often yields worse results in comparison than the previous method, on account of its greater sensitivity to the lengths of the vectors to be compared; notice that $\|x - y\|^2 = \|x\|^2 + \|y\|^2 - 2(x, y)$. On the other hand, if the lengths of the vectors are normalized, the results obtained are identical with those obtained by the previous methods. Often ρ_E is applicable to comparisons made in *parameter spaces*.

Measures of Similarity in the Minkowski Metric. Obviously (2.79) is a special case of distance which defines the *Minkowski metric*. This measure has been used in experimental sciences.

$$\rho_M(x, y) = \left(\sum_{i=1}^{n} |\xi_i - \eta_i|^\lambda \right)^{1/\lambda}, \ \lambda \in R \,. \tag{2.80}$$

The so-called *"city-block distance"* is obtained with $\lambda = 1$.

Tanimoto Similarity Measure. Some experiments have shown [2.12 – 16] that determination of similarity between x and y in terms of a measure introduced by *Tanimoto* [2.17] yields good results; it may be defined as

$$S_T(x, y) = \frac{(x, y)}{\|x\|^2 + \|y\|^2 - (x, y)} . \tag{2.81}$$

The origin of this measure is in the comparison of sets. Assume that A and B are two unordered sets of distinct (nonnumerical) elements, e.g., identifiers or descriptors in documents, or discrete features in patterns. The similarity of A and B may be defined as the ratio of the number of their common elements to the number of all different elements; if $n(X)$ is the number of elements in set X, then the similarity is

$$S_T(A, B) = \frac{n(A \cap B)}{n(A \cup B)} = \frac{n(A \cap B)}{n(A) + n(B) - n(A \cap B)} . \tag{2.82}$$

Notice that if x and y above were binary vectors, with components $\in \{0, 1\}$ the value of which corresponds to the exclusion or inclusion of a particular element, respectively, then (x, y), $\|x\|$, and $\|y\|$ would be directly comparable to $n(A \cap B)$, $n(A)$, and $n(B)$, correspondingly. Obviously (2.81) is a generalization of (2.82) for real-valued vectors.

The Tanimoto measure has been used with success in the evaluation of relevance between documents [2.15]; the descriptors can thereby be provided with individual weights. If a_{ik} is the weight assigned to the kth descriptor of the ith document, then the similarity of two documents denoted by x_i and x_j is obtained by defining

$$(x_i, x_j) = \sum_k a_{ik} a_{jk} = \alpha_{ij} , \tag{2.83}$$

and

$$S_T(x_i, x_j) = \frac{\alpha_{ij}}{\alpha_{ii} + \alpha_{jj} - \alpha_{ij}} .$$

Weighted Measures for Similarity. The components of x and y above were assumed independent. In practical applications they may be generated in a stochastic process which defines a statistical dependence between them; it can be shown that for vectors with normally distributed noise the optimal separation is obtained if instead of the scalar product, the *inner product* is defined as

$$(x, y)_\psi = (x, \psi y) , \tag{2.84}$$

or the *distance* is defined as

$$\rho_\psi(x, y) = \|x - y\|_\psi = \sqrt{(x-y)^\mathrm{T} \psi(x-y)} , \tag{2.85}$$

in which the weighting matrix ψ is the *inverse of the covariance matrix* of x and y, and T denotes the *transpose*. This measure is also named *Mahalanobis distance*.

Since ψ is assumed symmetric and positive semidefinite, it can be expressed as $\psi = (\psi^{1/2})^\mathrm{T} \psi^{1/2}$, whereby x and y can always be preprocessed before their analysis using the transformations $x' = \psi^{1/2}x$, $y' = \psi^{1/2}y$. Now comparison can be based on Euclidean measures (scalar product or distance) on x' and y'.

Unfortunately there are some drawbacks with this method: (i) In order to evaluate the covariance matrix for patterns of high dimensionality (n), an immense number of samples $(\gg n^2)$ have to be collected. (ii) Computation of matrix-vector products is much heavier than formation of scalar products.

Comparison by Operations of Continuous-Valued Logic. The basic operations of multiple-valued logic were first introduced by *Lukasiewicz* [2.18] and *Post* [2.19], and later extensively utilized in the theory of fuzzy sets by *Zadeh* [2.20], as well as others. Here we shall adopt only a few concepts, believed to be amenable to fast and simple computation in comparison operations.

The application of continuous-valued logic to comparison operations is here based on the following reasoning. The "amount of information" carried by a scalar signal is assumed proportional to its difference from a certain reference level. For instance, consider a continuous scale in which ξ_i, $\eta_i \in (0, +1)$. The signal value $1/2$ is assumed indeterminate, and the representation of information is regarded the more reliable or determinate the nearer it is to either 0 or $+1$. The *degree of matching* of scalars ξ_i and η_i is expressed as a generalization of the *logical equivalence*. The equivalence of Boolean variables a and b is

$$(a \equiv b) = (\bar{a} \wedge \bar{b}) \vee (a \wedge b) . \tag{2.86}$$

In continuous-valued logic, the logic product $(\wedge)$ is replaced by minimum selection (min), the logic sum $(\vee)$ is replaced by maximum selection (max), and the logical negation is replaced by complementation with respect to the scale $(\bar{a} = 1 - a)$. In this way, (2.86) is replaced by "equivalence" $e(\xi, \eta)$,

$$e(\xi, \eta) = \max\{\min(\xi, \eta), \min[(1 - \xi), (1 - \eta)]\} . \tag{2.87}$$

If (2.87) is applied to the comparison of ξ_i and η_i, the next problem is how to combine the results $e(\xi_i, \eta_i)$. One possibility is to generalize the logic product using the operation min. However, the effect of mismatching at a single element would be too fatal. Another possibility is the linear sum of $e(\xi_i, \eta_i)$ as in (2.79). A compromise would be to define the similarity of x and y with the aid of some function which is symmetrical with respect to its arguments, e.g.,

$$S_M(x, y) = \varphi^{-1} \left\{ \sum_{i=1}^{n} \varphi[e(\xi_i, \eta_i)] \right\}, \tag{2.88}$$

where φ is a monotonic function, and φ^{-1} its inverse. For instance,

$$S_M(x, y) = \sqrt[p]{\sum_{i=1}^{n} [e(\xi_i, \eta_i)]^p}_+, \tag{2.89}$$

with p some real value is one possibility. Notice that with $p = 1$ the linear sum is obtained, and with $p \to -\infty$, $S_M(x, y)$ will approach $\min_i [e(\xi_i, \eta_i)]$.

This method has two particular advantages when compared with, say, the correlation method: (i) Matching or mismatching of low signal values is taken into account. (ii) The operations max and min are computationally, by digital or analog means, much simpler than the formation of products needed in correlation methods. For this reason, too, $p = 1$ in (2.89) might be preferred.

It has turned out in many applications that there is no big difference in the comparison results based on different similarity measures, and so it is the computational simplicity which ought to be taken into account in the first place.

2.2.2 Measures of Similarity and Distance Between Symbol Strings

Written text is a high-level source of information, and words can be understood as patterns, too. Words are expressed as strings of symbols but such patterns can hardly be regarded as vectors in vector spaces. Other examples of strings are *codes* of messages which have been studied a long time in information theory. Further cases of symbol strings occur in structural pattern analysis (Sect. 7.7). We shall not discuss how these strings are formed; on the other hand, it may be understandable that they can be contaminated with errors which may have been generated in the conversion process itself, or in subsequent handling and transmission. In the statistical comparison of strings, the first task is to define some reasonable distance measure between them.

Hamming Distance. Perhaps the best-known measure of similarity, or in fact dissimilarity between coded representations is the *Hamming distance*. Originally this measure was defined for binary codes [2.21], but it is readily applicable to comparison of any *ordered sets* which consist of discrete-valued elements.

Consider two ordered sets x and y, which consist of discrete, nonnumerical symbols such as the logical 0 and 1, or letters from the English alphabet. Their comparison for dissimilarity may be based on the *number of different symbols in them*. This number is known as the *Hamming distance* ρ_H which can be defined for sequences of equal length only: e.g.,

$$x = (1, 0, 1, 1, 1, 0)$$
$$y = (1, 1, 0, 1, 0, 1)$$
$$\rho_H(x, y) = 4$$

and

$$u = (p, a, t, t, e, r, n)$$
$$v = (w, e, s, t, e, r, n)$$
$$\rho_H(u, v) = 3.$$

For binary patterns $x = (\xi_1, \ldots, \xi_n)$ and $y = (\eta_1, \ldots, \eta_n)$, assuming ξ_i and η_i as Boolean variables, the Hamming distance may be expressed formally as a logic operation:

$$\rho_H(x, y) = \text{bitcount}\{(\bar{\xi}_i \wedge \eta_i) \vee (\xi_i \wedge \bar{\eta}_i) \,|\, i = 1, \ldots, n\} \tag{2.90}$$

where $\wedge$ is the logical conjunction (AND) and $\vee$ is the disjunction (OR); $\bar{\xi}$ is the negation of ξ. The function bitcount $\{S\}$ determines the number of elements in the set S which attain the value logical 1; the Boolean expression occurring in the set variables is the *EXCLUSIVE OR* (EXOR) function of ξ_i and η_i.

The restriction imposed on the lengths of representations, or numbers of elements in sets, can be avoided in many ways (cf., e.g., the definitions of Levenshtein distances a bit later on). As an introductory example, consider two *unordered sets* A and B which consist of distinct, identifiable elements; if they had to represent binary codes, then for these elements one could select, e.g., the indices of all bit positions with value 1. Denote the number of elements in set S by $n(S)$. The following distance measure has been found to yield a simple and effective resolution between unordered sets:

$$p(A, B) = \max\{n(A), n(B)\} - n(A \cap B). \tag{2.91}$$

This measure is related to the Tanimoto similarity measure discussed above.

Variational Similarity. The following principle can be combined with many comparison criteria. Its leading idea is that patterned representations are allowed to be marred by deformations or local scale transformations, and the comparison for similarity is then performed by considering only small pieces of patterns at a time. The pieces are shifted relative to each other to find their maximum degree of matching. As the partial patterns must be connected anyway, the matching must be done sequentially, whereby this becomes a kind of *variational problem.*

The matching procedure, here termed *variational similarity*, is illustrated by a symbol string matching example. The three possible types of error that can occur in strings are: (i) Replacement or substitution error (change of a symbol into another one). (ii) Insertion error (occurrence of an extra symbol). (iii) Deletion error (dropping of a symbol). Errors of the latter two types stretch or constrict the string, respectively, and their effect is analogous with scale transformations.

Assume that one of the strings is a reference, and for simplicity, in the other one to be compared, two or more errors of the same type are not likely to occur in adjacent symbols. (Several errors may, however, occur in the string distant from each other.) Consider two strings written at the sides of a lattice as shown in Fig. 2.5. A line shall connect lattice points which are selected by the following rule:

> *A Dynamic Matching Procedure.* Assume that the line has already been defined to go through the lattice point (i, j); the next point shall be selected from $(i+1, j)$, $(i+1, j+1)$, and $(i+1, j+2)$. Compare the symbol pairs corresponding to these three points. If there is one match only, take the corresponding point for the next point on the line. If there is no match, select $(i+1, j+1)$ for the next point on the line. If there are matches at $(i+1, j+1)$ and some other point, select $(i+1, j+1)$. If there are matches only at $(i+1, j)$ and $(i+1, j+2)$, select for the next point $(i+1, j+2)$.

A *matching score* is now determined by counting the number of matching pairs of symbols along the above line.

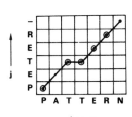

Fig. 2.5. Two examples of variational matching

The two examples shown in Fig. 2.5 are self-explanatory. Naturally, many other and more effective local matching criteria can be used; this example will only convey the basic idea. For instance, instead of exact match, some measure of similarity between nonidentical symbols may be defined; this principle is usual in the matching of phonemic strings [2.22]. Sequences of numerical values can also be matched in an analogous way, by dividing the sequences into smaller segments, and comparing the respective segments.

Levenshtein or Edit Distance. Closely related to the variational similarity is a dissimilarity measure for symbol strings introduced in the theory of coding errors by *Levenshtein* [2.23]. It is assumed that string y can be derived from string x by application of a sequence of *editing operations*; assume that this is done by p_i replacements, q_i insertions, and r_i deletions. The *Levenshtein distance* (LD) or *edit distance* between x and y is defined as

$$LD(x, y) = \min_i (p_i + q_i + r_i) . \qquad (2.92)$$

Since the different types of error may occur with different frequencies, an improved measure is the *weighted Levenshtein distance* (WLD) defined as

$$WLD(x, y) = \min_i (ap_i + bq_i + cr_i) \qquad (2.93)$$

with $a, b,$ and c suitable constants, depending on application.

Determination of WLD can be made by a dynamic programming method (cf., e.g., [2.24]).

3. Classical Learning Systems

For the implementation of information processes, some kind of fundamental physical systems which transform signals and patterns are needed. In the simplest cases the relationship between representations of information at input and output, respectively, can be described in terms of a transformation function. Such systems are often named filters. *The classical learning networks are signal-transforming systems the parameters of which are slowly changed by the effect of signal energy.* Such systems are also named *adaptive*, and they may automatically adjust themselves to become optimally selective with respect to certain signal or pattern statistics.

It may be necessary to mention at this point that learning processes, especially those taking place in artificial systems, are sometimes discussed on a more abstract or mathematical (algorithmic) level; mathematical statistics has become the general setting of such problems. Many complex and sophisticated control systems nowadays make use of so-called adaptive algorithms; the best known of these is the *Kalman filter* [3.1] which has been used, e.g., in radar tracking, space flights, and industrial control. The general structure of such algorithms resembles the recursive expressions which are used to describe the learning systems; such forms are very suitable for computation by digital computers. One ought to realize, however, that the computations are then made in a highly centralized way for which a complicated programming system is needed. Such computerized implementations fall outside the scope of this book, because they are not directly related to *physical models*. In the original sense, adaptive systems did not involve computerized information processing; all processing was intended to be done in a highly distributed and parallel fashion, based on simple physical components solely.

This chapter describes some classical approaches to the learning problem, and it seems that many of the constructs were introduced for models of the elementary brain functions, too; one may also regard them as the first steps towards the implementation of machine intelligence. We are not aiming at a complete survey of all related works but rather at setting a perspective of the

main lines of earlier research on these topics. Another attempt to systematically formalize the basic adaptive functions will then be made in Chap. 4.

The system models presented in Sects. 3.1 – 3 have the following main
characteristics:

1) In the *Adaline*, a linear mapping is formed adaptively (by a supervised
   training method) which produces a wanted response signal to different input patterns; the result is optimal in the sense of least squares.
2) In the *Perceptron*, there is an additional preprocessing network for the extraction of signal combinations (features) from the input pattern. The output circuits are made to discriminate between different input patterns, each
   one responding to a different class of patterns.
3) In the *Learning Matrices*, the internal structures of the networks are simpler, but the discrimination ability for patterns is not optimal; the dependence between pattern elements is not taken into account.

Further we shall introduce the principle of *holography* in this chapter since it
too has been suggested for a paradigm of associative memory.

3.1 The Adaptive Linear Element (Adaline)

The simplest "learning" adaptive systems have linear transfer properties; on
the other hand, their parameters are changed nonlinearly. The adaptive linear
element, also named *Adaline* (Adaptive Linear Element), suggested by
Widrow [3.2] is a classical example of them. In a simple physical implementation (Fig. 3.1) this device comprises a set of controllable resistors connected to
a circuit which can sum up currents caused by the input voltage signals.

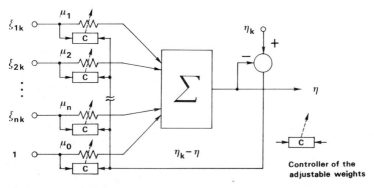

Fig. 3.1. The Adaline

Although the adaptive process is here exemplified in a case when there is only one output, it may be clear that a system with many parallel outputs is directly implementable by multiple units of the above kind.

If the input conductances are denoted by μ_i, $i = 0, 1, 2, \ldots, n$, and the input and output signals by ξ_i and η, respectively, then the system transfer equation reads:

$$\eta = \sum_{i=1}^{n} \mu_i \xi_i + \mu_0 . \tag{3.1}$$

The purpose of this device is to yield a given value η_k at its output when the set of values $\{\xi_{ik}\}$, $i = 1, \ldots, n$, is applied at the inputs. The problem is to determine the coefficients μ_i, $i = 0, 1, \ldots, n$ in such a way that the input-output-response is correct for a large number of arbitrarily chosen signal sets. If an accurate mapping is not possible, η has to approximate the η_k, for instance, in the sense of least squares. An adaptive operation means that there exists a mechanism by which the μ_i can be adjusted, usually iteratively, to attain the correct values.

One particular problem is connected with the representation of *negative values* of the η_i. A straightforward solution for it is to rescale η such that the sum expression in (3.1), with positive ξ_i and μ_i, never becomes negative. Another possibility is to use *antagonistic encoding* of signals, i.e., to represent positive and negative weights by different lines the signals of which are then subtracted in the output circuit (Sect. 3.3).

Although the basic physical system is time-continuous, it is often simpler to discuss the adaptive changes of the μ_i approximately as a so-called discrete-time process. If the signals and parameters are examined at a series of instances of time $\{t_k; k = 1, 2, \ldots\}$ and the same subscript k is used for variables, one of the simplest cases is obtained if it is assumed that the parameter changes can be defined by the recursion

$$\mu_{i,k+1} = \mu_{ik} + \alpha_k (\eta_k - \eta) \xi_{ik} \tag{3.2}$$

with α_k a sufficiently small positive scalar. In the simplest case, especially if the t_k are equidistant, α_k may be taken constant, equal to α. This is clearly a *corrective* process in which, if the response η was wrong, the values of μ_i are adjusted in a direction in which the error $\eta - \eta_k$ is apparently diminished.

It can be shown that if the input patterns are linearly independent, the μ_{ik} will converge to unique limits. More often, however, the corrections would remain oscillatory. To prevent this, α should be made to decrease as shown in the following.

3.1.1 Description of Adaptation by the Stochastic Approximation

Next, adaptation of the above linear system is described by a formalism which has been developed for regression problems. Solution methods called *stochastic approximation* as exemplified here are especially useful in more complicated regression problems when other means do not apply, for instance, when nonlinearities are present in the model, or the stochastic processes have complicated or unknown statistics. A rigorous discussion of stochastic approximation and nonlinear regression can be found elsewhere [3.3 – 6].

Without loss of generality, μ_0 may now be omitted since this term would correspond to a constant pattern element ($= 1$) acting at an input weight μ_0. It would then be equivalent to increase the dimensionality of the model by one.

Let us denote the set of input signals by a vector $x = [\xi_1, \xi_2, \ldots, \xi_n]^T$ and let $m^T = [\mu_1, \mu_2, \ldots, \mu_n]$. If $x \in R^n$ and $\eta \in R$ are stochastic variables, and a linear dependence is assumed between them, $\eta = m^T x + \varepsilon$, with ε a stochastic error with zero expectation value, a quadratic error criterion is defined by a functional

$$J = E\{(\eta - m^T x)^2\},\tag{3.3}$$

where $E\{\cdot\}$ is the mathematical expectation. The problem is to find a value m^* for m which minimizes the functional J; the condition of extremality is

$$\nabla_m J|_{m=m^*} = \left[\frac{\partial J}{\partial \mu_1}, \frac{\partial J}{\partial \mu_2}, \ldots, \frac{\partial J}{\partial \mu_n} \right]^T \bigg|_{m=m^*} = 0.\tag{3.4}$$

The local extremum of functional J can be found by the *gradient method* (e.g., [3.3]); starting with an arbitrary initial value for m denoted by m_0, a sequence of discrete values $\{m_k^T\}$ is defined by

$$m_k^T = m_{k-1}^T - G_k \nabla_m J|_{m=m_{k-1}},\tag{3.5}$$

where G_k is a gain matrix. It has been shown that a condition for the convergence of m_k is that matrix G_k be positive definite. The norm of G_k has some bounds, too. One important choice is $G_k = \alpha_k I$ (this complies with the method of steepest descent when α_k is suitably chosen).

If it is not a priori assumed that the statistics of the signals are known, the least-square optimal value must be computed from a series of realizations of x and η. The idea followed in stochastic approximation is to replace $\nabla_m J$ by its approximate values, or the gradient of the integrand $(\eta - m^T x)^2$ which is then a stochastic vector, its value depending on the realizations $x = x_k$ and $\eta = \eta_k$. Now it is obtained, when a new value for m_k is computed every time when a pair (x_k, η_k) is observed:

$$m_k^T = m_{k-1}^T + \alpha_k(\eta_k - m_{k-1}^T x_k)x_k^T . \qquad (3.6)$$

This is apparently identical with the reinforcement rule (3.2) written in vector notation. It has been shown that this sequence converges (with probability one) towards the optimal value $(m^*)^T$ for which J is minimum, if the following conditions are valid for the sequence $\{\alpha_k\}$:

$$\sum_{k=1}^{\infty} \alpha_k = \infty, \quad \sum_{k=1}^{\infty} \alpha_k^2 < \infty . \qquad (3.7)$$

For instance, $\alpha_k = k^{-1}$ satisfies these conditions. The following choice for the gain [3.5] has been found to yield a rather fast convergence in many applications:

$$\alpha_k = \left(\sum_{p=1}^{k} \|x_p\|^2 \right)^{-1} . \qquad (3.8)$$

We shall still revert to the determination of the optimal solution for m in Chap. 6.

3.2 The Perceptron

Another adaptive construct with components resembling those of the biological sensory systems has been suggested by *Rosenblatt* [3.7]. He analyzed several variants of the basic system of which the one shown in Fig. 3.2 has become to known as the "Perceptron". It is a combination of different units of which those in the first layer (S) simply comprise sensors of the environment. The signals produced by the sensors are combined in the second layer of units named "association elements" (A). If the S signals were binary, then the A could simply operate in the same way as the logic gates do, i.e., decoding their input signal patterns: an active response would be obtained if and only if the binary combination of the input signal values is a given one. The third layer of the 'response elements' (R) constitutes the proper learning system: connections from the A to the R are made through variable connections, similar to the controllable resistors of the Adaline.

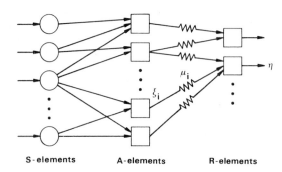

Fig. 3.2. The Perceptron (control of adjustable weights is not shown)

S-elements   A-elements   R-elements

It is difficult to know how much the works of Widrow and Rosenblatt were influenced by each other; it seems that the Adaline was later applied in communication engineering (especially in adaptive antennas) while the Perceptron has enjoyed a doctrinal status in theoretical neuroscience. The most apparent dissimilarity in the adaptive function of Perceptron when compared with Adaline is that every R element is a threshold trigger; it has only two stable output states (denoted, e.g., 0 and 1) which depend on the inputs according to a discriminant function. If the signals produced by the A elements are denoted by ξ_i, the weights of the respective adaptive input connections by μ_i, and the output of an R unit by η, then it is assumed that

$$\eta = 0 \quad \text{if} \quad \sum_{i=1}^{n} \mu_i \xi_i < \delta \,,$$

$$\eta = 1 \quad \text{if} \quad \sum_{i=1}^{n} \mu_i \xi_i \geq \delta \,,$$

(3.9)

where δ is a discrimination threshold.

The learning process at the R elements may take many different forms. Assuming that a given set of "training signals" is $\{\xi_{ik}\}$ whereby the ξ_{ik} signals produced by the A elements are first restricted to binary values, $\xi_{ik} \in \{0, 1\}$, and if the wanted binary response is η_k, then one of the suggested training rules is to change only those input weights for which $\xi_{ik} = 1$ (active); the μ_{ik} are increased or decreased by a constant amount λ according to the rule

for $\xi_{ik} = 1$, $\mu_{i,k+1} = \mu_{ik} - \lambda$ if $\eta = 1$ and $\eta_k = 0$,

$\mu_{i,k+1} = \mu_{ik} + \lambda$ if $\eta = 0$ and $\eta_k = 1$,

for $\xi_{ik} = 0$ or $\eta = \eta_k$, $\mu_{i,k+1} = \mu_{ik}$.   (3.10)

This set of formulas has been called the "α-reinforcement rule". They can also be put into the form of a single equation

$$\mu_{i,k+1} = \mu_{ik} + \lambda \cdot (\eta_k - \eta) \cdot \xi_{ik} , \qquad (3.11)$$

whereby a close analogy with (3.2) can be recognized; here we have to remember that η_k, η, and ξ_{ik} are binary. Apparently one can easily generalize the Perceptron for nonbinary ξ_{ik}, too. It may further be pointed out that if $\lambda = \alpha_k$ like in the Adaline, stochastic approximation methods lend themselves to the analysis of convergence conditions.

It has been proved in many different ways (e.g., [3.8]) that the wanted input-output response relations, if they at all are possible, can be achieved in a finite number of steps. This, of course, is due to the discrimination limit, and in general would not succeed in linear machines.

3.3 The Learning Matrix

Another early construct which was introduced for the explanation of brain functions and implementation of artificial intelligence is the *Learning Matrix* due to *Steinbuch* [3.9, 10]. It is a system of crossing signal lines, with an adaptive connection at each crossing (Fig. 3.3); each vertical line could also be thought of as forming a functional unit which sums up the signals coupled through the interconnections to this line. Fig. 3.3 has been drawn in a slightly different way than the original Learning Matrix, to better compare it with the previous models.

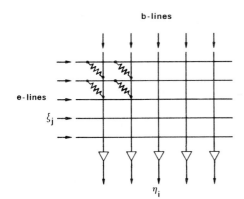

Fig. 3.3. The Learning Matrix (only four of the cross-connections are shown)

There is, however, a significant difference between the earlier principles and the Learning Matrix: the latter does not involve any difference-forming operations which would cause a corrective action towards a wanted response.

Instead this network, at least in its original form [3.9], was intended for the simulation of *classical conditioning* (i.e., a set of parallel conditioned reflexes induced by the same set of stimuli). Signals on the e-lines ("Eigenschaften"; characteristics, attributes) may be regarded to constitute a stimulus pattern, and signals on the b-lines ("Bedeutungen"; meanings, outcomes, responses) a classification result; each b-line could further be provided with a nonlinear threshold-trigger. In the *learning phase*, signals corresponding to wanted responses are simply forced or impressed on the b-lines, concomitant with a conditioning pattern which acts on the e-lines. In the *recall phase,* active signals are applied only on the e-lines, whereby signals on the b-lines are obtained through the cross-connections.

The original strategy for modification of the variable connections was supposed to imitate the classical conditioning; to this end the input signals on the e- and b-lines were assumed binary, η_i, $\xi_j \in \{0, 1\}$. If the connection between these lines is denoted by μ_{ij}, and the (continuous-valued) recollection on the corresponding b-line, in the recall phase, by $\hat{\eta}_i$, then the wanted output signals can be computed, e.g., using an electrical-circuit analogy where the μ_{ij} are conductances and each b-line has been connected to an output buffer amplifier with input impedance z.

For

$$\mu_{ij} \ll z^{-1},$$

$$\hat{\eta}_i = z \sum_{i=1}^{n} \mu_{ij} \xi_j . \tag{3.12}$$

The μ_{ij} should change according to the rule of Table 3.1. (There was a confusion of this rule in the original work; cf., e.g., [Ref. 3.9, p. 216].)

Table 3.1. Reinforcement rule for the Learning Matrix

		ξ_j	
		0	1
μ_i	0	*	μ_{ij} decreases
	1	*	μ_{ij} increases

* μ_{ij} does not change

This is exactly the reinforcement rule of the conditioned reflex since if the corrections are small and of equal magnitude, the expectation value of μ_{ij} after a great number of corrections can easily be seen to approach (Sect. 6.8.2)

$$\mu_{ij} = E\{\eta_i | \xi_j = 1\}.$$ (3.13)

As reversible changes in the μ_{ij} might have caused some technical difficulties, then a simpler learning rule (Table 3.2) was adopted in later works; this is the same rule which appears in a subsequent neural model named "associative net" of *Willshaw* et al. [3.11], and it will be termed "conjunction learning" here:

Table 3.2. The conjunction-learning rule

		ξ_j	
		0	1
η_i	0	*	*
	1	*	μ_{ij} increases

* μ_{ij} does not change

The values of μ_{ij} can be made to saturate. In particular, in the associative net they reach the saturation value in one step.

An analysis of the latter strategy can now be made assuming no saturation limits. If the increments of μ_{ij} are $\{0, \Delta\mu\}$, then, after exposure to a set of pairs of patterns $\{(\eta_i^{(k)}, \xi_j^{(k)}) | k = 1, 2, \ldots, N\}$ the connections and recollections, respectively, will become

$$\mu_{ij}^{(N)} = \Delta\mu \sum_{k=1}^{N} \eta_i^{(k)} \xi_j^{(k)},$$ (3.14)

$$\hat{\eta}_i = z \sum_{j=1}^{n} \mu_{ij}^{(N)} \xi_j = \sum_{k=1}^{N} \gamma_k \eta_i^{(k)},$$

where

$$\gamma_k = z\Delta\mu \sum_{j=1}^{n} \xi_j \xi_j^{(k)}.$$

The coefficient γ_k is found to be proportional to the *inner product* of two patterns on the e-lines, namely, they key pattern $\{\xi_j\}$ used for excitation in the recall phase, and the key pattern $\{\xi_j^{(k)}\}$ which was associated with the $\{\eta_i^{(k)}\}$ in the learning phase. This result then complies with the *correlation matrix approximation of associative mappings* discussed in Sect. 6.8.1.

Finally it should be noted that the signals η_i and ξ_j can assume continuous values, too, whereby (3.14) is still valid for the description of the learning process. The selectivity of correlation matrix networks in this case, as well as a "graceful degradation" of its performance when already existing connections are destroyed at random, has been studied by the present author [3.12].

Variations of the above adaptive principle, with relation to different network structures, have been presented by *Uttley* [3.13], *Caianiello* [3.14], and some subsequent researchers (Sect. 8.3).

It can be shown that the selectivity of a recollection from the Learning Matrix-type network would be improved significantly if the μ_{ij} could acquire negative values, too. As the realization of negative conductance, for instance, in electrical networks would be difficult, another straightforward way to solve the problems has been suggested: it is possible to use an *antagonistic encoding* of the signals whereby, for instance, every ξ_j-signal is represented by double signals, $+\xi_j$ and $-\xi_j$, respectively. If the coefficient μ_{ij} is positive, a conductance directly proportional to it is connected between the ith horizontal line and the line for $+\xi_j$. If the coefficient μ_{ij} is negative, a conductance which is directly proportional to its magnitude is connected between the ith horizontal line and the line for $-\xi_j$. Currents merging at every output amplifier are thereby added and transformed into output voltages according to (3.14).

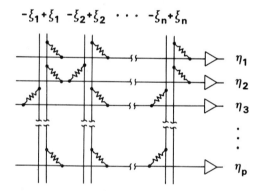

Fig. 3.4. Antagonistic encoding

3.4 Physical Realization of Adaptive Weights

3.4.1 Perceptron and Adaline

The most straightforward implementation of controllable input weights is to use servo-driven potentiometers according to Fig. 3.5. If for every input signal ξ_j, its negation $-\xi_j$ is available, too, then the potentiometers are able to compute the products $\mu_{ij} \cdot \xi_j$ in all quadrants, i.e., for all sign combinations of μ_{ij} and ξ_j. The difference $\mu - \mu_i$ is directly formed at the differential input of the servo amplifier.

This solution is practicable only for a relatively small number of signals. For large adaptive systems it would be desirable to find cheaper elements, at least for the resistors. Very few continuously adjustable components have

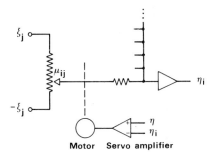

Fig. 3.5. Servo potentiometer

been invented, however. A classical solution is the *Memistor* shown in Fig. 3.6. There, a variable resistor the value of which can be increased or decreased by external control voltage is implemented using a plating bath arrangement. A conductive film (e.g., Cu) is formed on the plating cathode which is used (transversally) as the input resistor. The thickness of the film is controlled by plating current between anode and cathode; the direction of this current, and thus changes in the film are reversible. The input signals and the plating process can further be made more independent of each other if *ac* modulation is used for the former.

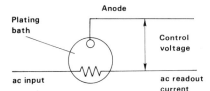

Fig. 3.6. The Memistor

If *ac* modulated signals with a sufficiently small amplitude can be used to represent the input signal values, a rather elegant method resembling, e.g., the automatic volume control of audio amplifiers is to use a fixed component with nonlinear voltage-current characteristic curve; field-effect transistors, the current through which is proportional to the square of the applied voltage might be used. Such a device can then be biased to a certain operating point by a control current which is a function of $\eta - \eta_i$. The μ_{ij} corresponds to the dynamic conductance, or $\partial i / \partial u$ where i is the current through the device and u the voltage over it.

3.4.2 Classical Conditioning

The following simple memory principle, suggested by this author, directly implements the conditioned reflexes according to (3.13). In its basic form it uses capacitors as storage elements which warrants a high degree of linearity over a wide range of stored values; the time constant of the arrangement, however, can then hardly exceed a few hours.

In this method the memory elements do not act as variable switches; instead they are used as "sample-and-hold" devices, i.e., they buffer part of the signal energy to deliver it later in the recall phase. Consider Fig. 3.7 which shows an array of capacitors, each one connected to the b-lines via a voltage-controllable resistor, e.g., field-effect transistor. These devices usually have a very high value of resistance (say, over 10 MΩ) in the passive state while their value is decreased (say, to $R \cong 1 \text{ k}\Omega$) whenever the corresponding e-line is activated by an input signal (with binary value 1).

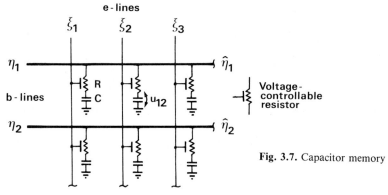

Fig. 3.7. Capacitor memory

If $\xi_j = 0$, all capacitors on the corresponding row are switched off (except for a small leakage) from the b-lines, and they hold their voltage values. For $\xi_j = 1$ the combination of R and C acts as a low-pass filter: if the time constant RC is much larger than the interval of time at which a new pattern is switched on the e-lines, then the voltage built up in the capacitor is the (exponentially weighted) time-average of the corresponding η_i signal, *taken over those intervals for which* $\xi_j = 1$. If the η_i signals are ergodic (their statistics are independent of time), then

$$u_{ij} \cong \frac{T}{RC} E\{\eta_i | \xi_j = 1\}, \tag{3.15}$$

where T is the length of the sampling interval of input patterns. On the other hand, if the b-lines are connected to amplifiers with a low input impedance Z, then in the *recall phase* the output signals attain the value

$$\hat{\eta}_i \cong \frac{Z}{R} \sum_{j=1}^{n} u_{ij} \xi_j, \tag{3.16}$$

and (3.15, 16) can be found similar to those of the earlier defined conditioned-reflex model, with the voltages u_{ij} now corresponding to the weights μ_{ij}.

This model represents one of the many forms in which the conditioned reflex may be realized; e.g., essentially similar equations would be obtained for some electrochemical processes which then would have higher time constants.

3.4.3 Conjunction Learning Switches

In the learning matrix and the associative net, the strength of the connections between lines ought to remain steady in the recall phase, at least during a short time span. On the other hand, the conductance value of an interconnection ought to change very nonlinearly in the learning phase when there is a conjunction of two signals converging upon this element.

For all-or-none switching, as the case is with the associative net, several electronic and magnetic components with these characteristics are known from digital computer technology. There are much fewer choices for components whose conductance would change gradually, directly proportional to the product (correlation) of the two signals. *Steinbuch* and *Piske* [3.10] devised several phenomena to this end: e.g., silver wires submerged into an AgBr bath were able to develop a variable galvanic contact between them.

3.4.4 Digital Representation of Adaptive Circuits

The above physical implementations of adaptive elements were mainly introduced in order to show that a rather simple materialization of adaptive components is feasible, in principle at least. If learning machines had found widespread applications, a new manufacturing technology for them might have been developed, e.g., using large-scale integration. Now it is to be emphasized that if the learning principle will show useful for highly parallel computations, and the technological applications are the main goal, then development of such a new analog technology is really not necessary since the signals and adaptive weights can easily be represented *digitally,* i.e., by numerical codes in special parallel arithmetic circuits, whereby the adaptation equations are readily computable digitally, too. Such digital circuits are inherently more complex but their accuracy and stability is superior to the analog ones; they can be integrated cheaply as microcircuits.

Combination of analog filter principles and digital representation seems to open new avenues to highly parallel computation in signal and pattern processing.

3.4.5 Biological Components

An important aspect of the learning theories introduced in this book is that they probably relate to neural circuits, too. It is nowadays rather generally thought that adaptation to sensory signals is mainly due to variable connections between nerve cells; the most common types of these contacts are named *synapses*. We shall revert to them in Chap. 8.

A nerve signal, at least on the higher levels of the central nervous system, is a train of equal-amplitude pulses with a repetition frequency signified as the signal value. When signals from several sources converge upon a nerve cell, the voltage across its membrane (the so-called post-synaptic potential) changes by a fixed increment for every incoming signal pulse.

When the membrane potential reaches a characteristic threshold, the cell becomes unstable and triggers pulses into the outgoing fibre, the *axon*. The dynamics of this process are rather complicated; nonetheless it may be approximately stated that the averaged frequency of output pulses is a weighted sum or another more general function of the input pulse frequencies, and the weights referring to the various inputs depend on the strengths and locations of the input synapses. A passive synapse can turn into an active one and vice versa; it is also possible that the strengths change gradually, at least over a limited dynamic range. The transfer function of a neuron is usually bounded by saturation limits, but at least in the active triggering state (around the 'operating point') one may use the approximation

$$\eta_i = \sum_{j=1}^{n} \mu_{ij}\xi_j, \qquad (3.17)$$

where now η_i is the output frequency, ξ_j is the frequency of the jth input signal, and the μ_{ij} denote proportionality factors due to the various synapses. As said above, the μ_{ij} are alterable on account of the signals whereby the neurons become adaptive.

3.5 Holographic Memories

It may be assumed that the reader is already familiar, superficially at least, with the basic principle of optical holography [3.15]. In this section we shall discuss it once again in more detail, relating to the context of the associative memory function.

In information technology, holographic memories have been developed for the storage of masses of pictorial information such as photographs, and in some special applications they offer an additional advantage of being tolerable to partial damage of memory media. Before a detailed discussion of the holographic principle for memories, it will be necessary to point out that spatial distributedness of memory traces, the central characteristic of holograms, may mean either of the following two facts: (i) Elements in a data set are spread by a transformation over a memory area, but different data sets are always stored in separate areas. (ii) Several data sets are superimposed on the same medium in a distributed form.

Examples of the first type are holographic memories in which pieces of information, for instance photographs of documents, are stored on a photographic film in the form of their holograms, usually in a microscopic size; a typical density of information is one million bits per square millimeter. Nevertheless, all holograms are kept spatially separate, and to retrieve one document, a mechanical or optoelectronic control is necessary by which a beam of light used for reading is directed towards a particular area. An example of the second type of memory is a hologram which utilizes the crystalline properties of matter. The hologram is formed on a substrate which in effect is a lattice of atoms, and when waves of light pass through it, they can form images only at certain diffraction angles. If during exposure of the holograms, the direction of the reference ray necessary to form the hologram is different for every image, memory traces from many (up to some tens with the present techniques) images can be superimposed on the same photosensitive substrate, and one of the images can be chosen for readout, if the reference beam during reading is selected correspondingly. However, neither of the above methods can yet be named *associative memory* because the set of possible reference beams is fixed and must be controlled by a selector mechanism; consequently, these are still *addressable* memories. One has to realize that *if a holographic memory has to implement the associative memory function, then reading must be content-addressable*; the wanted response or recollection must be obtained using a *patterned key*, either a separate one, or a fragment of the recollection, *without any extra control information*.

The capacities of optical holography in implementing *highly parallel computing operations* on images and patterns have been realized long ago, too (cf., e.g., the work of *Stroke* [3.16]). It is mainly the optical two-dimensional *convolution* of two patterns which is readily computable by the so-called Fourier optics. As for adaptive filters and associative memories, optical holograms would otherwise offer many interesting solutions if only there would exist a fast and reversible, or at least erasable photosensitive medium. Lacking this, optical holographic computing has remained at the experimental level.

It has further been suggested that the operation of neural networks which in the central nervous systems are often densely interconnected might be describable by the principle of holography (Sect. 8.1.1). Let it briefly be mentioned here that the diffraction principles which are utilized in optical holography are very exacting, and no physiological experiments or anatomical facts support the idea that holography could be directly implementable by neural signals, at least in the form that uses monochromatic, sinusoidally varying wave fronts. We shall suggest another more straightforward and natural formalism for their description in the next chapter; nonetheless the introduction of holographic principles may be justified here since they offer one framework for the understanding of collective (integrated) phenomena.

We shall restrict ourselves to the formation of cross-correlation of two images in holographic recording, mainly because this is an extension of classical conditioning between scalar-valued signals and it then leads to results which are implementable by network principles, too.

3.5.1 A Simple Principle of Holographic Associative Memory

Consider Fig. 3.8 which depicts a photographic plate P and two beams of coherent (phased) light, obtained, e.g., from the same laser lamp by splitting its beam in two by half-reflecting mirrors. One partial beam is falling upon the plate from direction A, and the other from direction B. Let the sources of light be modulated spatially, for instance, by their transmission through templates.

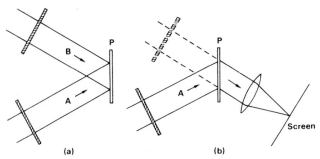

(a)   (b)

Fig. 3.8a, b. Principle of Fresnel holography: (a) recording, (b) recall

By diffraction, the wavefronts from A and B form a spatial interference pattern at P. The transparency of the plate, by exposure to the light, will then be changed. After development and fixing, the photographic plate will store information from the pair of patterns which were simultaneously displayed at A and B, respectively, in this *hologram*.

When the photographic plate P is later illuminated by the pattern from A or B alone, the wavefronts behind P, due to diffraction which occurs during their passage through the hologram, will assume information from the missing pattern, too. In particular, if P were illuminated by the A pattern only, then the diffracted waves could be collected by a lens system to form a projection image of B on the screen placed behind the photographic plate. Alternatively, an observer looking through the hologram would see a "virtual image" of the A pattern.

A theoretical explanation of this phenomenon can be made, for instance, in the following way. If the complex amplitudes of the electromagnetic fields at plate P, corresponding to the light sources at A and B are denoted by $F_A(r)$ and $F_B(r)$, respectively, where r is the spatial coordinate vector at P, then the transmittance $T(r)$ of the plate is assumed to change directly proportionally to the resultant light intensity, or

$$\Delta T(r) = -\lambda [F_A(r) + F_B(r)] [F_A^*(r) + F_B^*(r)] , \tag{3.18}$$

where λ is a proportionality factor depending on the sensitivity of the film as well as exposure time, and the asterisk denotes the complex conjugate. If the plate P is assumed to be very thin, then, upon illumination of the hologram by waves from A alone, the complex field immediately behind P is

$$\begin{aligned} F(r) &= [T(r) + \Delta T(r)] F_A(r) \\ &= T(r) F_A(r) - \lambda [F_A(r) F_A^*(r) + F_B(r) F_B^*(r)] F_A(r) \\ &\quad - \lambda [F_A(r) F_B^*(r) F_A(r) + F_B(r) F_A(r) F_A^*(r)] . \end{aligned} \tag{3.19}$$

Now $F_A(r) F_A^*(r)$ and $F_B(r) F_B^*(r)$ are the wave intensities which are assumed constant with r over plate P, and for simplicity, they both can be normalized to unity. On the other hand, $-\lambda [F_A(r) F_B^*(r)] F_A(r)$ is a term in which the expression $F_A(r) F_B^*(r)$ represents a so-called destructive interference and is not able to produce any image. The noise caused by this term may be neglected. It is further possible to assume that the initial transmittance of the plate is $T(r) = T$, i.e., constant with r. For the field behind the hologram it is, therefore, possible to write

$$F(r) \approx (T - 2\lambda) F_A(r) - \lambda F_B(r) . \tag{3.20}$$

In other words, the wavefronts behind the hologram are as if an attenuated image of the A pattern, as well as a reconstruction of the B pattern multiplied by $-\lambda$ were seen.

Assume now that exposures from several pairs of different patterns (A, B) are recorded (superimposed) on the same photographic plate. One might expect that the different holograms were confused and information would be lost. This is in general true. It can be shown, however, that under certain conditions, an information pattern associated with a particular key pattern can be reconstructed from this mixture with reasonable selectivity. Assume that several pairs of patterns with field strengths $F_{Ak}(r)$ and $F_{Bk}(r)$, respectively, with $k = 1, 2, \ldots, N$, have been recorded on plate P in successive exposures. Later illumination of the hologram by a pattern with field $F_A(r)$ then results in field intensity behind P which, on similar grounds as before, can approximately be written as

$$F(r) \approx (T - 2N\lambda) F_A(r) - \lambda \sum_{k=1}^{N} [F_{Ak}^*(r) F_A(r)] F_{Bk}(r) . \tag{3.21}$$

The *recollection,* represented by the sum over N terms, is then a *linear mixture* of images of the B patterns, with relative intensities that depend on the degree of matching of the field patterns $F_{Ak}(r)$ with the field pattern $F_A(r)$ that occurs during reading. So if the A pattern used during reading as the *search argument* would be identical with one of the earlier A patterns used as *"key word"*, then for one value of k, $F_{Ak}^*(r)F_A(r)$ would be equal to unity, and the corresponding term in the sum, representing the associated field $F_{Bk}(r)$, would dominate. The other terms in the mixture in general have variable phases and represent superimposed noise due to "crosstalk" from the other patterns. If the various A patterns were independent random images or randomized by modulation with irregular "speckles" [3.17], or if they had their nonzero picture elements at different places, the noise content would probably remain small. When the information patterns must represent arbitrary information, however, this assumption is in general not valid.

3.5.2 Addressing in Holographic Memories

As mentioned above, when a content-addressable memory is used to store arbitrary (normally binary) patterns, a large storage capacity cannot be achieved by the previous superposition method on account of the crosstalk noise between the patterns. It will then become necessary to store the partial holograms that represent different entries on locally separate areas on the film, corresponding to *addressed storage locations.* The addressed writing and reading of the small holograms can be made by the same technique that has been applied with conventional holographic memories; this will briefly be reviewed below. When it comes to content-addressable reading, however, special provisions are necessary.

A holographic memory plane may comprise, for example, an array of 100 by 100 small holograms, each with an area of 1 mm by 1 mm. Every small hologram stores typically an amount of information equivalent to 10^4 bits; thus the total capacity is 10^8 bits. In order to write a small hologram in one of these 10^4 storage locations, the holographic memory needs a delicate light switching system to make the beams A and B point at the location. This is equivalent to the *address decoding system* existing in all normal memories. The switching of the light beams, controlled by electric signals which define the address, is made by so-called *deflectors,* the operation of which can be based, for instance, on polarization switching in electro-optic crystals, and subsequent passage of the beam through birefringent prisms. For a more detailed discussion of the principles of beam deflection, see the article of *Kulcke* et al. [3.18].

The storage density, referring to surface area of the photographic plate, can be increased at least by a factor of 10 to 20 by making the hologram three-dimensional; it is then named *volume hologram.* The fields of the waves from beams A and B, of course, interfere anywhere where the waves meet, and in particular within a *thick* photosensitive emulsion used for recording. It can be shown [3.19, 20] that if several holograms are recorded in the same volume using A and B beams with different tilts, then, provided that the differences between the incident angles used in different exposures are greater than a certain limit depending on the thickness of the hologram, the stored information can be reconstructed without any crosstalk from the other patterns.

Thus, using multiple sources of light with different incident angles, *every small hologram can be made to correspond to several storage locations.* The control circuits used to select a particular angle naturally belong to the address decoding system.

In the following, the CAM principle will be exemplified with thin holograms only.

Addressed Writing and Content-Addressable Reading. The small holograms, corresponding to the various stored entries, had to be written using narrow coherent beams confined to them only. Content-addressable reading of the memory, on the other hand, has to be made in an all-parallel fashion, by interrogating all entries simultaneously and in parallel. Consider first the *addressed writing* of information. Since with the normal photosensitive materials the holographic memory operates in the read-only mode, it is possible to record the small holograms using a mask with a small aperture in front of the plate during writing, and the position of the mask can then be adjusted mechanically. If it were possible to make the memory traces erasable, then the aperture, too, ought to be electrically controllable. Two different principles to implement a movable aperture have been suggested [3.21, 22]. In both of them the fields of beams A and B are made broad enough to cover the whole memory plate, but during writing, only a portion of them corresponding to a small hologram is activated. In the first principle, the photosensitive plate is covered by another plate which in ambient light and in that due to the A and B beams only is opaque, but becomes transparent at light intensities exceeding a certain threshold. Such materials exist [3.23] although their technology has not been developed for this application. It is then possible to hold the broad A and B beams steady and to use a third, narrow beam with constant intensity which is deflected towards the location in which a small hologram has to be written. If the intensity of the third beam is sufficient, it will exceed the threshold and make the cover plate transparent to the A and B beams. In the second principle a magnetizable film is used as the storage medium. The interference pattern of the light waves is only used as a heat source which warms up the film locally. In the presence of a constant magnetic field the film will be magnetized at cool places, whereas if an area is heated above the Curie temperature, the magnetic polarization will be destroyed. A third beam of light is then used to bias the temperature over the small hologram to the vicinity of the Curie temperature. Reading of magnetic holograms is effected by polarized light the reflectivity of which depends on magnetic polarization of the surface.

The *content-addressable reading* of the holographic memory is done by exposing all small holograms in parallel to a broad A beam which corresponds to the prevailing *search argument*. The matching of this beam with information in the small holograms can be detected as explained below. A particular problem arises, however, with how to deal with multiple matches which are commonplace in all content-addressable memories. In the following it shall be explained in detail how the matching results are recollected, and how the associated data in the matching locations are again read out in entirety. This discussion contains in it ideas from the works of *Sakaguchi* et al. [3.21 – 24] and *Knight* [3.22 – 25], but the particular solutions presented here have been selected mainly for clarity of explanation.

To begin with, it will be necessary to discuss the imaging in Fig. 3.9, in order to clarify the basic optical matching operation. Assume that the field strength corresponding to the recollection of the B pattern (in the output plane) is integrated using a detector, one device per small hologram. Assume first that the B beam had no information written in it, having a field strength which is constant (with amplitude 1) over its cross section. It is then known from the theory of holography that, at least when the tilts of the A and B beams are small, the distribution of the electromagnetic field over the hologram corresponds to the two-dimensional Fourier transform of the spatial distribution of the field amplitude in the A pattern. Assume, without loss of generality, that the field amplitude of the A pattern is a real function $A(x)$, where x is the spatial coordinate vector of the plane in which the A pattern is defined. In other words, it is assumed that (for a unit area)

$$F_A(r) = \int_{S_x} e^{-jrx} A(x) dS_x; \quad j = \sqrt{-1}, \tag{3.22}$$

where S_x denotes the plane corresponding to x. Assume now that the field of an A pattern recorded on the hologram is $A_k(x)$, with corresponding field at plate P equal to $F_{Ak}(r)$. When the field on the output plane, corresponding to the recollection of the B beam, is integrated spatially and its intensity is detected as shown in Fig. 3.9 (notice that during reading the real B beam has been switched off), for the output it is obtained

$$I_B = \lambda^2 \left| \int_{S_r} F_{Ak}^*(r) F_A(r) dS_r \right|^2 = \lambda^2 \left| \int_{S_x} A_k(x) A(x) dS_x \right|^2, \tag{3.23}$$

where the last expression results from general properties of Fourier transforms. When it was assumed that $A_k(x)$ and $A(x)$ are real amplitude distributions, (3.23) then states that the output is directly proportional to the square of the *inner product* of the patterns $A_k(x)$ and $A(x)$.

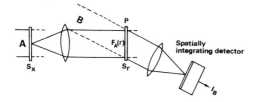

Fig. 3.9. Response from a hologram with spatial integration of the output beam intensity

In practice, the patterns $A_k(x)$ and $A(x)$ are formed of binary picture elements corresponding to one of two light intensities; one of the values is usually zero. The output I_B is then zero if and only if all light spots of $A(x)$ match with dark spots in $A_k(x)$.

It was assumed in the above analysis that the B pattern had a constant intensity. It can be shown that the same analysis basically applies to a system in which the B beam carries an information pattern.

There was also another feature which on purpose was neglected above, namely, that the small holograms were formed by interference from three beams. The narrow control beam, however, has no effect in the readout, since in this example its "recollection" points at a direction where a detection of light intensity is not made.

A *masked equality search* is a logic operation used in content-addressable memories. It simply means that the keyword must match exactly with the stored word in those parts which fall outside a *mask* whereas within the mask, the stored word can have any contents. Every bit position in $A_k(x)$ and $A(x)$ must be provided by two squares, one which is light and one which is dark. Let us call these values 0 and 1. The *logic value* of the bit positions is '0' if the value combination in the squares is, say, $(1, 0)$, whereas the bit value is '1' if $(0, 1)$ is written into the squares. If the value combination is $(0, 0)$, then it corresponds to the masked bit position. The value combination $(1, 1)$ shall be forbidden.

Consider now the integral in I_B; the integrand is zero at all places in which either $A_k(x)$ or $A(x)$ has a masked value. If and only if the bit values of $A_k(x)$ and $A(x)$ at all unmasked positions are logic complements of each other, will the output I_B be zero. This suggests a straightforward implementation of equality match operation: the bit values of the pattern to be used as search argument are *inverted* logically, and these values, together with the masking markings, then constitute the pattern $A(x)$. A match in unmasked portions is indicated by absence of light in the output detector corresponding to this small hologram.

In holography, the coherent light beam corresponding to $A(x)$ is spread during the reading simultaneously over all small holograms. If in the output plane there is an intensity detector for each of the small holograms, their responses then correspond to *multiple response detection,* and may be buffered by flip-flop states in a *results store.* The responses can in turn be handled by a multiple response resolver, and the address code thereby obtainable is used to control the final readout process.

Addressed Reading. During the writing, a constructive interference between *three* beams, namely, the A beam, the B beam, and the narrow control beam was formed. The combination of the A and control beams, or either beam

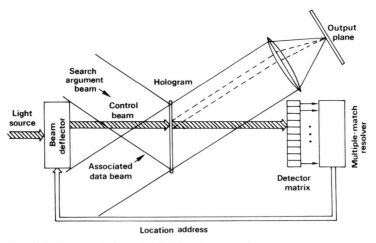

Fig. 3.10. Complete holographic CAM system organization

alone, is then effective to be used for holographic readout. In fact, it was the A beam alone which was used to implement the content-addressable readout. For the addressed reading, the control beam can be used, respectively. Since it was assumed to be provided with a controllable deflector mechanism, it is only necessary to control it by the address code obtained from the multiple-match resolver. The complete holographic CAM system is delineated in Fig. 3.10.

4. A New Approach to Adaptive Filters

The early works around 1960 on learning machines may be characterized as attempts to implement artificial intelligence using formal models of neurons and Perceptron networks, obviously in the hope that more and more complex functions would gradually evolve from such structures. There is no doubt about the biological organisms having that fundamental organization. Why was the success in artificial constructs not straightforward as expected? Below I am aiming at a critical analysis, mainly with an objective to find amendments to the early ideas.

4.1 Survey of Some Necessary Functions

Definition of a simple transfer function to the basic operational unit is obviously a sound starting point; in other words, there is no need to look at the neurons as complex, "intelligent" micro-organisms, as sometimes believed. The basic operation of a neural unit is *selective response* to a received signal pattern (value combination), and in this way a neural cell, or tightly co-operating group of cells is comparable to a *lock*, to which the input signal pattern must fit like a *key*. This view may be shared by most neurophysiologists, especially those performing single-cell recordings. The output responses from several cells, again, comprise a key to other cells, and so on. The selective properties, or the "codes" of these "locks" are changed in learning processes. This feature was also present in the models discussed in Chap. 3.

One criticism of the simplest neuron models may concern their being defined for spatial patterns (parallel values of signals at a certain time) only. It is true that many phenomena recorded from brain structures such as the EEG (electro-encephalogram) or evoke potentials are expressible as characteristic *temporal* activity patterns; their forms, however, mainly come from the recording method. It is self-evident that signal delays of varying lengths are associated with neural circuits, and quite characteristic temporal patterns are then generated by dynamic phenomena taking place at the cell membranes, as well as in recurrent signal loops. One purpose of signal loops is to facilitate the generation of *sequences* of signal patterns in mental processes as well as automatic control of actions, and this temporal dimension of information processing was discussed in a general form in Sect. 1.3.2.

A much more fundamental temporal phenomenon associated with learning is the alteration of the selective response of a neural unit due to the received signals, or *adaptation*. In view of the discussion that will be carried out in this chapter, it seems that the earlier models did not capture the most important characteristics of these laws. A systematic analysis carried out below in Sect. 4.3 will reveal that different statistical representations of the input signals will be imprinted on the system parameters with different choices for the functional law describing the adaptive changes. The choice of a law must guarantee *dynamic stability* of the system, a requirement which is generally satisfied in systems engineering, but seldom taken into account, not even in the most trivial way, in neural modelling.

In a couple of places in this work, it has already been referred to a property of the Perceptron, Adaline, and similar networks, which seems to exclude these models from the set of possible basic neural functions. They always include a *comparison* with the wanted response, or *supervised learning* at every unit. It is obvious that teaching can be a way to modify the overall behaviour of a learning system, but this should not mean that for every basic unit there must be a private teacher. This, however, is just the case with the above models. It is amazing that such a restriction has not been realized by most modellers of neural circuits; during 20 years, a great number of learning models have been presented which totally rely on supervised learning, even in their most detailed functions. The above models must therefore be regarded as *behavioral* models, describing learned stimulus-response relations *on a rather high organizational level*.

The worst handicap of the earlier neural models, however, seems to be that every basic unit is considered to operate essentially independently (although in parallel). In spite of certain claimed collective or cooperative properties, the only cooperative effect in these models has been in the neuron itself which in some way integrates the incoming signals spatially and temporally. One ought to realize that the neural networks, at least in the central nervous system, are densely interconnected, with an abundance of recurrent signal loops. In other words, a neural network model cannot reflect genuine collective phenomena, unless in its analysis, the *feedback* through many different paths is taken into account: in a collective model, the activity of every component in a system then depends on the activities of many other components. It seems impossible to analyze the dynamic behaviour of large feedback models unless some simplifying assumptions are made about their structure for typification. It seems that a very important type of feedback models, frequently encountered in brain networks, is the *lateral feedback model* or *laminar network model* delineated in one of its simplest forms in Fig. 4.1.

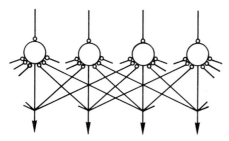

Fig. 4.1. Laterally interconnected array

We shall devote plenty of attention to the analysis of lateral feedback models in this book, because only with their aid it will become possible to ascend to the next organizational level in network structures; it will be necessary to understand the basic lateral feedback phenomena in their purest idealized form, even if the real neural systems would never exactly comply with them. This approach is like description of complex waveforms by their fundamental harmonics. One must realize that the behaviour of a collective system, due to feedback, may be completely different from that of the basic components, and this may then facilitate the extension of our understanding to the higher organizational phenomena underlying intelligence, too. Incidentally, a great number of brain functions is already explainable in terms of the lateral feedback models.

Finally, with the addition of a very special detailed feature ("teaching the neighbours locally"), the collective network models can be shown to switch into the *self-organizing mode* which is already able to create abstractions and symbolic representations. This phenomenon will be discussed separately in Chap. 5.

4.2 On Physical and Biological Modelling

Consider Fig. 4.2 which represents a physical nonrecurrent signal network.

Every output signal is a function of all the input signals. An output signal $\eta_i(t)$ which is a continuous function of time depends, not only on the input

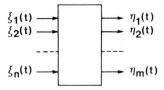

Fig. 4.2. Physical signal network

signals $\xi_j(t)$ at the same time, but on all earlier signal values $\xi_j(t')$, $t' < t$, too. In other words, the network integrates its input signals in the spatial as well as temporal domain. This is a usual case in systems theory, especially with engineering systems. A very simple example is shown in Fig. 4.3: the output voltage $U_o(t)$ is a functional of the input voltages $U_{i1}(t)$ and $U_{i2}(t)$ according to the formulas

$$U_o(t) \cong \frac{r}{R} [U_{c1}(t) + U_{c2}(t)], \quad \text{where}$$

$$U_{c1,2}(t) \cong \frac{1}{2RC} \int_{-\infty}^{t} [U_{i1,2}(t') - U_{c1,2}(t')] \, dt' + U_{c1,2}(-\infty),$$

(4.1)

which can easily be derived by elementary system analysis.

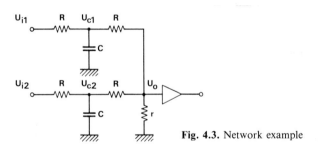

Fig. 4.3. Network example

In Fig. 4.3, the resistances R and r, and the capacitance C constitute the *system parameters*; in engineering systems, the system parameters are normally time-invariant. This is usually not the case with biological systems; not only are the parameters changed gradually due to metabolism, growth processes, and adaptation to the changing environment, but most biological system parameters are further actively controlled by chemicals (e.g., endocrinology) as well as by separate neural control loops. For instance, in many neural circuits performing a certain operation using one neurotransmitter system (e.g., acetylcholine), this operation is further modulated by another neurotransmitter system using different chemicals (e.g., norepinephrine). Such effects frequently correspond to fluctuations of *attention*.

The biophysical systems are often very complex, which makes a conventional exact mathematical approach impossible. There are many interactive phenomena with very different dynamics, ranging from membrane triggering phenomena lasting some milliseconds (with many types of chemicals involved) to complex system behaviour through signal loops which may take minutes. This may be followed by growth phenomena which take weeks or even years. In order to be able to define basic paradigms of system behaviour, one necessarily has to consider the effect of various factors separately, thereby assuming some factors constant or time-averaged.

In particular, in the discussion of *adaptive network behaviour* which is the central topics in this book, one has somehow to average or approximate the fast phenomena associated with the triggering of neural membranes. A classical approach is to consider the time-averaged frequencies of the neural pulses as constituting the signal values which carry significant information. Some specific pulse patterns which may occur in peripheral circuits, e.g., control of locomotion are thereby not considered. Although this approach was already justified by the founders of neurodynamics such as McCulloch and Rosenblatt, it is surprising that many contemporary biophysicists believe that inclusion of more accurate membrane dynamics would bring significant improvements to the models. Such suggestions are indeed amazing, since in engineering there has seldom existed any need of mixing, say, quantum phenomena or semiconductor physics with circuit analysis. If one realizes that many adaptive phenomena are actually very slow compared with membrane dynamics (with time constants of the order of 10^5 times those of the latter), then there ought to be no difficulties in accepting that signal values can be averaged over fractions of a second. This will simplify the writing and solution of system equations since the integral operators like the expression in (4.1) can be replaced by *stationary* signal transfer equations, e.g., of the form

$$\eta_i = \eta_i(\xi_1, \ldots, \xi_n, \mu_{i1}, \ldots, \mu_{in}) \qquad (4.2)$$

with the μ_{ij} now as slowly changing *adaptive parameters* for which another system of differential equations can be written. Since the μ_{ij} are continuous functions of time, their dynamics is describable by differential equations of the form

$$d\mu_{ij}/dt \stackrel{\text{def}}{=} \dot{\mu}_{ij} = \dot{\mu}_{ij}(\xi_1, \ldots, \xi_n, \eta_i, \mu_{ij}) . \qquad (4.3)$$

This formalism is also applicable to artificial adaptive systems constructed along with biological models.

4.3 Models for Basic Adaptive Units

4.3.1 Formulation of the Transfer Function

The basic network unit which underlies all systems discussed in this book shall implement a *selective response*. In biological networks it would correspond to a single neural cell.

In computer systems, the logic gates constitute such basic units. Since logic gates are time-invariant, one may realize that there exists a fundamental difference between digital computers and biological systems already on the lowest level of organization. In order to develop machines with nonsupervised learning capabilities, the basic units already ought to be made adaptive.

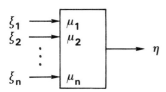

Fig. 4.4. The basic adaptive unit

Consider Fig. 4.4 which illustrates the basic network unit. It has a single output with the signal η obtained from it (the index i has been dropped) and an arbitrary number of inputs with respective signals ξ_j applied to them. Referring to the argumentation of Sect. 4.2, we shall not load the basic unit with dynamic phenomena other than the adaptive changes of its most significant transfer parameters. Even then there remain many choices for the functional law which determines the transfer function.

In some circuits which perform processing of primary sensory signals, nonlinearities may be found necessary for the implementation of certain specific feature analysis operations (e.g., [4.1]). On the other hand, it is possible to perceive a rule in the nature which implies that the newer the neural structures are, the closer their transfer functions are to linearity; the most nonlinear functions are found in phylogenetically oldest (and simplest) organisms. It further seems that the more plastic the functions are, i.e., the more adaptation is involved with them, the more important it is that the responses during learning are proportional to signal values.

In this discussion we shall mainly concentrate on the systematic analysis of phenomena that result from different choices for the adaptation equation, whereby the transfer function plays a secondary role. The following discussion therefore relates to a transfer function which, without significant loss of generality, can be chosen linear for most cases. If this is made, then the asymptotic states obtained in adaptation represent certain fundamental statistical measures, which seems a very reasonable result.

One further motivation in favour of linearization of the basic transfer function is that the only type of nonlinearity which is actually met in the cells of the central nervous system is *saturation* of triggering frequencies at a low and a high limit. The transfer function of the unit would then be of the form

$$\eta_i = \sigma \left[\sum_{j=1}^{n} \mu_{ij}(t)\, \xi_j(t) \right], \tag{4.4}$$

whereby the notation $\sigma[\cdot]$ describes a "sigmoid" function which takes care of saturation (Fig. 4.5).

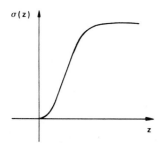

Fig. 4.5. "Sigmoid" function

As long as saturation limits are not reached, the linearization approximation

$$\eta_i = \sum_{j=1}^{n} \mu_{ij}(t)\, \xi_j(t) - \eta_{oi} \tag{4.5}$$

is applicable in the analysis. Without any loss of generality at all, the bias η_{oi} can further be put to zero; in other words, these phenomena are independent of the origin selected for the signal scale. Equation (4.5), with $\eta_{oi} = 0$, can then be expressed in vector notations as

$$\eta_i = m_i^{\mathrm{T}} x, \tag{4.6}$$

where

$$m_i = [\mu_{i1}, \ldots, \mu_{in}]^{\mathrm{T}} \quad \text{and} \quad x = [\xi_1, \ldots, \xi_n]^{\mathrm{T}}$$

are column vectors; m_i^{T} is a row vector. The output η_i is the *inner product* of the signal and parameter vectors, respectively, which is one measure of their *similarity*.

The adaptive parameters now constitute a *weight vector* m_i which is directly related to input "conductances", or strengths of signal coupling. In neural cells this would correspond to the set of individual synaptic efficacies (Chap. 8).

4.3.2 Various Cases of Adaptation Laws

Relative to the linear transfer function, a study of various functional laws for the adaptation equation is now carried out in this subsection.

There are many possible mathematical forms for (4.3) of which we shall now select the class

$$dm/dt \overset{\text{def}}{=} \dot{m} = \phi(\cdot)x - \gamma(\cdot)m \tag{4.7}$$

for closer examination; here $\phi(\cdot)$ and $\gamma(\cdot)$ are some (possibly nonlinear) scalar functions of x, m, and η. In other words, the magnitudes of the changes in m may be general nonlinear functions of the system variables, whereas these changes are restricted to occur only in the direction of x, m, or their linear combination. If this restriction were not made, then ϕ and/or γ should have been expressed as matrix operators. The choice for the form (4.7) may be justified by the following arguments: (i) If the latter term were tentatively neglected, then ϕx would represent a change in the input parameters whereby each parameter is changed in proportion to the respective input signal; the rate of change, however, would still be an arbitrary nonlinear function of the integrated input activity and the previous values of the input parameters. (ii) The latter term represents a typical form of *forgetting*, and the minus sign in front of it is used to emphasize the direction of changes. Pure forgetting or decay effects in natural phenomena are usually proportional to the prevailing values of variables, although, again, the rate may be a general function of all system parameters which includes nonlinear effects.

We have already in (4.6) defined the output activity $\eta = m^T x$ which thus contains both of the system variables m and x. Let us now see what follows if we assume that *the changes are proportional to certain functions of activity:*

$$\phi = \phi(\eta) \quad \text{and} \quad \gamma = \gamma(\eta);$$

many interesting and useful results will emerge from these forms and this may already be a sufficient motivation for their use as theoretical cases in modelling. Notice that the assumption concerning the linearity of the transfer function will now be reflected in a simple way in the adaptation law via η.

The most reasonable property required from a physical system law is *dynamic stability* which implies that if $x(t)$ is bounded for all t, the solution $m(t)$ shall remain finite; the solution in the present models would neither be meaningful physically if for nonzero $x(t)$, the parameter vector $m(t)$ would converge to zero when $t \to \infty$. Solutions which pass these criteria will then be regarded as *acceptable* in the sequel.

Let us now carry out a systematic study of cases with different degrees of nonlinearity of $\phi(\eta)$ and $\gamma(\eta)$. It would, of course, be more mathematical to proceed with the discussion of general functional properties of these forms; however, the nature of the processes will become more lucid if we first consider the lowest integral powers of η as special cases.

Various Cases of the Adaptation Law

Case 1. $\dot{m} = \alpha x - \beta m,$ α, β constants, $\beta > 0$.   (4.8)

This is a trivial case which does not generate any particularly interesting effects in the sequel. The general solution is

$$m(t) = e^{-\beta t}[m(0) + \alpha \int^t e^{\beta t'} x(t')dt'], \ m(0) = \text{constant vector} ,\qquad (4.9)$$

and for $t \to \infty$ this process will only produce the copy of an *exponentially weighted moving average* of $x(t)$ into the parameter vector m; the initial condition of m will be forgotten with time.

Case 2. $\dot{m} = \alpha \eta x - \beta m$.   (4.10)

This form will lead to the lowest-order nontrivial models of adaptation and memory. It is obtained first

$$\dot{m} = (\alpha x x^T - \beta I)m = -\beta \cdot (I - \lambda x x^T)m, \ \lambda = \alpha/\beta .\qquad (4.11)$$

The peculiar properties of (4.11) can be seen better if the differential equation is expressed in discrete-time approximation:

$$m(t+1) = [(1-\beta)I + \alpha x(t)x^T(t)]m(t) = P(t)m(t) ,\qquad (4.12)$$

whereby the solution reads

$$m(t+1) = \left[\prod_{k=0}^{t} P(k) \right] \cdot m(0) .\qquad (4.13)$$

For most typically occurring cases $m = m(t)$, the solution of (4.11) either diverges ("blows up"), or converges to the zero vector. Such solutions would then be unacceptable. There are some reasons, however, for which this form may still be useful on account of its simplicity. During a relatively short time, namely, the simple system law may approximate a more complicated (asymptotically stable) process, and we shall utilize this property in network models of Sect. 4.4.1. Especially if we would ignore the "forgetting" effect altogether by setting $\beta = 0$, and if the integrating time were relatively short (or α relatively small, respectively), then (4.11) could be approximated by

$$m(t) = \left[I + \alpha \int_0^t x(t')x^T(t')dt' \right] \cdot m(0), \tag{4.14}$$

where the latter term in the parenthesis is directly proportional to the *correlation matrix* of $x(t)$. This approximation has been used in many "neural models" reported so far, and for its simplicity we shall utilize it in more complex network models, too. It ought to be clearly realized that this simplification represents an ideal memory in which all forgetting effects are absent; on the other hand, if $x(t)$ has no zero mean when $t \to \infty$, the expression (4.14) would then tend to infinity, and the model would be unrealistic in a long run without modification of system laws, e.g., due to *saturation*.

We may also refer to a result analyzed in Sect. 4.3.3: even though the process were not stable, the direction of $m(t)$ would tend to that of the eigenvector of the correlation matrix of x, belonging to the largest eigenvalue.

There is one special case for which the solution has very interesting and important properties, and it is obtained with $\alpha < 0$, $x(t)$ being piecewise constant in time; if the values $x(t)$ are selected from a finite set, then $m(t)$ converges to a finite, nonzero vector which is of the form $P \cdot m(0)$, the matrix P being an *orthogonal projection operator*. This case, the *novelty detector*, will be discussed in Sect. 4.3.4 in more detail.

Case 3. $\dot{m} = \alpha x - \beta \eta m = (\alpha I - \beta mm^T)x, \quad \alpha, \beta > 0 . \tag{4.15}$

This is a nonlinear differential equation of m, of the form known as a *Riccati equation*, which for general $x = x(t)$ cannot be integrated in closed form. This will be the property of the following higher-order equations, too. Now it has to be pointed out that in all cases which have practical importance, x is assumed to have certain well-defined *statistical properties*, on account of which the most probable, "averaged" trajectories of $m = m(t)$ can be solved. (For a general setting of such problems, cf. [4.2].)

Before proceeding with the statistical problem, we shall derive an important auxiliary result which will be utilized in Chap. 5. It is possible to analyze the convergence of $\|m\|$, the norm of m, for rather general values of $x = x(t)$ multiplying both sides of (4.15) by $2m^T$, whereby it is obtained

$$2m^T \dot{m} = \frac{d}{dt}(\|m\|^2) = 2\eta(\alpha - \beta\|m\|^2). \tag{4.16}$$

Notice that this equation is still expressed in the deterministic form. If we now had $\eta > 0$, it would be immediately clear that $\|m\|^2$ would converge to $\alpha/\beta \stackrel{\text{def}}{=} \|m^*\|^2$. In other words, $\|m\|$, or the length of vector m, would tend to the value $\|m^*\|$ for any $x = x(t)$, such that $\eta > 0$. Mathematically, of course, the expression $\eta = m^T x$ could be ≤ 0, too. In models, however, it is possible to restrict the operation to the case $\eta \geq 0$ by a suitable choice of $\|x\|$ and the initial conditions of m. We may also refer to the result obtained below which states that if x is nonzero, m tends to be *rotated* towards x. It should further be noticed that if η were determined by a transfer function which had a low saturation limit at zero, $\eta = \sigma(m^T x)$, then we could avoid the case $\eta < 0$ altogether, and $\|m\|^2$ would change only for values $\eta > 0$.

Statistical problems are in general very cumbersome mathematically; even after reasonable simplifications, the discussion would be disguised by complicated proofs, unless we rest content with the understanding of the basic operation. The first reasonable simplification is to consider only such input vectors $x(t)$ the statistical properties of which are constant in time, i.e., stationary stochastic processes, and the subsequent values of which are statistically independent. In practice, this means that the "averaged" trajectories of $m = m(t)$ are obtained by taking the expectation value of the sides of (4.15) conditional on m,

$$E\{\dot{m}|m\} \stackrel{\text{def}}{=} \langle \dot{m} \rangle = E\{\alpha x - \beta\eta m|m\}. \tag{4.17}$$

Because x and m were assumed independent, we have

$$E\{x|m\} = \bar{x} \quad \text{(mean of } x). \tag{4.18}$$

Since now $\bar{x}$ is a constant vector in time, we can analyze how the direction of m will change with respect to that of $\bar{x}$. Let us denote the angle between m and $\bar{x}$ by θ, whereby it is obtained

$$E\{d(\cos\theta)/dt|m\} = E\left\{\frac{d}{dt}\left(\frac{\bar{x}^T m}{\|\bar{x}\| \cdot \|m\|}\right)|m\right\}$$

$$= E\left\{\frac{d(\bar{x}^T m)/dt}{\|\bar{x}\| \cdot \|m\|} - \frac{(\bar{x}^T m)d(\|m\|)/dt}{\|\bar{x}\| \cdot \|m\|^2}|m\right\}. \tag{4.19}$$

The first term can be calculated multiplying both sides of (4.15) by $\bar{x}^T/(\|\bar{x}\| \cdot \|m\|)$, and the second term is obtained from (4.16) taking into account that $d(\|m\|^2)/dt = 2\|m\| \cdot d(\|m\|)/dt$. Then

$$E\{d(\cos\theta)/dt \,|\, m\} = \frac{\alpha\|\bar{x}\|^2 - \beta(\bar{x}^T m)^2}{\|\bar{x}\| \cdot \|m\|} - \frac{(\bar{x}^T m)^2(\alpha - \beta\|m\|^2)}{\|\bar{x}\| \cdot \|m\|^3}. \qquad (4.20)$$

After simplification this equation can be written

$$E\left\{\frac{d\theta}{dt} \,\Big|\, m\right\} = -\frac{\alpha\|\bar{x}\|}{\|m\|}\sin\theta; \qquad (4.21)$$

for nonzero $\|\bar{x}\|$, the "averaged" direction of m can be seen to monotonically tend to that of $\bar{x}$.

Since by (4.16), the magnitude of m approaches the value $\|m^*\| = \sqrt{\alpha/\beta}$, the asymptotic state must then be

$$m(\infty) = m^* = \frac{\sqrt{\alpha}}{\sqrt{\beta} \cdot \|\bar{x}\|} \cdot \bar{x}, \qquad (4.22)$$

a vector which has the direction of $\bar{x}$, and length normalized to $\sqrt{\alpha/\beta}$.

This value is also obtained by determining the so-called *fixed point* of m, denoted m^*, for which $\langle \dot{m} \rangle = 0$. Notice that mm^T is a matrix; then

$$\alpha\bar{x} - (\beta m^* m^{*T})\bar{x} = 0. \qquad (4.23)$$

A trial of the form $m^* = \rho\bar{x}$, with ρ a scalar constant will yield

$$\alpha\bar{x} = \beta\rho^2\bar{x}(\bar{x}^T\bar{x}),$$
$$m^* = \frac{\sqrt{\alpha}}{\sqrt{\beta}\|\bar{x}\|}\bar{x}. \qquad (4.24)$$

Case 4. $\dot{m} = \alpha\eta x - \beta\eta m = \alpha x x^T m - \beta m m^T x, \quad \alpha, \beta > 0. \qquad (4.25)$

Denoting

$$E\{x \,|\, m\} = \bar{x},$$

$$E\{xx^T \,|\, m\} = C_{xx} \quad \text{(correlation matrix of } x\text{)}$$

we get

$$\langle \dot{m} \rangle = \alpha C_{xx} m - \beta (\bar{x}^T m) m, \tag{4.26}$$

which is of the form known as a *Bernoulli differential equation* (of second degree). The behaviour of the solution is more complicated than in the previous cases. If we set $\langle \dot{m} \rangle = 0$, it is possible to see that $m^* = 0$ is a solution; further any of the eigenvectors of C_{xx} is a fixed point. This can be seen by substitution: let c_i be an eigenvector with eigenvalue λ_i, and make a trial $m^* = \rho c_i$, with ρ a scalar constant; then

$$C_{xx} c_i = \lambda_i c_i,$$

$$0 = \rho \alpha \lambda_i c_i - \rho^2 \beta (\bar{x}^T c_i) c_i,$$

$$\rho = \frac{\alpha \lambda_i}{\beta (\bar{x}^T c_i)},$$

$$m^* = \frac{\alpha \lambda_i}{\beta (\bar{x}^T c_i)} c_i. \tag{4.27}$$

Not all of the fixed points represent a stable solution, however. This can be seen by considering the angles between m and the eigenvectors c_i, denoted by θ_i, respectively. In analogy with Case 3 we then obtain

$$E\{d(\cos \theta_i)/dt \,|\, m\} = E\left\{ \frac{d}{dt} \left(\frac{c_i^T m}{\|c_i\| \cdot \|m\|} \right) | m \right\}$$

$$= E\left\{ \frac{d(c_i^T m)/dt}{\|c_i\| \cdot \|m\|} - \frac{(c_i^T m) d(\|m\|)/dt}{\|c_i\| \cdot \|m\|^2} | m \right\}. \tag{4.28}$$

This expression is now handled in the already familiar way; in the first term, obtained by multiplication of (4.25) by $c_i^T m / (\|c_i\| \cdot \|m\|)$, one should notice that by definition of eigenvectors, we can put

$$c_i^T C_{xx} = \lambda_i c_i^T. \tag{4.29}$$

After simplification, we obtain

$$E\{d(\cos \theta_i)/dt \,|\, m\} = \alpha \cos \theta_i \left(\lambda_i - \frac{m^T C_{xx} m}{\|m\|^2} \right). \tag{4.30}$$

There is a well-known result in matrix algebra, known as the *Rayleigh quotient*, which states that if A is any square matrix with the largest eigenvalue λ_{max}, and a is an arbitrary vector, then

$$\frac{a^T A a}{\|a\|^2} \leqslant \lambda_{max}. \tag{4.31}$$

If now $A = C_{xx}$, with λ_{max} its largest eigenvalue, if subscript "max" is used for variables belonging to λ_{max}, and $c_{max}^T m(0) \neq 0$, then θ_{max} can be seen to decrease monotonically until the stable equilibrium is reached, m thereby having the same or opposite direction as c_{max}.

When analyzing the trajectories, one may notice that $m = m(t)$ tends to be "slowed down" at the fixed points; however, if at any time $c_{max}^T m > 0$, the solution will finally converge to the direction of the eigenvector of C_{xx} having the largest eigenvalue. On the other hand, there is a finite probability for m converging to the zero vector, too, as may be seen in numerical simulations performed on this model.

Case 5. $\dot{m} = \alpha \eta x - \beta \eta^2 m = \alpha x x^T m - \beta(m^T x x^T m) m, \quad \alpha, \beta > 0. \tag{4.32}$

If this case is again handled as a statistical problem, we obtain

$$\langle \dot{m} \rangle = \alpha C_{xx} m - \beta(m^T C_{xx} m) m. \tag{4.33}$$

This model is actually easier to analyze than some of the previous ones; the results are also intriguing. Let us consider the magnitude of m first.

$$E\{d(\|m\|^2)/dt \,|\, m\} = 2m^T C_{xx} m(\alpha - \beta\|m\|^2); \tag{4.34}$$

now $m^T C_{xx} m$ is a scalar, $\geqslant 0$, which is assumed to be nonzero for a sufficient time; then it is immediately clear that $\|m\|$ converges to $\sqrt{\alpha/\beta}$ when $t \to \infty$. This result is similar to that of Case 3.

The next step is again to consider the angles between m and the c_i, the eigenvectors of C_{xx}. After simplification we obtain

$$E\{d(\cos\theta_i)/dt \,|\, m\} = \alpha \cos\theta_i \left(\lambda_i - \frac{m^T C_{xx} m}{\|m\|^2}\right); \tag{4.35}$$

so, if we consider λ_{max}, c_{max}, and θ_{max}, we have as result that if the initial conditions are selected suitably, i.e., $c_{max}^T m(0) \neq 0$, and because $\lambda_{max}\|m\|^2 - m^T C_{xx} m \geqslant 0$, then $m = m(t)$ will converge to a value which has the length $\sqrt{\alpha/\beta}$ and direction coinciding with that of c_{max}.

Another proof for this case has been presented in [4.3].

4.3.3 Two Limit Theorems

A discussion of the general form $\dot{m} = \phi(\eta)x - \gamma(\eta)m$ seems, if not impossible, at least very cumbersome; some results have been obtained only for x which is constant in time. We shall refer to this briefly at the end of the present subsection.

We shall now first derive two limit theorems *relating to a generalized forgetting law*. These results reflect the most important property of the asymptotic solution $m(\infty)$, namely, its *direction*.

Now there is a very delicate relationship between the time derivative of a single solution, denoted $\dot{m}$, and the "averaged" derivative $\langle \dot{m} \rangle$; this distinction has been discussed by *Geman* [4.2]. In Theorems 4.1 and 4.2 we are allowed to discuss single trajectories, with $x = x(t)$ being a stochastic variable all the time. Therefore the results of these Theorems are even more general than those of the previous cases.

Theorem 4.1. Let $\alpha > 0$, $\eta = m^T x$, and let $\gamma(\eta)$ be an arbitrary scalar function of η such that $E\{\gamma(\eta) \mid m\}$ exists. Let $x = x(t) \in R^n$ be a stochastic vector with stationary statistical properties, and let x be independent of m. Let $\bar{x}$ be the mean of x. If the equations of the form

$$\dot{m} = E\{\alpha x - \gamma(\eta) \cdot m \mid m\}$$

at all have nonzero bounded asymptotic solutions, then these must have the same direction as that of $\bar{x}$.

Proof. Let us denote $E\{\gamma(\eta)\}$ by $\langle \gamma(\eta) \rangle$. Denote the angle between m and $\bar{x}$ by θ. The following steps are formally similar as in the introductory cases:

$$\dot{m} = \alpha\bar{x} - \langle \gamma(\eta) \rangle \cdot m,$$

$$\bar{x}^T \dot{m} = \alpha\|\bar{x}\|^2 - \langle \gamma(\eta) \rangle \cdot (\bar{x}^T m),$$

$$\frac{1}{2}\frac{d\|m\|^2}{dt} = \|m\|\frac{d\|m\|}{dt} = \alpha\bar{x}^T m - \langle \gamma(\eta) \rangle \cdot \|m\|^2,$$

$$\frac{d\cos\theta}{dt} = \frac{\frac{d}{dt}(\bar{x}^T m)}{\|\bar{x}\| \cdot \|m\|} - \frac{(\bar{x}^T m)\frac{d\|m\|}{dt}}{\|\bar{x}\| \cdot \|m\|^2}$$

$$= \frac{\alpha}{\|\bar{x}\| \cdot \|m\|^3}[\|\bar{x}\|^2 \cdot \|m\|^2 - (\bar{x}^T m)^2] \geqslant 0, \qquad (4.36)$$

the strict equality holding only if $\bar{x}$ and m have the same direction (Schwarz inequality). Since $\|\bar{x}\|$ and $\|m\|$ can be assumed finite, θ will converge to zero monotonically. This is the sought result.   Q.E.D.

Theorem 4.2. Let α, η, $\gamma(\eta)$, and x be the same as in Theorem 4.1. Let C_{xx} be the correlation matrix of x. If the equations of the form

$$\dot{m} = E\{\alpha\eta x - \gamma(\eta) \cdot m \,|\, m\}$$

at all have nonzero bounded asymptotic solutions, then these must have the same direction as that of c_{max}, where c_{max} is the eigenvector of C_{xx} corresponding to the largest eigenvalue λ_{max}, provided that $c_{max}^T m(0) \neq 0$.

Proof. Denote the angle between m and c_i by θ_i where c_i is any eigenvector of C_{xx}. The following steps may be self-explanatory:

$$\dot{m} = \alpha C_{xx} m - \langle \gamma(\eta) \rangle \cdot m,$$

$$c_i^T \dot{m} = \alpha \lambda_i (c_i^T m) - \langle \gamma(\eta) \rangle \cdot (c_i^T m),$$

$$\frac{1}{2} \frac{d\|m\|^2}{dt} = \|m\| \frac{d\|m\|}{dt} = \alpha m^T C_{xx} m - \langle \gamma(\eta) \rangle \cdot \|m\|^2,$$

$$\frac{d \cos \theta_i}{dt} = \frac{\frac{d}{dt}(c_i^T m)}{\|c_i\| \cdot \|m\|} - \frac{(c_i^T m) \frac{d\|m\|}{dt}}{\|c_i\| \cdot \|m\|^2}$$

$$= \alpha \cos \theta_i \left(\lambda_i - \frac{m^T C_{xx} m}{\|m\|^2} \right). \tag{4.37}$$

On similar grounds as earlier, if $c_i^T m(0) \neq 0$, and taking $\lambda_i = \lambda_{max}$, $c_i = c_{max}$, $\theta_i = \theta_{max}$, the angle θ_{max} is seen to converge to zero or 2π monotonically; thereby m has a direction coinciding with that of c_{max}.   Q.E.D.

The following result, as mentioned before, holds only for x which is *constant in time*; however, it can be used to obtain a rough conception of stability of the solutions.

Lemma (due to Oja (unpublished)): Let

$$\dot{m} = \phi(\eta) \cdot x - \gamma(\eta) \cdot m,$$

$$\eta = m^T x,$$

where x is constant in time; without loss of generality let $\|x\| = 1$. Let $\phi(\eta)$ and $\gamma(\eta)$ be scalar-valued functions. If there exists ρ such that

i) $\phi(\rho) = \rho \gamma(\rho)$,

ii) ϕ and γ can be expanded in Taylor series which converge in a domain D around $\eta = \rho$,

$$\phi(\eta) = \phi_0 + \phi_1(\eta - p) + \phi_2(\eta - p)^2 + \ldots,$$

$$\gamma(\eta) = \gamma_0 + \gamma_1(\eta - p) + \gamma_2(\eta - p)^2 + \ldots, \qquad \text{where}$$

$$\gamma_0 > 0,$$

$$\phi_1 - p\gamma_1 < \gamma_0, \quad \text{then}$$

$$\lim_{t \to \infty} m(t) = px,$$

provided that $m(0)$ is sufficiently close to px.

Corollary. If the above series converge in a domain D' around $\eta = 0$, then

$$\lim_{t \to \infty} m(t) = 0$$

if $m(0)$ is sufficiently close to zero, and

i) $\phi(0) = 0$;

ii) $\gamma_0 > 0,$

$$\phi_1 < \gamma_0 .$$

The proofs of the lemma and the corollary will be omitted here. The reader may check the validity of the conditions imposed on the coefficients for the Cases $1 - 5$ above.

Comment. In analogy with the examples discussed in Chap. 3, we might expect that the solutions of all equations would converge, not only in the "averaged" sense but to unique limit values if the system parameters were made suitable functions of time. For instance, numerical simulations have shown that if both α and β in Cases $1 - 5$ are made directly proportional to $1/t$, convergence properties similar to those obtained in other examples of stochastic approximation are obtained.

4.3.4 The Novelty Detector

Among the basic adaptive units there is a particular one which has quite special properties, and which therefore deserves a separate discussion. In its purest form this unit is governed by the equation of Case 2, with $\alpha < 0$ and $\beta = 0$. The most characteristic property of such a unit is that if any input pattern x applied to it is held stationary, the output η will monotonically tend to zero. The input weights, on the other hand, do not tend to zero, but the positive and negative weights μ_j thereby produced tend to be *balanced* in relation to the ξ_j signals in such a way that the resulting output becomes zero. What is still more intriguing is that such an asymptotic balance can simultaneously be achieved for many different input patterns, the number of which is less than n, the number of input terminals. On the other hand, if the input pattern were a novel one, then a nonzero output would normally be obtained from the unit. If this phenomenon were discussed within the context of experimental psychology, it would be termed *habituation*.

As mentioned above, we shall now consider an idealized adaptive unit the system equations of which are written

$$\eta = m^{\mathrm{T}}x,$$
$$dm^{\mathrm{T}}/dt = -\alpha\eta x^{\mathrm{T}} = -\alpha m^{\mathrm{T}}xx^{\mathrm{T}}. \tag{4.38}$$

(Here, due to the minus sign in front of the right side, α must be redefined to be >0.)

The adaptive behaviour of the above system can easily be analyzed in the case of stationary input patterns. Assume first that the input vector x is constant with time for $t \geq t_0$; then, by substitution, the following expression can be found to constitute the solution of (4.38):

$$m^{\mathrm{T}}(t) = m^{\mathrm{T}}(t_0)[I - \omega(t)xx^{\mathrm{T}}], \quad \text{where}$$
$$\omega(t) = \|x\|^{-2}(1 - e^{-\alpha\|x\|^2(t-t_0)}). \tag{4.39}$$

Notice that $0 \leq \omega(t) \leq \|x\|^{-2}$.

Consider now a finite set of patterns $S = \{x_1, x_2, \ldots, x_m\}$ which are made to appear at the system input as an infinite sequence

$$\{x_{i_k}\}_{k=1}^{\infty}, \quad i_k \in \{1, 2, \ldots, m\},$$

with an arbitrary frequency and in an arbitrary order. Consider further a series of instants of time $\{t_k\}_{k=1}^{\infty}$ between which the input patterns are assumed to be stationary. In other words, the input signal patterns are constant in time during arbitrarily long half-open intervals $[t_{k-1}, t_k)$ but otherwise their appearance is almost arbitrary. When the above system equations are integrated over the intervals $[t_{k-1}, t_k)$, always replacing t_0 by t_{k-1}, there follows

$$m^{\mathrm{T}}(t_k) = m^{\mathrm{T}}(t_{k-1})(I - \alpha_k x_{i_k}x_{i_k}^{\mathrm{T}}) = m^{\mathrm{T}}(t_{k-1})Q_k, \tag{4.40}$$

where the scalars α_k have a close bearing on the $\omega(t)$ in (4.39), and the Q_k are matrices which have the form of an *elementary matrix* (Sect. 2.1.3). Recursive application of (4.40) yields

$$m^{\mathrm{T}}(t_k) = m^{\mathrm{T}}(t_0) \prod_{i=1}^{k} Q_i = m^{\mathrm{T}}(t_0) T_k. \tag{4.41}$$

The central mathematical problem is now to study the convergence conditions of the product matrix T_k as k tends to infinity. It will be shown that if, in general, the α_k are scalars within certain limits and each of the vectors of S occurs infinitely often in T_k, then T_k will converge to a projection matrix P, such that $m^{\mathrm{T}}(t_0)P$ is orthogonal to all vectors of S. In other words, if one of these pattern vectors or their arbitrary linear combination is shown as input to the converged system, the corresponding output will be zero. On the other hand, if an arbitrary new pattern not belonging to the subspace $\mathscr{L}$ spanned by the vectors of S is chosen for input, the output in general will be nonzero, unless, in a highly improbable case, the new pattern happens to be orthogonal to the weighting vector of the converged system.

The following results have been analyzed in detail in [4.4] and [4.5].

A Limit Theorem for a Product of Elementary Matrices. Let $S = \{x_1, \ldots, x_m\}$ be a set of arbitrary (not necessarily linearly independent) vectors in R^n. Consider the product matrix T_k of (4.41) in which the scalar sequence $\{\alpha_k\}$ and the index sequence $\{i_k\}$ satisfy the following assumptions:

A1) $\delta \leqslant \alpha_k \leqslant 2\|x_{i_k}\|^{-2} - \delta$,

where δ is an arbitrarily small fixed number satisfying

$$0 < \delta < 2(\max_j \|x_j\|^2)^{-1}.$$

A2)   For every fixed $r \in \{1, \ldots, m\}$ and every $p \in N$ (N is the set of natural numbers) there exists an index $k \geqslant p$ such that $i_k = r$.

In fact, the first assumption guarantees that the norms of the elementary matrices

$$[I - \alpha_k x_{i_k} x_{i_k}^{\mathrm{T}}]$$

do not exceed unity and $\{\alpha_k\}$ does not converge to zero, while the second assumption expresses the fact that each vector x_k appears in the product infinitely often. The following result [4.5] is here given without proof.

Theorem 4.3. Let A1 and A2 hold. Then the sequence $\{T_k\}$ converges (in any matrix norm) to the projection matrix on the subspace $\mathscr{L}^\perp(x_1, \ldots, x_m)$.

If the set $S = \{x_1, \ldots, x_m\}$ spans R^n, then the projection matrix on $\mathscr{L}^\perp(x_1, \ldots, x_m)$ is the zero matrix and the following corollary holds true.

Corollary. Let the assumptions of the theorem hold and let $\mathscr{L}(x_1, \ldots,$ $x_m) = R^n$. Then $\lim\limits_{k \to \infty} T_k$ is the zero matrix.

Numerical Example. In order to obtain a concrete conception about the speed of convergence in the above process, the following result is reported. Ten 35-component binary patterns, to be depicted in Fig. 6.3, comprised the set S, and they were cyclically applied at the input. Denoting $m^* = \lim\limits_{k \to \infty} m_k$, then, as the measure of convergence $\|m_k - m^*\| / \|m^*\|$ was selected. The scalar α_k was selected constant, with a value from the middle of its allowed range which provided the fastest convergence.

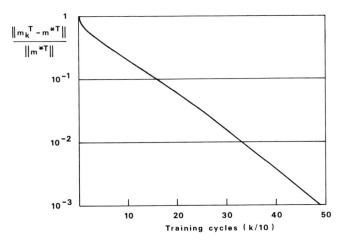

Fig. 4.6. Speed of convergence in a novelty detector process

The diagram in Fig. 4.6 shows that the convergence was almost exponential. Other results, not shown here, have indicated that in general the speed of convergence in this process is roughly inversely proportional to the dimensionality of the patterns n. The speed of convergence in general depends strongly on the ratio m/n with radical slowdown when $m \to n$.

The novelty detector alone has less importance than an array formed of several units of this kind. We shall return to the function of such organizations in Sect. 4.4.2.

4.4 Adaptive Feedback Networks

Adaptive phenomena may occur at different levels of organization. Above, adaptive processes (interactions between state variables) were considered *within* the functional units; the latter were thus discussed as isolated systems. The next higher level of interaction comes from *mutual connections between units.*

We have to point out already in the beginning that if the cross-connections are only made between the inputs, no genuine collective phenomena are produced: each unit could be analyzed independently of the others, as seen from Fig. 4.7. In other words, collective phenomena must result from *feedback*, i.e., connection of *outputs.*

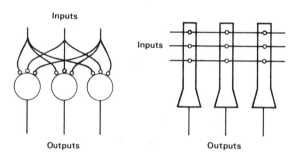

Inputs

Inputs

Outputs

Outputs

Fig. 4.7. Two configurations of single-cell systems

All the systems discussed in this section have a basically similar structure which demonstrates the effect of *multiple feedback*. Due to such feedback connections, every unit is made to depend on the state of many other units. In an extreme case (the autocorrelation matrix memory and the novelty filter) every unit receives a feedback from all the other units; the feedback system can thereby be described by a *matrix operator.*

Another type of feedback which creates very interesting self-organizing mappings, utilizes lateral feedback connections the distribution of which is a function of distance between the units. We shall discuss this case in Chap. 5.

In order to analyze the effect of feedback in a pure, isolated form, we first assume that every basic adaptive unit receives *a single external input signal,* and *feedback signals from all the other units* (Fig. 4.8).

For further simplicity, the external inputs can be assumed to have a fixed input weight, normalized to unity for convenience. It is thereby also assumed that the effect of each individual feedback connection is much weaker; these cross-connections, denoted by μ_{ij}, are *adaptive*. Without the feedback connections, the external signals would only be propagated unaltered to the output ports. The effect of feedback is to modify this one-to-one transformation.

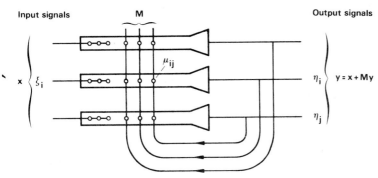

Input signals M **Output signals**

μ_{ij}

x { ξ_i

η_i } $y = x + My$

η_j

Fig. 4.8. Feedback network

Due to the assumed simple input structure, there is a one-to-one geo-metrical correspondence between the input and output terminals. Both sets of terminals can be imagined to have a one- or two-dimensional geometrical ar-rangement. In the latter case we may think that the ordered sets of input and output signals, described by the pattern vectors

$$x = [\xi_1, \xi_2, \ldots, \xi_n]^T \quad \text{and} \quad y = [\eta_1, \eta_2, \ldots, \eta_n]^T,$$

respectively, represent two-dimensional images in a "dot matrix".

4.4.1 The Autocorrelation Matrix Memory

If we apply functional laws of the basic adaptive units to the present organiza-tion, in the first approximation we may then assume that every unit has a linear transfer function. The results from systematic analysis of the adaptive phenomena carried out in Sect. 4.3 now facilitate significant simplifications. If we concentrate on the system models of the form considered with Theorem 4.2, we can see that the various alternative forms for the "forgetting" term which mainly provide for long-term stability may be neglected, if only minor increments in the μ_{ij} are caused during a short period of time.

The system equations (without the forgetting term) may then be written as

$$\eta_i = \xi_i + \sum_{j=1}^{n} \mu_{ij}\eta_j , \tag{4.42}$$

$$d\mu_{ij}/dt = \alpha\eta_i\eta_j .$$

The set of all the adaptive weights $\{\mu_{ij}\}$ can now be expressed as a matrix operator $M \in R^{n \times n}$, whereby the system equations read

$$y = x + My \, ,$$

$$dM/dt \overset{\text{def}}{=} \dot{M} = \alpha y y^{\mathsf{T}}. \tag{4.43}$$

It is now possible to solve the *overall transfer function*, denoted Ω; from the first equation above we get

$$y = (I - M)^{-1} \cdot x \overset{\text{def}}{=} \Omega x \, . \tag{4.44}$$

It is also assumed that $(I - M)^{-1}$ exists which is normally true. The differential equation for Ω is now obtained using the methods introduced in Sect. 2.1.6:

$$\frac{d\Omega^{-1}}{dt} = -\Omega^{-1} \frac{d\Omega}{dt} \Omega^{-1} = -\dot{M} \, ,$$

$$d\Omega/dt = \alpha \Omega^2 x x^{\mathsf{T}} \Omega^{\mathsf{T}} \Omega \, . \tag{4.45}$$

This is a *matrix Bernoulli equation of fourth degree;* for general $x = x(t)$ it is difficult, if not impossible to solve in closed form. Approximate solutions can be derived, e.g., using matrix series, as will be seen in Sect. 4.4.2. In this case, however, there may be no sense to strive for exact solutions because they will anyway "blow up" with time; this is because the stabilizatory forgetting phenomena were omitted in this simplified discussion. (We shall carry out a more exact treatment of the related novelty filter in Sect. 4.4.2.) For the present purpose it may be sufficient to consider the conventional lowest-order approximation, assuming on the right-hand side of (4.45) that $\Omega \approx I$ (or $y \approx x$):

$$d\Omega/dt \cong \alpha x x^{\mathsf{T}}, \tag{4.46}$$

whereby the first-order "perturbation solution" for the system transfer operator is seen to be

$$\Omega(t) \cong I + \alpha \int^{t} x(t') x^{\mathsf{T}}(t') \, dt', \tag{4.47}$$

the latter term (the contribution due to the adaptive feedback connections) being proportional to the *autocorrelation matrix of x*. Assume now that the value for the operator Ω has been formed during some period $0 \leqslant t' \leqslant t$, i.e., Ω has "memorized" the $x(t)$ by its state changes; assume $\Omega(0) = I$. If the system is later, at a time $t_0 > t$ *excited* by an input signal pattern x_0, the set of following responses y is obtained:

$$y = \Omega x_0 = x_0 + \alpha \int_0^t [x^{\mathrm{T}}(t') \cdot x_0] \cdot x(t') dt'. \tag{4.48}$$

If we regard the first term x_0 on the right-hand side as a "memoryless" response which would be obtained *without* adaptive interconnections, then the second term

$$\alpha \int_0^t [x^{\mathrm{T}}(t') \cdot x_0] \cdot x(t') dt' \tag{4.49}$$

represents the contribution to the output pattern coming from the interconnections, or the *"recollection"* of information from memory. We can see that $x^{\mathrm{T}}(t') \cdot x_0$ is a scalar "kernel", and thus the recollection is a *weighted sum* of all the memorized values $x(t')$.

The recollection can further be seen to have a very important structure. Notice that the inner product $x^{\mathrm{T}}(t') \cdot x_0$ directly expresses the *similarity* of x_0 to the earlier values of input $x(t')$, $0 \leqslant t' \leqslant t$. If x_0 would be regarded as a *key excitation* by which the recollection is *read out*, then we can easily find out that *in the recollection, those components $x(t')$ dominate which (at least partially) match with the key pattern*. Thus the recollection is a selective replica of the memorized information relative to the applied key excitation. This is why the system under discussion has been termed *Autocorrelation Matrix Memory* (ACMM). The ACMM is a fundamental paradigm of *linear (analog) auto-associative memory systems*. It has been analyzed in some previous articles (e.g., [4.6, 7]).

A more lucid view of the function of the ACMM can be obtained if we consider only such pattern vectors $x(t')$ which are *piecewise constant* in time over intervals which without loss of generality can be assumed to be of unit length; moreover, there shall be only a finite number k of them. In other words, this system has then been "exposed" to k "pictures" which are memorized in the state of Ω. It immediately follows from (4.48) that

$$y = x_0 + \alpha \sum_{k'=1}^{k} (x_{k'}^{\mathrm{T}} x_0) \cdot x_{k'};$$

$$= x_0 + \sum_{k'=1}^{k} \sigma_{k'} x_{k'}, \tag{4.50}$$

where $\sigma_{k'}$ is a *similarity measure* between x_0 and the respective memorized pattern. If the $x_{k'}$ are statistically independent, then it can be seen that if x_0 has a high correlation with one of the memorized patterns, it is this pattern which predominantly will be recalled.

Incomplete ACMM. Especially with the two-dimensional geometric arrangement of the input and output signals, one might feel uneasy with the great number of matrix elements of M (or Ω) that enter the analysis. Therefore it will be necessary to remark that if one is striving for a certain degree of accuracy in the recollection, it is not necessary to retain all the matrix elements μ_{ij}; it will suffice to have a *randomly selected subset of them* as really existing interconnections. The recollection is then an approximation of the exact one. The performance of such an incomplete ACMM has been analyzed thoroughly in [4.7]. Let it suffice to present here a computer simulation, since the analytical matrix formalism does not work well with such incomplete arrays. We shall also emphasize that *the number of matrix elements (interconnections) need then only be directly proportional to the number of signals, as contrasted with the square of this number in a complete ACMM.* In the following simulation, the number of interconnections was 40 times the number of input or output signals, and this ratio seems already sufficient for a modest statistical accuracy, at least related to the simple binary patterns used in this simulation.

There were 510 cells in this simulation, arranged in a rectangular array, and corresponding to the display in Fig. 4.9.

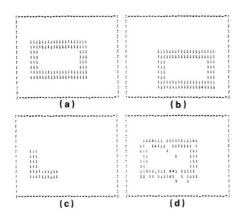

(a)   (b)   (c)   (d)

Fig. 4.9a – d. Demonstration of associative recall from a randomly interconnected network model. (a) First activity pattern. (b) Second activity pattern. (c) Key pattern. (d) Recollection

Signal values which were zero were shown by blanks, and other values that occurred were indicated by signs in a three-shade scale. A total of 20,000 interconnections (corresponding to about 40 per each unit) was defined between randomly selected pairs of the units. These interconnections correspond to the elements of matrix M of which part is missing.

The first two of these illustrations, Fig. 4.9a and b, depict patterns that were memorized. The third pattern shows a key in which a few signals from one of the stored patterns were present. The fourth picture indicates the recollection according to (4.49). ●

Since the key had a higher correlation with the first pattern, this is what predominates in the recollection. However, apparently the performance of this model is not yet of particularly high standard, as a consequence of some crosstalk from the second pattern. If the number of patterns were very large, the amount of crosstalk noise might become intolerable. A simple remedy is now *preprocessing* of the patterns before they enter the memory network; by a suitable transformation (e.g., edge-enhancement using convolution operators (Sect. 6.5.1)), the crosstalk from processed patterns will then be eliminated.

"Brain-State-in-a-Box." This name was coined by *Anderson* [4.8] to a mode of use of the previous model, whereby the output signals during the recall phase are made to saturate at $\eta_i = 0$ and $\eta_i = 1$; notice that due to the divergent properties of the simplified process, the $y = y(t)$ would otherwise tend to infinity. With saturation, the process then converges to some stable output state, whereby y becomes a binary vector, related to the eigenvectors of C_{xx}. In order to make this process operate correctly, saturation effects should not occur during the period when C_{xx} is formed. It seems that this process needs some extra stabilizing control during the long period of memorization.

We shall discuss somewhat related phenomena in Chap. 5; the output activity in saturating models, due to distance-dependent feedback, will there be further *localized* in a feature map.

4.4.2 The Novelty Filter

From the example given in Sect. 4.3.4 it can be deduced that convergence in a novelty detector-type process is rather slow. It is therefore believed that physical processes with accelerated adaptation, as discussed here, might be of considerable interest in machine learning. Acceleration of convergence is achieved by the inclusion of negative feedback in the system. There have been presented several adaptive models with different types of feedback connection which, accordingly, have varying degrees of convergence. In this section it is pointed out that there exists one particular type of feedback which guarantees extremely prompt convergence: the asymptotic state of the optimal novelty filter can be achieved in one single cycle of application of the input patterns.

The System Model of the Novelty Filter. Instead of taking a set of independent novelty detectors, an adaptive filter is here constructed assuming mutual interactions between the units, i.e., this model is based on collective phenomena. A theoretically simplified model which generates orthogonal projections is discussed first; after that, a more realistic variant is discussed in which the process involves the effect of forgetting.

Consider the system model of Fig. 4.10 with $x \in R^n$, its input pattern vector, and $\tilde{x} \in R^n$, the vector of output signals. A feedback taken from the output is again assumed to recurrently affect the output through variable weights. In the simplest case the feedback is assumed to be direct. However, the dynamics is not significantly changed if feedback is taken through low-pass filters; it can be shown that the asymptotic properties are not affected.

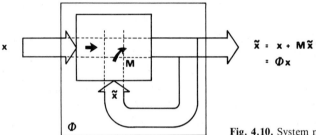

Fig. 4.10. System model of the novelty filter

Every element of the output vector $\tilde{x}$, denoted by $\tilde{\xi}_i$, is thus assumed to receive a feedback from the other elements $\tilde{\xi}_j$ through variable weights μ_{ij}. The output signals $\tilde{\xi}_i$ are assumed to be linear combinations of the input signals ξ_i and the feedback signals as

$$\tilde{\xi}_i = \xi_i + \sum_j \mu_{ij} \tilde{\xi}_j. \tag{4.51}$$

The feedback connections μ_{ij} are assumed adaptive. In pursuance of the system principles discussed with the linear adaptive unit and the novelty detector, these weights are discussed in the case where they change as

$$d\mu_{ij}/dt = -\alpha \tilde{\xi}_i \tilde{\xi}_j. \tag{4.52}$$

In matrix notation, the feedback "gain" may be denoted by a time-variable matrix M. On the other hand, the *overall* transfer operator for the input patterns is described by a square matrix ϕ that can be solved from the implicit feedback equations:

$$\tilde{x} = x + M\tilde{x} = (I - M)^{-1} x = \phi x. \tag{4.53}$$

It is tentatively assumed that $(I - M)^{-1}$ always exists. As long as the process is physically realizable, this is the case.

The feedback matrix $M = (\mu_{ij})$ has a state equation

$$dM/dt = -\alpha \tilde{x}\tilde{x}^T. \tag{4.54}$$

The differential equation for ϕ is obtained as follows:

$$\frac{d\phi^{-1}}{dt} = -\phi^{-1}\frac{d\phi}{dt}\phi^{-1} = -\frac{dM}{dt}; \tag{4.55}$$

$$d\phi/dt = -\alpha\phi^2 xx^T\phi^T\phi. \tag{4.56}$$

This is a *matrix Bernoulli equation*. It will be shown that it has stable asymptotic solutions if $\alpha \geqslant 0$.

Extensive study of all matrix Bernoulli equations has been confined to the Riccati differential equations, in which the right-hand side is of second degree in ϕ, and which naturally originate in various applications of control and systems theory (cf. [4.9]). Bernoulli equations of higher degree in ϕ do not seem to have been treated in literature, although the asymptotic solutions of some of them have proved to be extremely interesting.

The solution of (4.56) seems difficult if $x = x(t)$ is an arbitrary function of time. However, if x is constant, or piecewise constant in time, it is then readily observable that (4.56) becomes autonomous (globally or piecewise), and a solution in the form of a series expansion is demonstrable, say, by the Picard-Lindelöf method [4.10]. Since it is desirable to have at least some basic results in closed form, it is hereafter assumed that the initial condition of ϕ is *symmetric* (for instance, if M was initially a zero matrix, then $\phi(0) = I$). If this is the case, then ϕ can be seen to remain symmetric at all times, and the differential equation is written

$$d\phi/dt = -\alpha\phi^2 xx^T\phi^2. \tag{4.57}$$

Although the general solution is not needed in the rest of this discussion, it is outlined as follows. The successive approximations of the Picard-Lindelöf method yield an expression for $\phi(t)$ which is a series containing rising powers of $\phi(0)$. Because all vectors $\phi(0)^j x$, with $j > 0$, can be expressed as linear combinations of the vectors $\phi(0)x$, $\phi(0)^2 x$, $\ldots$, $\phi(0)^r x$, where r is less than or equal to the degree of the so-called minimum polynomial of $\phi(0)$ (e.g., [Ref. 4.11, pp. 60–61]), only a finite number of terms is retained in the series expansion which is then of the general form

$$\phi(t) = \phi(0) + \sum_{i=1}^{r}\sum_{j=1}^{r}\phi(0)^i xx^T\phi(0)^j f_{ij}(t), \tag{4.58}$$

on an interval where x is constant. The sequence $f_{ij}(t)$ is a symmetrical double sequence of continuous scalar-valued functions which could, in principle at least, be solved by the substitution of $\phi(t)$ from (4.58) into (4.57).

The lack of further knowledge in regard to the functions f_{ij} means that the asymptotic properties of $\phi(t)$ are not obvious. However, in one important class of initial matrices $\phi(0)$ the solution is enormously simplified, i.e., that of projection matrices (Sect. 2.1.5). In particular, $\phi(0) = I$ constitutes a special case of them. *This corresponds to the case in which the memory was originally empty,* $M(0) = 0$, as mentioned above. If x is now constant everywhere, then (4.58) is reduced to

$$\phi(t) = \phi(0) + \phi(0)xx^{T}\phi(0)f(t) , \tag{4.59}$$

which by substitution into (4.57) yields

$$f(t) = \alpha h^{-1}[(3ht+1)^{-1/3} - 1], \quad \text{if} \quad \phi(0)x \neq 0 ,$$
$$h = \alpha x^{T}\phi(0)x ; \tag{4.60}$$
$$f(t) = 0, \quad \text{if} \quad \phi(0)x = 0 .$$

Unfortunately, if x is only piecewise constant, then this simple method no longer applies; it can be seen that $\phi(t)$, $t > 0$, is not generally idempotent; consequently, on successive intervals of constant x, resort has to be made to the more general solution.

Successive Adaptations. It can now be shown that if the input vector x is constant for a sufficiently long time, the system output $\tilde{x}$ approaches the zero vector, although ϕ does not approach the zero matrix. If a set of input patterns $\{x_k\}$ is successively applied at the input, and each one is displayed for an adequate time, it is demonstrable that this system will then be adapted to each one *in one cycle of presentation.*

There is another characteristic mathematical difficulty associated with the above matrix Bernoulli equation (in which $d\phi/dt$ is of rank 1). Even in the simplest case when $\phi(0) = I$, the asymptotic solution $\phi(\infty)$ will be *singular* which also implies that $M(\infty)$, or some of its elements, do not remain finite. In practice, the integration times are always finite, whereby ϕ remains nonsingular and M finite. Certain saturation limits can also be set on the elements of M. Then, however, the successive "asymptotic" solutions discussed below are only more or less good approximations.

The adaptation process can now be studied in greater detail, with the result of considerable simplification of the solution of (4.57). Define a series of successive instances of time $\{t_k\}_{k=0}^S$. During each half-open interval $[t_{k-1}, t_k)$, a new constant pattern is applied at the input, and the state matrix ϕ is allowed to approximately converge towards the asymptotic value during each interval. The accuracy with which ϕ converges towards the asymptotic value can be made arbitrarily good by the selection of intervals that are sufficiently long. An approximate recursive expression for the successive state changes is then derivable in the following way. We are primarily interested in the asymptotic solution of (4.57), which for idempotent $\phi(0)$ reads

$$\phi(\infty) = \phi(0) - \frac{\phi(0)x_1 x_1^T \phi(0)}{x_1^T \phi(0) x_1} \quad \text{if} \quad \phi(0)x_1 \neq 0 ,$$

$$\phi(\infty) = \phi(0) \quad \text{if} \quad \phi(0)x_1 = 0 . \tag{4.61}$$

If the interval $[0, t_1)$ is long, then $t = \infty$ is approximately replaceable by $t = t_1$. Next, use is made of the fact which is easily proven by squaring both sides of (4.61), viz., that $\phi(\infty)$ is idempotent, too.

Since $\phi(0)$ is idempotent, then $\phi(t_1)$ is also approximately idempotent. It can now be shown that (4.59) and (4.61) remain valid if t_1 is taken for the time of initialization: it is sufficient to assume that $\phi(t_1)$ is idempotent. Continuation of the induction results in a recursive expression being obtained for successive state changes, with use being made of the fact that all of the $\phi(t_k)$ remain approximately idempotent:

$$\phi(t_k) \approx \phi(t_{k-1}) - \frac{\phi(t_{k-1})x_k x_k^T \phi(t_{k-1})}{x_k^T \phi(t_{k-1}) x_k} \quad \text{if} \quad \phi(t_{k-1})x_k \neq 0 ;$$

$$\phi(t_k) = \phi(t_{k-1}) \quad \text{if} \quad \phi(t_{k-1})x_k = 0 , \quad (k = 2, 3, \ldots) . \tag{4.62}$$

This set of equations resembles a very important mathematical expression: it has the same structure as the recursive formulas for the *orthogonal projection operator* (Sect. 2.1.5). Thus the $\phi(t_k)$ are approximately projection matrices.

Iterative Convergence in the Fast Adaptive Process. The above approximate treatment can be replaced by a mathematically more strict discussion. In discrete-time formalism the matrix Bernoulli equation is written

$$\phi_p = \phi_{p-1} - \alpha_p \phi_{p-1}^2 x x^T \phi_{p-1}^2 , \quad p > 0 . \tag{4.63}$$

If, for each p, $\alpha_p = \alpha \cdot \Delta t$, and we interpret the ϕ_p-matrices as $\phi_p = \phi(p \cdot \Delta t)$, then (4.63) yields (4.57) as $\Delta t \to 0$, $p \cdot \Delta t \to t$. In this manner, (4.63) can be regarded as a one-step (Euler) numerical quadrature of (4.57). However, as

(4.63) has some value in its own right, the results are discussed with the more general gain sequence $\{\alpha_p\}$.

As a complete discussion [4.12] is too lengthy to be reviewed here, only the results are given in the form of three lemmas, a theorem, and a corollary.

Let x be constant during each step. Let us define an integer sequence $\{i_p\}_{p=1}^{\infty}$, where each i_p belongs to the discrete set $\{1, 2, \ldots, m\}$. With the help of i_p, the input vector is expressible as $x = x_{i_p}$; it is then understood that x is one of the vectors $x_1, \ldots, x_m$, with no specification of which one.

In Lemma 2, a restriction will be imposed on $\{i_p\}$, telling something about the frequency with which each vector of S is used as input.

With this convention, (4.63) becomes

$$\phi_p = \phi_{p-1} - \alpha_p \phi_{p-1}^2 x_{i_p} x_{i_p}^T \phi_{p-1}^2 . \tag{4.64}$$

The aim of this section is that of showing that the matrix ϕ_p, starting from a *projection matrix* ϕ_0, will converge to another projection matrix under fairly general conditions on $\{i_p\}$ and the gain sequence $\{\alpha_p\}$. (Note that $\phi_0 = I$ is also a projection matrix.) These conditions will now be presented in two lemmas followed by a theorem.

Lemma 1. Let ϕ_0 be a symmetric positive semidefinite (psd) matrix, and for every p

$$\varepsilon \leqslant \alpha_p \leqslant \lambda_p - \varepsilon \quad \text{with}$$

$$\lambda_p = (x_{i_p}^T \phi_{p-1}^3 x_{i_p})(x_{i_p}^T \phi_{p-1}^2 x_{i_p})^{-1}(x_{i_p}^T \phi_{p-1}^4 x_{i_p})^{-1}$$

and

$$0 < \varepsilon < \lambda_p ;$$

then every ϕ_p is symmetric and psd.

Lemma 2. Let ϕ_p be symmetric psd for every p. Let the sequence $\{i_p\}$ be such that every integer $1, 2, \ldots, m$ appears in it infinitely often. Then all the vector sequences $\phi_p x_1, \phi_p x_2, \ldots, \phi_p x_m$ converge to zero as $p \to \infty$.

Theorem 4.4. Let ϕ_0 be a projection matrix, and $\{\alpha_p\}$ and $\{i_p\}$ satisfy the conditions imposed by Lemma 1 and 2. The sequence of matrices $\{\phi_p\}$ then converges to the unique projection matrix $\bar{\phi}$ on the subspace $\mathcal{M} = \mathcal{R}(\phi_0) \cap \mathcal{L}^\perp$, where $\mathcal{R}(\phi_0)$ is the range space of ϕ_0, and $\mathcal{L}^\perp$ is the orthogonal complement of the subspace $\mathcal{L}$ spanned by the vectors $x_1, \ldots, x_m$.

By employment of the concept of matrix pseudoinverse an explicit form can be given to the limit matrix $\bar{\phi}$. Let X denote, as before, the $(n \times m)$ matrix with columns $x_1, x_2, \ldots, x_m$. It is then easy to confirm that

$$\bar{\phi} = \phi_0 - \phi_0 X (X^T \phi_0 X)^+ X^T \phi_0 \tag{4.65}$$

is the unique projection matrix on the subspace $\mathcal{M} = \mathcal{R}(\phi_0) \cap \mathcal{L}^\perp$.

If, in particular, we have $\phi_0 = I$, then (4.65) yields (by application of the well-known identity $(X^T X)^+ X^T = X^+$):

Corollary. If the assumptions of Lemma 1 and Lemma 2 hold, and ϕ_0 is the unit matrix, then ϕ_p converges to $\bar{\phi} = I - XX^+$ which is the projection operator on the subspace $\mathcal{R}(I) \cap \mathcal{L}^\perp = \mathcal{L}^\perp$.

So far, no reference has been made to the nature and the speed of convergence of ϕ_p. The concluding lemma of this section is the following.

Lemma 3. If α_p remains within the bounds defined in Lemma 1, and the input vector is held constant, then the norm of the output vector is monotonically decreasing. The larger α_p is, the faster is the convergence.

The assumptions of the above theorem may not be immediately clear in terms of the original feedback system. The main purpose of introducing the index sequence $\{i_p\}$ was that of elimination of any suggestions concerning the order in which the different input vectors are employed in the course of training. Thus many possible processes are covered, for example a cyclic training in which the vectors of S are used repeatedly, and particularly the process where they are used one at a time for long periods. In the latter process the index sequence might be the following: $\{i_p\} = \{1, 1, \ldots, 1, 2, 2, \ldots, 2, 3, \ldots, m, \ldots\}$ where it is understood that each interval of constant i_p is arbitrarily long. Then convergence is guaranteed if α_p is sufficiently small. By letting the step size which is now proportional to α_p become infinitesimal (which is allowed by Lemma 1), the discrete process is an arbitrarily close approximation of the continuous one. This question is intrinsically connected with the stability and convergence properties of one-step discretization formulas, as the step size becomes very small.

If the learning process of a pattern is interrupted, as is always the case when each input vector is used in the training for a limited period only, then an iterative improvement by repetitive use of the input vector is due in the above process. Lemma 3 then guarantees that the error must always decrease in a monotonous fashion.

Adaptation with Forgetting. Memory effects in physical systems are usually volatile. For this reason it is desirable to study adaptation equations when the memory traces are allowed to decay. The discussion of this type of process with "forgetting" is yet amenable to the matrix equation formalism if, in the case that the external signals are zero, every memory element is assumed to decay at a rate which is directly proportional to its value. This is the simplest law of "leakage" in most physical processes, and the equation for M is then written

$$dM/dt = -\alpha\tilde{x}\tilde{x}^T - \beta M \tag{4.66}$$

with α and β constant positive scalars. In discrete-time formalism, this equation would read

$$M_p = \gamma_p M_{p-1} - \alpha_p x_{i_p} x_{i_p}^T \tag{4.67}$$

with γ_p and α_p certain scalar-valued parameters and the subscripts p and i_p as explained in Sect. 3.4.2.

In place of the matrix Bernoulli equation, the following more general differential equation is now obtained, with ϕ the overall transfer matrix as before:

$$d\phi/dt = -\alpha\phi^2 xx^T\phi^T\phi + \beta(\phi - \phi^2) . \tag{4.68}$$

Again, a mathematical discussion becomes possible if the initial value $\phi(0) = \phi_0$ is assumed symmetrical and idempotent and x is taken constant from the time $t = 0$ on.

The following discussion is due to *Oja* [4.13]. A conjecture about the solution being of the form

$$\phi = \phi_0 + f(t)\phi_0 xx^T\phi_0 \tag{4.69}$$

is now made, where $f(t)$ is a time function to be determined. Using the fact that ϕ_0 is idempotent, the following scalar differential equation for $f(t)$ is obtained:

$$df/dt = -\alpha[1 + \lambda f(t)]^4 - \beta f(t)[1 + \lambda f(t)] ,$$
$$f(0) = 0, \quad \text{with} \quad \lambda = x^T\phi_0 x \text{ (a scalar)} . \tag{4.70}$$

In order that the above trial solution be applicable, it is necessary that $f(t)$ remain bounded. For convenience, the function

$$s(t) = 1 + \lambda f(t) \tag{4.71}$$

is introduced. The differential equation for it reads

$$ds/dt = -\alpha\lambda s^4 - \beta(s^2 - s), \ s(0) = 1 . \tag{4.72}$$

To the first it is shown that $s(t) > 0$ for $0 \leqslant t < \infty$. This follows from the fact that the right-hand side of (4.72) is continuous and continuously differentiable in s. The solution for $s(t)$ is then unique. On the other hand, because $s(t) \equiv 0$ is the solution for the initial value $s(0) = 0$, there follows that the solution for $s(0) = 1$ cannot become zero with finite t without contradiction of uniqueness. Therefore, with $s(0) = 1$, $s(t)$ remains positive.

The asymptotic properties of $s(t)$ can now be determined. Especially in the case that β can be selected arbitrarily small, all real roots of the equation $ds/dt = 0$ are also small, and it can be deduced (although a formal proof is omitted here) that the solution of $s(t)$ monotonically tends to a small positive number ε. Thereby

$$\lim_{t \to \infty} \phi(t) = \phi_0 + \frac{\varepsilon - 1}{x^\mathsf{T} \phi_0 x} \phi_0 x x^\mathsf{T} \phi_0 . \tag{4.73}$$

This is an approximation of the recursive formula (4.61). It is to be noted that the asymptotic solution with forgetting has the same form as a solution of the original matrix Bernoulli equation (without forgetting) when it was integrated over a finite interval of time.

Demonstration of the Novelty Filter. Although we shall revert to the novelty filter in the context of optimal associative mappings (Sect. 6.3), it may be expedient to have here a preliminary demonstration of the capacity of this model. The central phenomenon that takes place in this system is that the "filter", by and by, becomes "opaque" to the presented pattern: the output will gradually fade out. As this kind of adaptation occurs for a number of patterns, the operation is very much similar to various aftereffects that are met in the visual system; the model will become "habituated" to the inputs. One might also say that the presented patterns have been stored in the memory of the system.

If then a new pattern is shown at the inputs, and before the system has become adapted to it, there will appear a pattern component at the output which represents the "novel" or unfamiliar parts in the input, i.e., that contribution to the input pattern which cannot be explained as a linear combination of the "memorized" patterns. If the input pattern is x, and its projection on the space spanned by the "old" patterns is $\hat{x}$, then

$$\tilde{x} = x - \hat{x} = (I - XX^+)x, \tag{4.74}$$

where $\tilde{x}$ is the "novelty" component at the output. Here X is the matrix with the "old" patterns as its columns.

Figure 4.11 presents pictures which were taken of the same person with different facial expressions. There were ten "neutral" expressions, not shown here; they defined the matrix X, and the projector $I - XX^+$. The upper row shows the inputs x, and the lower row the outputs $\tilde{x}$. It may be self-explanatory which parts are "novel".

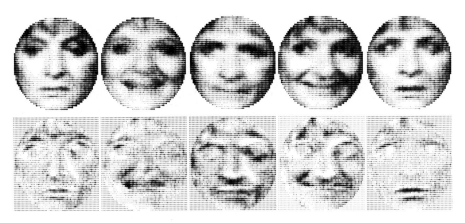

Fig. 4.11. Demonstration of the novelty filter function

5. Self-Organizing Feature Maps

A property which is commonplace in the brain but which has always been ignored in the "learning machines" is a meaningful order of their processing units. *"Ordering"* thereby usually does not mean *moving* of units to new places. The units may even be structurally identical; the specialized role is determined by their internal parameters which are made to change in certain processes. It then appears as if specific units having a meaningful organization were produced.

Although a part of such ordering in the brain were determined genetically, it will be intriguing to learn that an almost optimal spatial order, in relation to signal statistics, can completely be determined in simple self-organizing processes under the control of received information. The properties of these processes result from a few fundamental system principles discussed in this chapter. It seems that such a spatial order is necessary for an effective representation of information in the internal models. The various *maps* formed in self-organization are able to describe topological relations of input signals, using a one- or two-dimensional medium for representation. Such dimensionality-reducing mappings seem to be fundamental operations in the formation of abstractions, too.

5.1 On the Feature Maps of the Brain

Economic representation of data with all their interrelationships is one of the most central problems in information sciences, and such an ability is obviously characteristic of the operation of the brain, too. In thinking, and in the subconscious information processing, there is a general tendency to compress information by forming *reduced representations* of the most relevant facts, without loss of knowledge about their interrelationships. The purpose of intelligent information processing seems in general to be creation of simplified images of the observable world at various levels of abstraction, in relation to a particular subset of received data.

The above ability of the human information processing was earlier almost a mystery; only recently it has been possible to obtain concrete evidence for the ability of the brain to form neural representations which are images of various sensory experiences, projected onto the various cortical areas.

It has been known a long time that the various areas of the brain, especially of the cerebral cortex, are organized according to different sensory modalities: there are also areas performing specialized tasks, e.g., speech control and analysis of sensory signals (visual, auditory, somatosensory, etc.) (Fig. 1.1). Between the primary sensory areas which comprise only ten per cent of the total cortical area, there are less well known *associative areas* onto which signals of different modality converge. The planning of actions takes place in the frontal lobe. More recent experimental research has also revealed a *fine-structure* within the areas: the visual, somatosensory, etc. response signals are obtained in the same topographical order on the cortex in which they were received at the sensory organs; see the somatotopic map shown in Fig. 1.2.

A pure topographical order of the nerve connections might be explained rather easily: the axons of the neural cells, when growing towards their destination, may be kept separate by histological structures, and their destination is found by following the control action of chemical markers (e.g., [5.1 – 3]). Nonetheless, there is a somewhat confusing aspect that the connections are not always one-to-one, because there also exist in the signal-transmission path processing stations (nuclei) in which signals are mixed. This explanation breaks down completely in some maps where the primary signal patterns are ordered in a more abstract way. For instance, in the auditory cortex there exists the *tonotopic map* in which the spatial order of cell responses corresponds to the pitch or acoustic frequency of tones perceived (Fig. 1.3); although some researchers claim that this order also corresponds to the location of resonances on the basilar membrane of the ear, the neural connections are no longer direct due to many nuclei in the auditory tract of nerves. Some more confusion is caused by the fact that the neural signals corresponding to the lowest tones are neither encoded by the position of the resonance; nonetheless the map of acoustic frequencies on the auditory cortex is perfectly ordered and almost logarithmic with respect to frequency.

Some evidence is also available about more abstract maps being formed elsewhere in the brain system, even according to sensory experiences. Some maps of the geographic environment have been measured in the *hippocampus* which is part of the midbrain; when a rat had learned its location in a maze, then certain cells on the hippocampal cortex responded only when the animal was in a particular corner [5.4]. It is believed that many other kinds of maps exist in the hippocampus or other parts of the brain system.

Without doubt the main structures of the brain network are determined genetically. However, there also exists direct experimental evidence for sensory projections to be affected by experience. For instance, after ablation of sensory organs or brain tissue, or sensory deprivation at young age, some projections are not developed at all, and the corresponding territory of the brain is occupied by the remaining projections (e.g., [5.5 – 7]). Recruitment of cells to different tasks depending on experience is well-known. These effects should then be explained by neural plasticity and they exemplify simple self-organization that is mainly controlled by sensory information.

The possibility that the representation of knowledge in a particular category of things in general might assume the form of a feature map that is geometrically organized over the corresponding piece of the brain has motivated the series of theoretical investigations reported in this chapter. The results thereby obtained have gradually led this author to believe that one and the same functional principle might be responsible for self-organization of widely different representations of information. Furthermore, some results reported in this chapter point out that the very same functional principle which operates on a uniform, singly-connected, one-level medium is also able to represent *hierarchically related data,* by assigning different subareas of the medium to the different abstract levels of information. The representations over such maps then resemble the tree structures that are obtainable by conventional taxonomic and clustering methods (Sect. 7.6.2). This result is theoretically very fundamental, since it reveals a new aspect of hierarchical representations; it is not necessary, and it may always not even be possible to arrange the processing units in many subsequent levels, as usually thought; although such levels may still exist, a more fundamental hierarchical organization may follow from structured occupation and utilization of a uniform memory territory.

We shall approach the basic self-organizing processes as adaptive phenomena which take place in simple physical systems. Somewhat similar, although simpler phenomena occur in the so-called retinotectal mappings (e.g., [5.8 – 11]) which are obviously implemented by chemical labeling during the growth of the tissue. The present discussion, on the other hand, is related to an idealized hypothetical neural structure which is affected by sensory signals, and its purpose is to show which kind of structural and functional properties of systems are sufficient for the implementation of self-organization. It is thus the *process* in which we are primarily interested, not its particular implementation; if enough knowledge about accurate chemical phenomena would be available, the same principles might be demonstrable in a purely chemical model, too. However, it seems that the neural structures have many details which are particularly favourable for the formation of feature maps with very high resolution and at an arbitrary level of abstraction.

In some relatively recent investigations [5.12 – 17] it has turned out that certain laminar networks which consist of interconnected adaptive units have an ability of changing their responses in such a way, that the location of the cell in a network where the response is obtained becomes specific to a certain characteristic feature in the set of input signals. This specification, in particular, occurs *in the same topological order which is present in the metric (similarity) relations of the input signal patterns.* As pointed out above, the cells or units do not move anywhere; it is the set of their internal parameters that defines this specificity and which is made to change. Since such networks are usually planar (two-dimensional) arrays, this result also means that there exist mappings which are able to preserve the topological relations *while performing a dimensionality reduction of the representation space.*

This remarkable behaviour will now be demonstrated by means of some basic system models which resemble those discussed in Sect. 4.4. The most significant difference lies in the type of feedback which is made to depend on distance according to a characteristic *lateral feedback function* often met in neural networks.

5.2 Formation of Localized Responses by Lateral Feedback

Before introducing the new adaptive phenomenon, it will be necessary to demonstrate a processing function that modifies the primary input excitation by lateral feedback.

Most neural networks in the brain, especially those in the cerebral neocortex, are essentially two-dimensional layers of processing units (cells or cellular modules) in which the units are densely interconnected through lateral feedback. According to some estimates, in the neocortex there are 10 000 interconnections emerging from and converging upon every principal cell. Figure 5.1 delineates an array of model neurons, each of which receives the primary input ϕ_i and a great number of lateral connections from the outputs of other units. The array can also be two dimensional.

Assume that the lateral coupling is a function of distance in the following way. There is both anatomical and physiological evidence from the mammalian brains (cf. also Chap. 8) for the following type of *lateral interaction* to exist between cells: (i) Short-range lateral excitation reaching up to a radius of 50 to 100 μm (in primates); (ii) The excitatory area is surrounded by a penum-

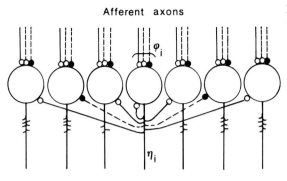

Afferent axons

Fig. 5.1. Laterally interconnected neurons

Efferent axons

bra of inhibitory action reaching up to a radius of 200 to 500 μm; (iii) A weaker excitatory action surrounds the inhibitory penumbra and reaches up to a radius of several centimeters. The degree of lateral interaction is usually described as having the form of a Mexican hat (Fig. 5.2).

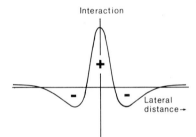

Fig. 5.2. The "Mexican-hat function" of lateral interaction

In the discussion relating to this chapter, the weaker excitatory surround is neglected; it has probably more relevance to autoassociative memory as discussed in Chaps. 6 and 8.

The form of the lateral interaction function used in simulations is depicted in Fig. 5.3. Signal transfer in the network is assumed to be describable by the following expression, written in the discrete-time form for computing.

$$\eta_i(t) = \sigma\left[\phi_i(t) + \sum_{k=-16}^{16} \gamma_k \eta_{i+k}(t-1)\right], \tag{5.1}$$

where each feedback has a small delay normalized to unity; the coefficients γ_k have been defined in Fig. 5.3. Here $\sigma[\cdot]$ stands for a "sigmoid"-type non-linearity for which we (rather arbitrarily) choose

$$\sigma[z] = 0 \text{ for } z < 0, \sigma[z] = z \text{ for } 0 \leqslant z \leqslant 10, \text{ and } \sigma[z] = 10 \text{ for } z > 10.$$

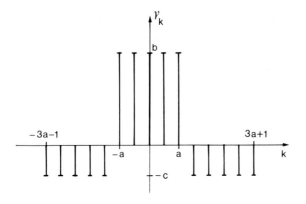

Fig. 5.3. Lateral interaction used in simulations

Assume now that the input excitation $\phi_i(t)$ is some smooth function of the array index i and it is made to last, e.g., for one unit interval of time. The distribution $\eta_i = \eta_i(t)$ may then be plotted for subsequent instants of time as done in Fig. 5.4.

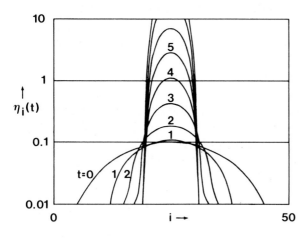

Fig. 5.4. Clustering of activity in a one-dimensional array

For instance, if it is taken $\phi_i(0) = A \sin^2(\pi i/50)$, and the parameters are as in the caption of Table 5.1, the activity, due to the lateral couplings, tends to a spatially bounded *cluster*, and due to saturation it is stabilized to a constant amplitude. The cluster is *centered around the local maximum* of the input excitation $\phi_i(t)$.

In this simple model the "clusters" are stabilized permanently. It is then easy to add some simple features to the model like "fatigue" effects, or temporary weakening of the connections under persistent activity; such effects are commonplace in neural circuits. If this is done, the clusters can be made to decay off after some time, and the network is free to receive new excitation.

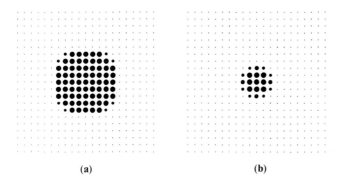

(a)   (b)

Fig. 5.5a, b. Clustering of activity in a two-dimensional array. (a) Positive feedback stronger; (b) Negative feedback stronger

Figure 5.5 represents another, two-dimensional case of clustering which has taken place in a 21 by 21 square array of processing units. The lateral interaction function was two dimensional, of the type shown in Fig. 5.3. Only the final activity state is shown. An *"activity bubble"* is again obtained at a location where the primary excitation had a maximum. This picture also demonstrates another important effect: the width of the bubble depends on the strength of the lateral coupling, in particular the ratio of the excitatory to inhibitory interconnections. In the simulation reported in Fig. 5.4, the integrals of the positive and negative feedback, respectively, were equal; on the other hand, in the two-dimensional simulations, a slight unbalance was used. If positive feedback was stronger, it made the "bubble" wider, whereas enhancement of the negative feedback tended to "focus" the bubble sharper. (Of course, if the net feedback is too negative, no "clustering" phenomena take place.)

The effects described above will be shown useful in the self-organizing processes. The degree of feedback can also be modified by the feedback parameters corresponding, e.g., to nonspecific chemical effects in the neural networks.

A word of caution concerning simulations may be due. Although none of the processes discussed in this book is very "brittle", i.e., the effects are not sensitive to minor changes in the parameters, nonetheless the processes do not work for arbitrary parameter values. Since there are many of them, some patience is needed to find the right combinations. For instance, the clustering phenomena can be realized with feedback gains which, in a relative scale of values, may vary as much as 1 to 10. On the other hand, for the control of the optimal resolution, the accuracy of the ratio between positive and negative gains may have to be defined by an accuracy of 10 to 20%.

In order to facilitate even a nonexperienced reader to experiment with this process, the following piece of program code which contains the central part of the one-dimensional process algorithm is given in Table 5.1. It must also be pointed out that the models must be restricted to spatially limited networks, whereby usually various kinds of boundary effects occur; in reality, the neural networks are very large and boundary effects need not be considered. This is the reason why the particular form of $\phi_i(t)$, with zero derivative at the borders, was used. The algorithms can also be made cyclic with respect to the array which then simulates the effect of an infinite array.

Table 5.1. BASIC program for Fig. 5.4
($A = a, B = b, C = c$ for a, b, c defined in Fig. 5.3; e.g.,
$A = 4, B = .06, C = .04; Y(I) = \eta_i$)

```
    . . .
1000 FOR I = 0 TO 50
1010 Y(I) = .1*SIN(PI*I/50)∧2
1020 PRINT Y(I)
1030 NEXT I
1040 FOR T = 1 TO 10
1050 FOR I = 0 TO 50
1060 U(I) = Y(I)
1070 NEXT I
1080 FOR I = 0 TO 50
1090 FOR J = − A TO A
1100 Y(I) = Y(I) + A*(B + C)*U(RMD(I − J + 102,51))
1110 NEXT J
1120 FOR J = − 3*A − 1 TO 3*A + 1
1130 Y(I) = Y(I) − A*C*U(RMD(I − J + 102,51))
1140 NEXT J
1150 Y(I) = MIN(10,MAX(0,Y(I)))
1160 PRINT Y(I)
1170 NEXT I
1180 NEXT T
    . . .
```

If the excitation function were not smooth, for instance, if the input gains varied randomly, then the "bubbles" would be shaped irregularly. Even in this case, it may be possible to obtain them at the maximum of $\phi_i(t)$. The "bubbles" become better if the transfer function $\sigma[\cdot]$ is not selected linear but *convex* in its middle portion.

For comparison, Fig. 5.6 shows what kind of "activity bubbles" in reality have been recorded from the neural realms: samples of the distribution of cell activity over a 4 by 7 mm^2 area in a raccoon's cortex were taken with a 400-electrode array [5.18]. It is very plausible that this picture does not represent any well-defined map; the activity distribution may then be rather diffuse.

Nonetheless one can compare the widths of the activity "clusters" with those obtained in simulations.

Fig. 5.6. Distributions of activity on raccoon's cortex

5.3 Computational Simplification of the Process

It seems that the "clustering" phenomenon can be made to take place using many alternative forms for the lateral feedback function; the linearized convolution of the previous example is only one of them. It is plausible that there exist even more effective processes in the neural structures; the brain is known to have many kinds of lateral feedback control, neural as well as biochemical. In the continuation of this study, it therefore seems unnecessary to express the feedback equations in any particular form. Another possibility is to assume that such "clusters" occur, and to simplify the computational algorithm to this end.

It also seems that the formation of an "activity bubble" somewhere in a restricted area is the most central phenomenon which is responsible for self-organization of that area; this can be justified mathematically, as we shall see later. As the "bubble" should obviously be formed at the local maximum of activity, it may be completely expedient to *define* the computational algorithm as consisting of the following steps: (i) Find the activity maximum. (ii) Define a subset of units in the array around this maximum, corresponding to the "bubble".

It will further be expedient to define the radius of the "bubble" as a function of time, being large in the beginning, and gradually decreasing with time. The accurate *form* of the "bubble" has never had a large effect on the ordering results.

5.3.1 Definition of the Topology-Preserving Mapping

In the self-organizing process, we are aiming at mappings which transform a signal pattern of arbitrary dimensionality onto a one- or two-dimensional array. Therefore the input to the array cannot be as simple as the direct connectivity shown in Fig. 5.1: that picture was only used to define an initial value of activity to every unit. In reality, the $\phi_i(t)$ ought to be replaced by a weighted sum of primary signals. Every unit has then its own input weights which, in order to implement self-organization, must be *adaptive*.

In the most general case, the array of adaptive units receives its input signals through a *relaying network* (Fig. 5.7); this corresponds to the various transformations that take place in the sensory pathways. The signals in the relaying network are allowed to be mixed; what is most important is that the output signals from this array remain *correlated*. For instance, if three input vectors x_1, x_2, and x_3 can somehow be ordered according to some metric, then the output vectors from the relaying network y_1, y_2, and y_3 ought to retain the same order relating to some other metric.

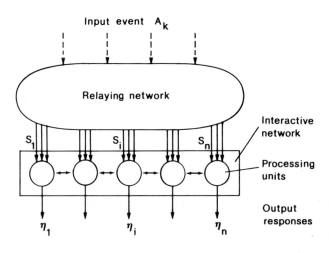

Fig. 5.7. Input connections in a self-organizing system

Consider now a physical system that receives a set of concomitant *input signals;* these are transformed into *output responses* (Fig. 5.8). (The system block may now be thought to contain the relaying network as well as the adaptive array.) Characteristic of the systems discussed in this work is that there operates some mechanism by which the active response is concentrated around some location in the output plane; for different sets of input signals this location is in general different. The *localized response* in Fig. 5.8 may be thought to represent the *center* of an "activity bubble".

One of the simplest systems which can be thought to produce localized responses is a linear array (row) of functional units, each of which receives the same set of input signals in parallel. Assume that such a unit i then produces a different response to the different input patterns: $\eta_i(x_1)$, $\eta_i(x_2)$, ... Next, we

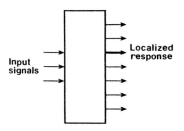

Fig. 5.8. Localized response

define a transformation that is characteristic of the present self-organizing systems, and obviously of many brain areas, too. Assume for simplicity that a set of input patterns $\{x_i: i = 1, 2, \ldots\}$ can be ordered in some metric or topologic way such that $x_1 R x_2 R x_3 \ldots$, where R stands for a simple ordering relation, e.g., with respect to a single feature that is implicit in the representations.

Definition 5.1. The system is said to produce a *one-dimensional topology-preserving mapping* if for $i_1 > i_2 > i_3 > \ldots$

$$\eta_{i_1}(x_1) = \max_i \{\eta_i(x_1): i = 1, 2, \ldots, n\},$$

$$\eta_{i_2}(x_2) = \max_i \{\eta_i(x_2): i = 1, 2, \ldots, n\},$$

$$\eta_{i_3}(x_3) = \max_i \{\eta_i(x_3): i = 1, 2, \ldots, n\} \quad \text{etc.}$$

The above definition is readily generalizable to two- and higher-dimensional arrays of processing units. In this case the *topology* of the array is simply defined by the definition of *neighbours* to each unit. As for the input signals, some metric or topological order may also be definable for the patterns x_k, induced by more than one ordering relation with respect to different features or attributes. If the units form, say, a two-dimensional array, and the unit with the maximum response to a particular input pattern is regarded as the *image* of the latter, then *the mapping is said to be ordered if the topological relations of the images and the patterns are similar.*

As the dimensionality of the signal space can be arbitrary, and even much higher than two (notice that there may be 10^4 inputs to the principal neurons of the cortex), some further explanations concerning topological equivalence may be due.

It may be helpful to imagine that the two-dimensional medium forms some kind of *projection image* of a higher-dimensional signal distribution, and if there are clusters or branches in the latter, they will obviously be projected as clusters or branches, respectively. The present mapping, however, can no longer be any parallel or orthogonal projection; instead, the mapping automatically (dynamically) seeks an optimal orientation in the signal space for every part of the map. To illustrate what is meant, consider Fig. 5.9. There a "twisted" signal distribution (this time three dimensional), demarcated by heavy solid lines, will be mapped onto a planar lattice of points, connected by auxiliary (thinner, dashed) lines.

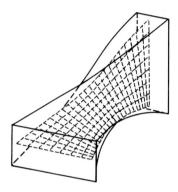

Fig. 5.9. Illustration of "projection"

5.3.2 A Simple Two-Dimensional Self-Organizing System

To concretize the basic self-organizing process, we shall use the array of Fig. 5.10 for illustration. The units can be arranged in any planar configuration, e.g., rectangular or hexagonal lattice.

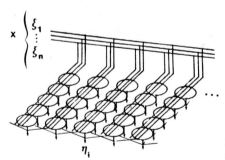

Fig. 5.10. Two-dimensional self-organizing system

Let each unit receive the same scalar signals $\xi_1, \xi_2, \ldots, \xi_n \in R$; in other words, the relaying network is neglected. Unit i, before "clustering", then forms a functional of these which in the simplest case can be linear:

$$\eta_i = \sum_{j=1}^{n} \mu_{ij} \xi_j \,, \tag{5.2}$$

where the $\mu_{ij} \in R$ are variable (adaptive) parameters. In fact, every ordered set $(\mu_{i1}, \mu_{i2}, \ldots, \mu_{in})$ may be regarded as a kind of *image* that shall be matched or compared against a corresponding ordered set $(\xi_1, \xi_2, \ldots, \xi_n)$; our aim is to devise adaptive processes in which the parameters of all units converge to such values that every unit becomes specifically matched or sensitive to a particular domain of input signals in a regular order.

Instead of considering the maximum output response, the location of the maximum can also be defined according to the *best match* between the *vectors* $x = [\xi_1, \xi_2, \ldots, \xi_n]^T$ and $m_i = [\mu_{i1}, \mu_{i2}, \ldots, \mu_{in}]^T$. The similarity criterion applied in (5.2) is the (unnormalized) correlation, or inner product of x and m_i.

It has already been shown in Chap. 4, and it will further be pointed out below that many adaptation laws tend to *normalize* the weight vectors m_i to *constant length*; one may recall Case 4 and Case 5 of Sect. 4.3.2. If this result is adopted here, then another equivalent matching criterion would be the Euclidean distance between vectors. If we define the best match to be due at unit with index c, then c can be determined, in the computational algorithm at least, by the condition

$$\|x - m_c\| = \min_i \|x - m_i\|. \tag{5.3}$$

A further advantage of using the form (5.3) for the definition of the process is that it allows a simple mathematical approach.

For the processing units of the array, some model law of the basic adaptive units could be chosen: for instance, Case 4 or Case 5 looks rather promising. Without loss of generality, one may take $\alpha = \beta$; a different value of the "forgetting constant" would only cause stabilization of the weight vectors into a different length. However, α should be made a decreasing function of time in order to guarantee convergence to a unique limit. The adaptation equations may be of the form

$$d\mu_{ij}/dt = \alpha(t)\{\eta_i(t) \cdot \xi_j(t) - \gamma[\eta_i(t)] \cdot \mu_{ij}(t)\}. \tag{5.4}$$

Next, the process which causes "clustering" or "bubbles" is taken into account. Around the maximally responding unit c, a topological neighbourhood N_c is defined such that all units which lie within a certain radius from unit c are included in N_c. Then, for all units which are inside N_c one can take $\eta_i(t) = 1$ (or some other constant value), and outside N_c, $\eta_i(t) = 0$. If, without loss of generality, we further assume $\gamma(0) = 0$, $\gamma(1) = 1$, then (5.4) can be dressed into the following simple form:

$$d\mu_{ij}/dt = \alpha(t)[\xi_j(t) - \mu_{ij}(t)] \quad \text{for} \quad i \in N_c,$$

$$d\mu_{ij}/dt = 0 \quad \text{for} \quad i \notin N_c . \tag{5.5}$$

Finally the complete computational algorithm is expressed in the discrete-time formalism and written in vector form as the following set of equations, where t_k now stands for the discrete-time index (usually integer):

Similarity Matching

$$\|x(t_k) - m_c(t_k)\| = \min_i \{\|x(t_k) - m_i(t_k)\|\} . \tag{5.6}$$

Updating

$$m_i(t_{k+1}) = m_i(t_k) + \alpha(t_k)[x(t_k) - m_i(t_k)] \quad \text{for} \quad i \in N_c ,$$
$$m_i(t_{k+1}) = m_i(t_k) \qquad\qquad\qquad\qquad \text{otherwise} .$$

As pointed out many times above, the algorithm chosen here for simulations is only representative of many alternative forms. We would like to demonstrate the phenomena as simply as possible; without simplifications, the computations become intolerably heavy.

The "topological neighbourhood" $N_c = N_c(t_k)$ (which is a function of the discrete-time index) may be defined in several ways, too. Numerous simulations have shown that the best results in self-organization are obtained if the neighbourhood is selected fairly wide in the beginning and then it is let to shrink with time (Fig. 5.11). Notice that at the borders of the array, N_c is not full.

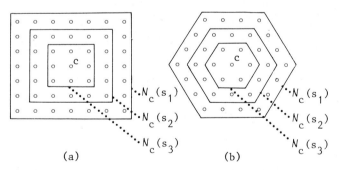

Fig. 5.11a, b. Two examples of topological neighbourhood ($s_1 < s_2 < s_3$)

The gain sequence $\{\alpha(t_k); t_k = 0, 1, \ldots; 0 < \alpha(t_k) < 1\}$ is usually a slowly decreasing function of time. It might be conjectured that $\alpha(t_k)$ should satisfy similar conditions as in stochastic approximation, e.g.,

$$\sum_{s=0}^{\infty} \alpha(s) = \infty, \ \sum_{s=0}^{\infty} \alpha(s)^2 < \infty ;$$

it has turned out, however, that the problem of optimal gain sequence is very subtle, especially in the initial phase of ordering. In practical computations, $\alpha(t_k)$ can be chosen as a linearly decreasing function of t_k, whereby the process then automatically stops when $\alpha(t_k) = 0$.

A proper choice for $\{\alpha(t_k); t_k = 0, 1, \ldots\}$ and $\{N_c(t_k); t_k = 0, 1, \ldots\}$ can best be determined by experience. Certain "rules of thumb" can be invented easily after some experience. Moreover, it may be useful to notice that there are two phases in the formation of maps that have a slightly different nature, viz., *initial formation of the correct order,* and *final convergence* of the map into asymptotic form. For good results, the latter phase may take 10 to 100 times as many steps as the former, whereby a low value of $\alpha(t_k)$ is used.

We would once more like to emphasize that many experiments have indicated the following general rules to form the basis of various self-organizing processes:

   i) Locate the best-matching unit.
   ii) Increase matching at this unit and its topological neighbours.

Mathematical Definition of the Ordering Result. What will then be achieved with this or a similar process? It may not be quite easy to deduce the result from the equations; it needs a mathematical proof. The result, however, is expressible in a precise form which further will be illustrated by the computer simulations given below: *if the input vector x is a random variable with a stationary probability density function p(x), then an ordered image of p(x) will be formed onto the input weights μ_{ij} of the processing units.* In other words, every unit becomes maximally sensitized to a particular x, but for different units this sensitization occurs in an orderly fashion, corresponding to the distribution $p(x)$. Let us put this result in still another way:

Proposition 5.1. The point density function of the m_i vectors tends to approximate the probability density function $p(x)$ of the input vectors, and the m_i vectors tend to be ordered according to their mutual similarity.

This result then has some very important consequences to information processing as will be seen later.

5.4 Demonstrations of Simple Topology-Preserving Mappings

5.4.1 Images of Various Distributions of Input Vectors

The first computer simulations shall illustrate the effect that the weight vectors tend to approximate the distribution of input vectors in an orderly fashion. In the first examples, the input vectors were chosen two dimensional for visual display purposes, and their probability density function was uniform over the area demarcated by its borderlines. The vectors $x(t_k)$ were drawn from this density function independently, at random, whereafter they caused adaptive changes in the weight vectors m_i.

The m_i vectors are shown as points in the same coordinate system where the $x(t_k)$ are represented; in order to indicate to which unit each m_i belongs, the end points of the m_i have been connected by a lattice of lines which conforms with the topology of the processing unit array. A line connecting two weight vectors m_i and m_j is thus only used to indicate that the two corresponding units i and j are adjacent in the array.

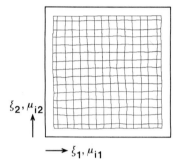

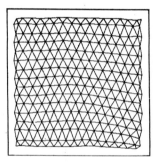

Fig. 5.12. Distribution of weight vectors, rectangular array. The input vectors had a uniform density within the framed area

Fig. 5.13. Distribution of weight vectors, hexagonal array

The two examples shown in Figs. 5.12, 13 represent the *final state* of the weight vectors, one for a rectangular, one for a hexagonal topology of the array. There is thus one weight vector at every crossing and end point of the lines. The different units have clearly become sensitized to the different training vectors in an orderly fashion. There is a boundary effect visible which causes a slight contraction of the map. Notice that the density of weight vectors is correspondingly higher at the borders. The contraction effect also diminishes with increasing size of the array.

In Figs. 5.14, 15 the input vectors had a uniform distribution over a triangular area. In Fig. 5.14 the array was two dimensional. The results, however, are particularly interesting if the distribution and the array have different dimensionalities: Fig. 5.15 illustrates a case in which the distribution was two dimensional, but the array one dimensional (linear). The linear arrays often tend to approximate higher-dimensional distributions by Peano curves (Sect. 5.8).

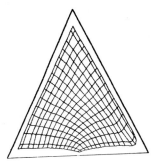

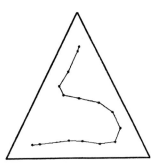

Fig. 5.14. Distribution of weight vectors, rectangular array

Fig. 5.15. Distribution of weight vectors, linear array

We might like to know the mathematical explanation of this self-ordering effect. The phenomenon is actually rather delicate and needs a lengthy discussion which in the one-dimensional case is given in Sect. 5.7. A simple proof follows from general properties of Markov processes, especially that of the *absorbing state* for which the transition probability into itself is unity. Here the ordered state corresponds to the absorbing state. If such a state is reached by some sequence of independent inputs which has a positive probability, starting from arbitrary initial values, then with a random sequence of inputs, the state is reached almost surely.

One should also make a remark which concerns all future demonstrations represented in this section: since there is no factor present which would define a particular orientation in the output map, the latter can be realized in the process in any mirror- or point-symmetric inversion. If a particular orientation had to be favoured, the easiest way to reach this result would be by an asymmetric choice of the initial values $m_i(0)$ of the system parameters. Since this effect may not be as interesting as the self-organizing behaviour itself, we shall ignore it in the forthcoming examples.

Examples of intermediate phases during the self-organizing process are given in Figs. 5.16, 17. The initial values $m_i(0)$ were selected at random from a certain (circular) support of values, and the structure of the network becomes visible only after some time. In these demonstrations, $\alpha(t_k)$ was also a function of the "bubble" radius, a Gaussian function with a width which was decreasing in time.

In Fig. 5.18 we have another example with a more complex density function; it shows that the weight vector distribution is very flexible in approximating structures. This example resembles the so-called *cladograms* of numerical taxonomy, and it may be used to explain the structures obtained in the examples of Sect. 5.6.

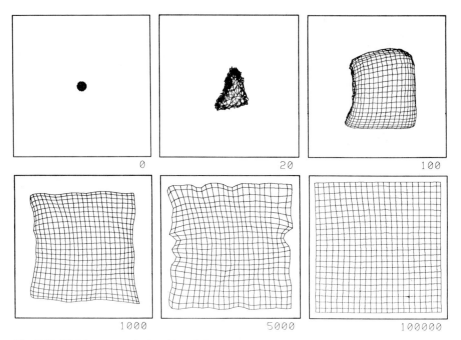

Fig. 5.16. Weight vectors during the ordering process

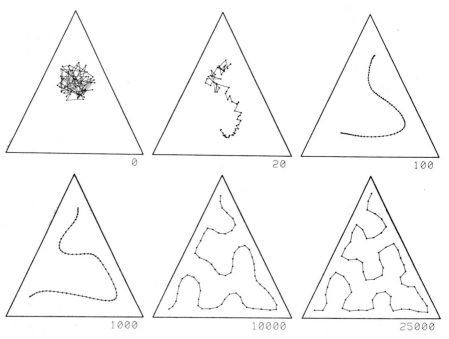

Fig. 5.17. Weight vectors during the ordering process

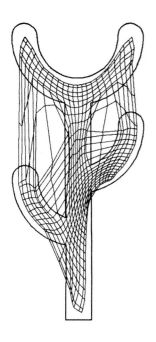

Fig. 5.18. Distribution of weight vectors for a structured density function of input vectors

5.4.2 "The Magic TV"

The following demonstration (Fig. 5.19) shows another, more realistic example of self-organization. It describes a hypothetical image-transferring system (dubbed here "The Magic TV") in which there are no control mechanisms for the encoding of the position of picture elements, but where the order of image points in the output display automatically results in the self-organizing learning process. The result is a one-to-one mapping of the points of the input plane onto the points in the output plane; in the transmission of the signals, however, this order was never specified explicitly. The system has to deduce the order gradually from the relations that are implicit in the transmitted signals. This system consists of a primitive "TV camera" and an adaptive system of the above type. The camera is thought to have a very poor optical system, such that whenever there appears a spot of light on the input plane, it forms a very diffuse focus onto the photocathode. Assume that the cathode has three sectors, each one producing a signal directly proportional to the area which is illuminated by the broad focus. Now let the light spot move at random in different points in the input plane, with a probability density function that is uniform over a square area. The resulting signals ξ_1, ξ_2, ξ_3 are then transmitted to the processing-unit array, where they cause adaptive changes. Let this process continue for a sufficient time, after which a test on the system is performed. This test is accomplished, e.g., by recording the output of each

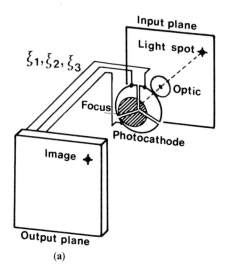

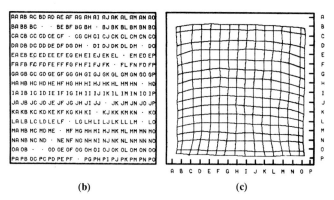

Fig. 5.19a–c. "The Magic TV"
(a) System. (b) Output plane. Pairs of letters correspond to processing units, labelled by the images of test vectors (with coordinates defined in (c)). (c) Input plane showing those points to which the various processing units (corresponding to nodes of the net) have become most sensitive

(a)

(b)   (c)

unit in turn and trying to locate that point in the input plane where a light spot must be in order to cause the maximum output response in the unit under discussion.

The resulting output maps can always be tested in either of the following ways: A) One can look at which processing unit each of the test vectors in turn makes the best match, and call this unit the image of the test vector. The array is labelled accordingly. B) One can test to which training vector (with known classification) each of the units has become most sensitive, making the best match.

Obviously these tests are related but the respective output maps look slightly different. With Test A, two or more test vectors may become mapped onto the same unit while the classification of some units may be left undefined. Test B always defines a unique matching input to every output unit but it eventually happens that some input vectors, especially near the edges, are "neglected".

5.4.3 Mapping by a Feeler Mechanism

The purpose of this example is to demonstrate that a map of the environment of a subject can be formed in a self-organizing process whereby the observations can be mediated by very rude, nonlinear, and mutually dependent mechanisms such as arms and detectors of their turning angles. In this demonstration, two artificial arms, with two joints each, were used for the feeling of a planar surface. The geometry of the setup is illustrated in Fig. 5.20. The tips of both arms touched the same point on the plane which during the training process was selected at random, with a uniform distribution over the framed area. At the same time, two signals, proportional to the bending angles, were obtained from each arm; these signals were led to a self-organizing array of the earlier type, and adaptation of its parameters took place.

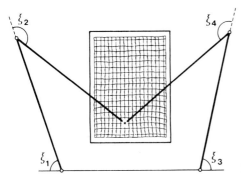

Fig. 5.20. Feeler mechanism

The lattice of lines which has been drawn onto the framed area in this picture represents a virtual image of the weight vectors, i.e., showing to which point on the plane each unit is most sensitive. When this point is touched, the corresponding processing unit gives the maximum response. One might also define the map so obtained as the map of the *receptive fields* of the array units. It can be tested for both arms separately, i.e., by letting each of them to touch the plane and looking at which point it had to be in order to cause the maximum response at a particular unit. These two maps coincide almost perfectly.

5.5 Tonotopic Map

This experiment demonstrates that the inputs can be nonidentical as long as
the signals to every unit are correlated, and the topological order of their input
vectors is the same. Consider Fig. 5.21 which depicts a one-dimensional array
of processing units. This system will receive sinusoidal signals and become ordered according to their *frequency*. Assume a set of resonators or bandpass
filters tuned at random; their outputs shall be proportional to signal power.
The filters may have a rather shallow resonance curve. The inputs to the array
units (five to each) are now picked up at random from the resonator outputs,
different samples for different array units, so that there is no order in any
structure or initial weight parameters. Next a series of adaptation operations
is carried out, every time generating a new sinusoidal signal with a randomly
chosen frequency. After a number of iteration steps, the units start to become
sensitized to different frequencies in an ascending or descending order. Final
results of two experiments are shown in Table 5.2.

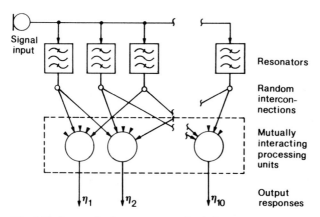

Fig. 5.21. System for frequency-map simulation

Table 5.2. Formation of frequency maps. There were twenty second-order filters with quality
factor $Q = 2.5$ and resonant frequencies distributed at random over the range $[1, 2]$. The training
frequencies were drawn at random from the range $[0.5, 1]$. The numbers in the table indicate
those test frequencies to which each processing unit became most sensitive

Unit	1	2	3	4	5	6	7	8	9	10
Experiment 1, 2000 training steps	0.55	0.60	0.67	0.70	0.77	0.82	0.83	0.94	0.98	0.83
Experiment 2, 3500 training steps	0.99	0.98	0.98	0.97	0.90	0.81	0.73	0.69	0.62	0.59

5.6 Formation of Hierarchical Representations

It will now be shown that the self-organizing mapping is able to represent rather complicated hierarchical relations of high-dimensional spaces in a two-dimensional display.

5.6.1 Taxonomy Example

In this example, the input data vector consisted of five components corresponding to some hypothetical characteristics of observable items. The data were designed artificially and they are shown in Table 5.3. Each column corresponds to an item, represented as a vector, and these vectors are further identified by the labels A, B, C, etc. The training vectors were picked up from this matrix at random.

Table 5.3. Input data matrix

Char.	A	B	C	D	E	F	G	H	I	J	K	L	M	N	O	P	Q	R	S	T	U	V	W	X	Y	Z	1	2	3	4	5	6
ξ_1	1	2	3	4	5	3	3	3	3	3	3	3	3	3	3	3	3	3	3	3	3	3	3	3	3	3	3	3	3	3	3	3
ξ_2	0	0	0	0	0	1	2	3	4	5	3	3	3	3	3	3	3	3	3	3	3	3	3	3	3	3	3	3	3	3	3	3
ξ_3	0	0	0	0	0	0	0	0	0	0	1	2	3	4	5	6	7	8	3	3	3	3	6	6	6	6	6	6	6	6	6	6
ξ_4	0	0	0	0	0	0	0	0	0	0	0	0	0	0	0	0	0	0	1	2	3	4	1	2	3	4	2	2	2	2	2	2
ξ_5	0	0	0	0	0	0	0	0	0	0	0	0	0	0	0	0	0	0	0	0	0	0	0	0	0	0	1	2	3	4	5	6

If a usual hierarchical clustering analysis (numerical taxonomy) were performed on the same data (Sect. 7.6.2), the *minimal spanning tree* shown in Fig. 5.22 would be obtained. The same data set was now processed by the self-organizing algorithm.

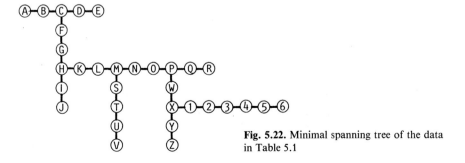

Fig. 5.22. Minimal spanning tree of the data in Table 5.1

The output map formed in the process was tested by looking at which unit each of the items caused the maximum response, and labelling the unit respectively (Fig. 5.23). We have here the same structures as in the minimal spanning tree, however, squeezed into the minimum space. Notice that in these diagrams, the topological relationships between neighbours are correct although the "legs" of the graph may be bent in different ways.

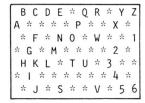

Fig. 5.23. Self-organized map of the data in Table 5.1

5.6.2 Phoneme Map

The following experiment was carried out with natural data which were collected in speech recognition experiments [5.19]. Its purpose is to visualize the topological or metric relations between phonemes picked up from continuous speech; in this demonstration, however, only those phonemes of the Finnish language were applied which were describable by their frequency spectra. The inputs to the processing units consisted of spectra of natural speech, taken at 15 different frequency channels.

The first map (Fig. 5.24a) shows at which processing unit each phonemic sample caused the maximum response. The second map (Fig. 5.24b) was tested by looking to which phoneme each unit became most sensitive, and labelling it accordingly.

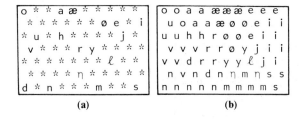

Fig. 5.24a – b. Phoneme maps

It can be seen from this example that the self-organized mapping does directly what would be hard for clustering methods, namely, to display the overall similarity relations in a metric way, two-dimensionally. For this reason, the self-organized mappings might be used to visualize topologies and hierarchical structures of high-dimensional pattern spaces.

5.7 Mathematical Treatment of Self-Organization

Although the basic principle of the above system is simple, the process behaviour, especially relating to the more complex input representations, has
been difficult to describe in mathematical terms. The present approach dis-
cusses the process in its simplest form, but it seems that fundamentally similar
results are obtainable with more complex systems, too.

We shall try to justify the self-organizing ability analytically. The reasons
for the self-ordering phenomena are actually very subtle and have strictly been
proved only in the simplest cases. In this presentation we shall delineate an explanation that should help to understand the basic nature of the process.

In the first place we shall restrict ourselves to a *one-dimensional* array of
functional units to each of which a *scalar-valued input signal* ξ is connected.
Let the units be numbered $1, 2, \ldots, l$. Each unit i has a single input weight μ_i,
whereby the similarity between ξ and μ_i is deduced according to their dif-
ference $|\xi - \mu_i|$; the best match is indicated by

$$|\xi - \mu_c| = \min_i |\xi - \mu_i|. \tag{5.7}$$

We shall define the set of units N_c selected for updating as follows:

$$N_c = \{\max(1, c-1), c, \min(l, c+1)\}. \tag{5.8}$$

In other words, every unit i has the neighbours $i-1$ and $i+1$, except at the
borders of the array, whereby the neighbour of unit 1 is 2, and the neighbour
of unit l is $l-1$, respectively. Then N_c is simply the set of units, consisting of
unit c and its immediate neighbours.

The general nature of the process is similar for very different values of α
$(0 < \alpha < 1)$; it is mainly the speed of the process which is varied with α. In the
continuous-time formalism, the equations read

$$d\mu_i/dt = \alpha(t)(\xi - \mu_i) \quad \text{for} \quad i \in N_c,$$
$$d\mu_i/dt = 0 \qquad\qquad \text{otherwise}. \tag{5.9}$$

Proposition 5.2. Starting with randomly chosen initial values for the μ_i,
these numbers will gradually assume new values in a process specified by
$(5.7 - 9)$, such that as $t \to \infty$, the set of numbers $(\mu_1, \mu_2, \ldots, \mu_l)$ becomes
ordered in an ascending or descending sequence. Once the set is ordered, it
remains so for all t. Moreover, the point density function of the μ_i will
finally approximate $p(\xi)$.

The discussion shall be carried out in two parts: formation of ordered sequences of the μ_i, and their converge to certain "fixed points", respectively.

5.7.1 Ordering of Weights

The degree of ordering is directly measurable if we define the *index of disorder D* of the μ_i in the following way:

$$D = \sum_{i=2}^{l} |\mu_i - \mu_{i-1}| - |\mu_l - \mu_1|. \tag{5.10}$$

Obviously $D \geqslant 0$, whereby the equality holds only if the values $\mu_1, \mu_2, \ldots, \mu_l$ are ordered in an ascending or descending sequence. (Due to the nature of this process the probability for some of the μ_i being equal is zero.) The self-organizing phenomenon now directly follows from the fact that if ξ is a random variable, then D more often decreases than increases in updating. Computation of dD/dt on the basis of $(5.7 - 10)$ can be performed in a straightforward way. For instance, if $3 < c < l - 2$, then only μ_{c-1}, μ_c, and μ_{c+1} can be changed in updating, and there are only five terms in D which can be affected. For any particular sign combination of the $\mu_i - \mu_{i-1}$ corresponding to these terms, the derivative dD/dt can then be expressed in closed form and simplified.

Our next task is to show that D is a good indicator of the advances made in the ordering process. In particular, D is expected to converge to zero and stay there.

To set up the central ordering theorem (Theorem 5.1), we first need some definitions which are descriptive of intermediate "states" of the process, i.e., various types of partial sequences of the μ_i. Every ordering step can be shown to depend only on ξ and the value combination of the μ_i in the immediate neighbourhood around the selected node. Illustrations of these definitions are given in Fig. 5.25.

Definition 5.1. *A fold of length $2k + 1$ at node m* is a sequence of values $(\mu_{m-k}, \mu_{m-k+1}, \ldots, \mu_{m-1}, \mu_m, \mu_{m+1}, \ldots, \mu_{m+k-1}, \mu_{m+k})$ in which one of the partial sequences $(\mu_{m-k}, \ldots, \mu_m)$, $(\mu_m, \ldots, \mu_{m+k})$ is monotonically increasing while the other is monotonically decreasing, respectively.

Definition 5.2. The value ξ lies *on the inside of the fold* if it lies in the intersection of $[\mu_{m-k}, \mu_m]$ and $[\mu_m, \mu_{m+k}]$; otherwise ξ lies *on the outside of the fold*.

Definition 5.3. An *edge fold of length k at $m = 1$* (resp. l) is a monotonically increasing or decreasing sequence of values $(\mu_l, \mu_1, \mu_2, \ldots, \mu_k)$ (resp. $(\mu_1, \mu_l, \mu_{l-1}, \ldots, \mu_{l-k+1})$).

Definition 5.4. ξ is said to lie *on the outside of an edge fold at m* if there is an edge fold at m and the signs of $\xi - \mu_1$ and $\xi - \mu_l$ are different.

Definition 5.5. A *double edge fold of length $k+1$ at $m = 2$* (resp. $l-1$) is a sequence of values $(\mu_1, \mu_2, \ldots, \mu_{k+1}, \mu_l)$ (resp. $(\mu_l, \mu_{l-1}, \ldots, \mu_{l-k}, \mu_1)$) in which the partial sequence $(\mu_2, \ldots, \mu_{k+1})$ (resp. $(\mu_{l-1}, \ldots, \mu_{l-k})$) is monotonically increasing or decreasing, *and* the signs of $\mu_1 - \mu_2$ and $\mu_2 - \mu_3$ (resp. $\mu_l - \mu_{l-1}$ and $\mu_{l-1} - \mu_{l-2}$) are different, *and* the signs of $\mu_1 - \mu_2$ and $\mu_1 - \mu_l$ (resp. $\mu_l - \mu_{l-1}$ and $\mu_l - \mu_1$) are identical.

Definition 5.6. ξ is said to lie *on the outside of a double edge fold at $m = 2$* (resp. $l-1$) if there is a double edge fold at m and the signs of $\xi - \mu_2$ and $\xi - \mu_l$ (resp. $\xi - \mu_{l-1}$ and $\xi - \mu_1$) are different.

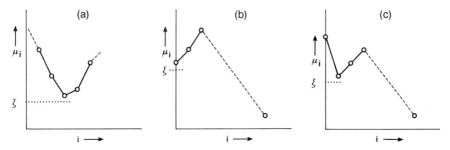

Fig. 5.25. (a) ξ lies on the outside of a fold of length 5. **(b)** ξ lies on the outside of an edge fold of length 3. **(c)** ξ lies on the outside of a double edge fold of length 4

Theorem 5.1 (The Ordering Theorem). A) Let m denote the selected node. If $3 \leqslant m \leqslant l-2$, then D decreases in updating except in the following two cases: (A1) D is not changed if the values $\mu_{m-2}, \mu_{m-1}, \mu_m, \mu_{m+1}, \mu_{m+2}$ form a monotonically increasing or decreasing sequence; (A2) D increases if ξ lies on the outside of a fold of length $\geqslant 5$ at the selected node.

B) If the selected node is $m = 1$ or $m = l$, then D decreases in updating except in the following two cases: (B1) D is not changed if the values μ_1, μ_2, μ_3, μ_l (or μ_l, μ_{l-1}, μ_{l-2}, μ_1, respectively) form a monotonically increasing or decreasing sequence; (B2) D increases if ξ lies on the outside of an edge fold of length $\geqslant 3$ at the selected node.

C) If the selected node is $m = 2$ or $m = l-1$, then D decreases in updating except in the following two cases: (C1) D is not changed if the values μ_1, μ_2, μ_3, μ_4, μ_l (or μ_l, μ_{l-1}, μ_{l-2}, μ_{l-3}, μ_1, respectively) form a monotonically increasing or decreasing sequence; (C2) D increases if ξ lies on the outside of a double edge fold of length $\geqslant 4$ at the selected node.

The proof of Theorem 5.1 is constructive and its central idea is to consider only those terms in D which can be changed at a time. The direction and magnitude of change depend on the sign combination of the successive differences $\mu_i - \mu_{i-1}$ of these terms. Corresponding to the parts A, B, and C of Theorem 5.1, its proof will similarly be shown separately for these parts.

Proof of Theorem 5.1: Part A. Since the selected node can affect its nearest neighbours only, all the other terms in D remain constant except those which constitute the partial sum

$$S = \sum_{i=m-1}^{m+2} |\mu_i - \mu_{i-1}|. \tag{5.11}$$

The expression S can be simplified for any particular combination of signs of the $\mu_i - \mu_{i-1}$. For instance, if $\mu_{m-1} - \mu_{m-2} > 0$, $\mu_m - \mu_{m-1} < 0$, $\mu_{m+1} - \mu_m > 0$, and $\mu_{m+2} - \mu_{m+1} < 0$, then $S = -\mu_{m-2} + 2\mu_{m-1} - 2\mu_m + 2\mu_{m+1} - \mu_{m+2}$. On the other hand, around the selected node m one has

$$\dot{\mu}_{m-2} \equiv 0,$$
$$\dot{\mu}_{m-1} = \alpha(\xi - \mu_{m-1}),$$
$$\dot{\mu}_m = \alpha(\xi - \mu_m), \tag{5.12}$$
$$\dot{\mu}_{m+1} = \alpha(\xi - \mu_{m+1}),$$
$$\dot{\mu}_{m+2} \equiv 0.$$

Therefore, in the above-mentioned example, $\dot{S} \overset{\text{def}}{=} dS/dt = 2\alpha(\xi - \mu_{m-1} + \mu_m - \mu_{m+1})$. Taking into account the assumed magnitude relations of the terms, it is easy to conclude that $\dot{S} < 0$.

There are 16 sign combinations of relevant terms in S. Of these, eight cases are symmetric with respect to the remaining eight so that one may restrict to those cases for which, e.g., $\mu_{m-1} > \mu_{m-2}$. The cases can be labeled by a0 through a7 according to Table 5.4:

Table 5.4.

Case	$\mu_m - \mu_{m-1}$	$\mu_{m+1} - \mu_m$	$\mu_{m+2} - \mu_{m+1}$
a0	>0	>0	>0
a1	>0	>0	<0
a2	>0	<0	>0
a3	>0	<0	<0
a4	<0	>0	>0
a5	<0	>0	<0
a6	<0	<0	>0
a7	<0	<0	<0

If these labels are used as subscripts for $\dot{S}$, then a straightforward calculation yields

$$\dot{S}_{a0} \equiv 0,$$

$$\dot{S}_{a1} = 2\alpha(\xi - \mu_{m+1}) < 0,$$

$$\dot{S}_{a2} = 2\alpha(\mu_{m+1} - \mu_m) < 0,$$

$$\dot{S}_{a3} = 2\alpha(\xi - \mu_m) \begin{cases} > 0 & \text{for} \quad \xi > \mu_m \ (\xi \text{ outside of fold at } m) \\ < 0 & \text{for} \quad \xi < \mu_m \end{cases} \tag{5.13}$$

$$\dot{S}_{a4} = 2\alpha(\mu_m - \mu_{m-1}) < 0,$$

$$\dot{S}_{a5} = 2\alpha(\xi - \mu_{m-1} + \mu_m - \mu_{m+1}) < 0,$$

$$\dot{S}_{a6} = 2\alpha(\mu_{m+1} - \mu_{m-1}) < 0,$$

$$\dot{S}_{a7} = 2\alpha(\xi - \mu_{m-1}) < 0.$$

Part B. The proof is similar for nodes 1 and l and will be carried out for 1 only. One can also restrict to the case $\mu_l > \mu_1$ since the case $\mu_l < \mu_1$ is symmetric to the other one. (Notice the term $|x_l - x_1|$ in D.) Now only four cases, defined in Table 5.5, need to be considered:

Table 5.5.

Case	$\mu_2 - \mu_1$	$\mu_3 - \mu_2$
b0	>0	>0
b1	>0	<0
b2	<0	>0
b3	<0	<0

$$\dot{D}_{b0} \equiv 0,$$

$$\dot{D}_{b1} = 2\alpha(\xi - \mu_2) < 0,$$

$$\dot{D}_{b2} = 2\alpha(\mu_2 - \mu_1) < 0,$$

$$\dot{D}_{b3} = 2\alpha(\xi - \mu_1) \begin{cases} > 0 & \text{if} \quad \xi > \mu_1 \ (\xi \text{ outside of edge fold}), \\ < 0 & \text{if} \quad \xi < \mu_1. \end{cases}$$

Part C. It will suffice to consider the case $\mu_l > \mu_1$. The following sign combinations shall then be discussed:

Table 5.6.

Case	$\mu_2-\mu_1$	$\mu_3-\mu_2$	$\mu_1-\mu_3$
c0	>0	>0	>0
c1	>0	>0	<0
c2	>0	<0	>0
c3	>0	<0	<0
c4	<0	>0	>0
c5	<0	>0	<0
c6	<0	<0	>0
c7	<0	<0	<0

In a similar way as before one obtains

$$\dot{D}_{c0} \equiv 0,$$
$$\dot{D}_{c1} = 2\alpha(\xi-\mu_3) < 0,$$
$$\dot{D}_{c2} = 2\alpha(\mu_3-\mu_2) < 0,$$
$$\dot{D}_{c3} = 2\alpha(\xi-\mu_2)\begin{cases} >0 & \text{if} \quad \xi>\mu_2 \quad (\xi \text{ outside of double edge fold}), \\ <0 & \text{if} \quad \xi<\mu_2, \end{cases} \tag{5.14}$$
$$\dot{D}_{c4} = 2\alpha(\mu_2-\mu_1) < 0,$$
$$\dot{D}_{c5} = 2\alpha\,(\xi-\mu_1+\mu_2-\mu_3) < 0,$$
$$\dot{D}_{c6} = 2\alpha(\mu_3-\mu_1) < 0,$$
$$\dot{D}_{c7} = 2\alpha(\xi-\mu_1) < 0.$$

This concludes the proof of Theorem 5.1.

There are many more cases above in which D decreases than in which D stays constant or increases. This is, indeed, the very reason for the observed self-ordering effects. Theorem 5.1, nonetheless, does not state anything about the frequency of occurrence of different cases during the ordering process; they depend on the whole history of updating operations. Only in the beginning, with random initial conditions, one is allowed to assume that the different cases are obtained with comparable probabilities, whereby also the rate of decrease of D is appreciable (and directly proportional to α). For instance, if the array were large, so that one could neglect the cases associated with its borders, and if the various cases would initially occur with equal probability, then, referring to Table 5.4, D would decrease in 13 cases out of 16 (notice that ξ can be smaller or greater than the value of μ_m at the selected node). However, when ordering starts to build up, one will observe that the cases in which D stays constant become more and more frequent, finally comprising most of the steps.

There is one very important consequence of Theorem 5.1, expressed in Corollary 5.1:

Corollary 5.1. If all the values $\mu_1, \mu_2, \ldots, \mu_l$ are ordered, they cannot become disordered in further updating.

The proof follows from the fact that if all partial sequences are ordered, then there are no cases in which D could increase.

One might like to have a more rigorous proof for that ordering occurs almost surely (i.e., with probability 1). Following the argumentation presented by *Grenander* for a related problem [5.20], a rigorous proof of ordering can be delineated as indicated below. Let $\xi = \xi(t) \in R$ be a random (scalar) input which has a density function $p(\xi)$ over a finite support, with $\xi(t_1)$ and $\xi(t_2)$ independent for $t_1 \neq t_2$.

Proposition 5.3. With probability one, the μ_i become ordered in ascending or descending order when $t \to \infty$.

The proof follows from general properties of Markov processes, especially that of the *absorbing region* for which the transition probability into itself is 1. It can be shown [5.21] that if such a region is reached by *some* sequence of inputs which has a *positive* probability, starting from arbitrary initial values, then allowing a random sequence of inputs, the region is reached almost surely (i.e., with probability one), when $t \to \infty$.

The absorbing region is now identified with an ordered sequence of the μ_i. On the line of real numbers, select an interval such that ξ has a positive probability on it. By repeatedly choosing values of ξ from this interval, it is possible to bring all μ_i within it in a finite time. After that it is possible to repeatedly choose values of ξ such that if, e.g., μ_{i-2}, μ_{i-1}, and μ_i are initially disordered, then μ_{i-1} will be brought between μ_{i-2} and μ_i, while the relative order in the other subsequences is not changed. Notice that if unit i is selected, then units $i-1$ *and* $i+1$ will change; if there is disorder on both sides of i, we may consider that side which is ordered first and call this an elementary sorting operation. For instance, if $\mu_{i-1} < \mu_{i-2} < \mu_i$, then selection of ξ from the vicinity of μ_i will bring μ_{i-1} between μ_{i-2} and μ_i (notice that μ_{i-2} is not changed). The sorting can be continued systematically. An overall order will then result in a finite number of steps. Since the above ξ values are realized with positive probability, the proof of Proposition 5.3 is concluded.

5.7.2 Convergence Phase

After the μ_i have become ordered, their final convergence to the asymptotic values is of particular interest since the latter represent the image of the input distribution $p(\xi)$.

In this subsection it is assumed that the μ_i, $i = 1, 2, \ldots, l$ are already ordered and, on account of Corollary 1, remain such in further updating processes. The aim is to calculate the asymptotic values of the μ_i. To be quite strict, asymptotic values are obtained in the sense of mean square or almost sure convergence only if the "gain coefficient" $\alpha(t)$ in (5.9) decreases to zero; the sequence $\{\alpha(t) \mid t = 0, 1, \ldots\}$ must obviously satisfy certain conditions similar to those imposed on stochastic approximation processes [5.22].

The convergence properties of the μ_i are discussed in this paper in a less restricted sense, namely, only the dynamic behaviour of the *expectation values* $E\{\mu_i\}$ is analyzed. These numbers will be shown to converge to unique limits. The variances of the μ_i can then be made arbitrarily small by a suitable choice of $\alpha(t)$, $t \to \infty$.

It may be useful to refer to Fig. 5.26 which represents the values μ_i on a line of real numbers. As stated above, the μ_i shall already be in order; we may restrict ourselves to the case of increasing values. It is also assumed that $[\mu_1, \mu_l]$ is a proper subset of $[a, b]$, the support of $p(\xi)$, which is obviously due if ordering has occurred through a process described above.

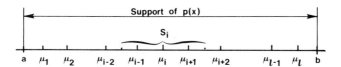

Fig. 5.26. Input weights after ordering

Since ordering of the μ_i was postulated, and because a selected node can only affect its immediate neighbours, it is obvious from (5.7−9) that any particular value μ_i can be affected only if ξ hits an interval S_i defined in the following way: assuming $l \geqslant 5$, we have

$$
\begin{aligned}
\text{for } 3 \leqslant i \leqslant l-2: \quad & S_i = [\tfrac{1}{2}(\mu_{i-2}+\mu_{i-1}), \tfrac{1}{2}(\mu_{i+1}+\mu_{i+2})], \\
\text{for } \quad i = 1 \quad : \quad & S_i = [a, \tfrac{1}{2}(\mu_2+\mu_3)], \\
\text{for } \quad i = 2 \quad : \quad & S_i = [a, \tfrac{1}{2}(\mu_3+\mu_4)], \\
\text{for } \quad i = l-1: \quad & S_i = [\tfrac{1}{2}(\mu_{l-3}+\mu_{l-2}), b], \\
\text{for } \quad i = l \quad : \quad & S_i = [\tfrac{1}{2}(\mu_{l-2}+\mu_{l-1}), b].
\end{aligned}
\tag{5.15}
$$

The conditional expectation values, with respect to $\mu_1, \ldots, \mu_l$, of the $d\mu_i/dt \overset{\text{def}}{=} \dot{\mu}_i$, according to (5.9), read

$$\langle \dot{\mu}_i \rangle \overset{\text{def}}{=} E\{\dot{\mu}_i\} = \alpha(E\{\xi | \xi \in S_i\} - \mu_i) . \tag{5.16}$$

Now $E\{\xi | \xi \in S_i\}$ is the center of gravity of S_i, see (5.15), which is a function of the μ_k when $p(\xi)$ has been defined. In order to solve the problem in simplified closed form, it is assumed that $p(\xi) \equiv \text{const}$, whereby one first obtains:

for $3 \leqslant i \leqslant l-2$:

$$\langle \dot{\mu}_i \rangle = \tfrac{\alpha}{4}(\mu_{i-2} + \mu_{i-1} + \mu_{i+1} + \mu_{i+2} - 4\mu_i) ,$$

$$\langle \dot{\mu}_1 \rangle = \tfrac{\alpha}{4}(2a + \mu_2 + \mu_3 - 4\mu_1) ,$$

$$\langle \dot{\mu}_2 \rangle = \tfrac{\alpha}{4}(2a + \mu_3 + \mu_4 - 4\mu_2) ,$$

$$\langle \dot{\mu}_{l-1} \rangle = \tfrac{\alpha}{4}(\mu_{l-3} + \mu_{l-2} + 2b - 4\mu_{l-1}) ,$$

$$\langle \dot{\mu}_l \rangle = \tfrac{\alpha}{4}(\mu_{l-2} + \mu_{l-1} + 2b - 4\mu_l) . \tag{5.17}$$

Starting with arbitrary initial conditions $\mu_i(0)$, the most probable, "averaged" trajectories $\mu_i(t)$ are obtained as solutions of an equivalent differential equation corresponding to (5.17), namely,

$$dz/dt = Fz + h , \tag{5.18}$$

where

$$z = [\mu_1, \mu_2, \ldots, \mu_l]^{\text{T}} ,$$

$$F = \frac{\alpha}{4} \begin{bmatrix} -4 & 1 & 1 & 0\ 0\ 0\ 0 \cdots \\ 0 & -4 & 1 & 1\ 0\ 0\ 0 \\ 1 & 1 & -4 & 1\ 1\ 0\ 0 \\ 0 & 1 & 1 & -4\ 1\ 1\ 0 \\ \vdots & & & & & & & \vdots \\ & & & & 0\ 1\ 1 & -4 & 1 & 1 & 0 \\ & & & & 0\ 0\ 1 & 1 & -4 & 1 & 1 \\ & & & & 0\ 0\ 0 & 1 & 1 & -4 & 0 \\ & & & & \cdots 0\ 0\ 0 & 0 & 1 & 1 & -4 \end{bmatrix}$$

and

$$h = \tfrac{\alpha}{2}[a, a, 0, 0, \ldots, 0, b, b]^{\text{T}} ,$$

with the initial condition

$$z(0) = [\mu_1(0), \mu_2(0), \ldots, \mu_l(0)]^{\text{T}} .$$

The averaging, producing (5.18) from (5.17), could be made rigorous along the lines given by *Geman* [5.23]. Equation (5.18) is a first-order differential equation with constant coefficients, and its solutions are well-established in system theory. It has a fixed-point solution, a particular solution with $dz/dt = 0$, which is

$$z_0 = -F^{-1}h, \tag{5.19}$$

provided that F^{-1} exists; this can be shown [5.16]. The general solution of (5.18) reads formally

$$z = z_0 + e^{Ft} \cdot [z(0) - z_0], \tag{5.20}$$

where the exponential function is a square matrix operator. It is a known fact that z will converge to z_0 if all eigenvalues of F have negative real parts [5.16].

The asymptotic values of the μ_i have been calculated for a few lengths l of the array and presented in Table 5.7 as well as in Fig. 5.27.

Table 5.7. Asymptotic values for the μ_i, with $a = 0$ and $b = 1$

Length of array (l)	μ_1	μ_2	μ_3	μ_4	μ_5	μ_6	μ_7	μ_8	μ_9	μ_{10}
5	0.2	0.3	0.5	0.7	0.8	–	–	–	–	–
6	0.17	0.25	0.43	0.56	0.75	0.83	–	–	–	–
7	0.15	0.22	0.37	0.5	0.63	0.78	0.85	–	–	–
8	0.13	0.19	0.33	0.44	0.56	0.67	0.81	0.87	–	–
9	0.12	0.17	0.29	0.39	0.5	0.61	0.7	0.83	0.88	–
10	0.11	0.16	0.27	0.36	0.45	0.55	0.64	0.73	0.84	0.89

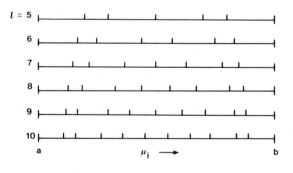

Fig. 5.27. Asymptotic values of input weights for different lengths of the array

It can be concluded that
- the outermost values μ_1 and μ_l are shifted inwards by an amount which is approximately $1/l$; consequently this effect vanishes with increasing l,
- the values μ_3 through μ_{l-2} seem to be distributed almost evenly.

5.7.3 The Magnification Factor

Let us express the result obtained above (which can also be proven easily more rigorously) by stating that, let alone the values near the edge, *the μ_i are distributed evenly* on the line of real numbers for $p(\xi) = $ const.

Reverting now to (5.16) with arbitrary $p(\xi)$, it still seems obvious (although a dynamic analysis would then become much more cumbersome) that *the asymptotic values of the μ_i coincide with the centers of gravity of the S_i, with respect to the weighting function $p(\xi)$*. In simple terms this means that *the densities of the μ_i values on the line of real numbers become approximately proportional to their weights $p(\mu_i)$, i.e., the point density function of the μ_i approximates $p(\xi)$, as asserted in Proposition 5.2.*

If, on the other hand, we consider the set of the original nodes and their associated values μ_i as a *map* of the input distribution $p(\xi)$, then a result equivalent to the above one is that *the number of nodes which have their μ_i values confined to a particular interval $[\mu', \mu'']$ is approximately proportional to the average of $p(\xi)$ over $\xi \in [\mu', \mu'']$*. This number may be termed the *magnification factor* of the map in the due location.

Asymptotic State with General Dimensionalities. It seems straightforward to generalize the one-dimensional result. For instance, if the array is linear but the distribution two dimensional, then x must be in a *selective region* defined by *discriminating surfaces* as illustrated in Fig. 5.28. Unit i is affected if x lies *in the union of the selective regions of units $i-1$, and $i+1$. Let us call this the influence region of unit i. At equilibrium, the asymptotic value of every weight vector will coincide with the center of gravity of $p(x)$ over the due influence region.* This, however, is only a necessary condition for asymptotic state, and does not warrant uniqueness of solution.

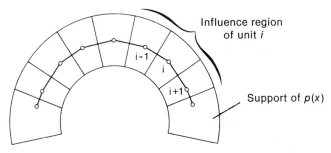

Fig. 5.28. Equilibrium state in self-organization

5.8 Automatic Selection of Feature Dimensions

There are two opposing tendencies in the self-organizing process. To the first, the set of weight vectors tends to approximate the density function of the input vectors. On the other hand, local interaction between processing units tends to preserve *continuity* in the double (two-dimensional) sequences of weight vectors. A result of these opposing "forces" is that the weight-vector distribution, tending into an approximate form like a surface, also seeks an optimal orientation and form in the pattern space which best imitates the structure of the input vector density.

A very important consequence of the above phenomenon is that the weight-vector distribution is automatically able to find those two dimensions of the pattern space where the input vectors have a high variance and which, accordingly, ought to be described in the map. As this effect otherwise might remain a bit obscure, the following extremely simple experiment is intended to illustrate, what is meant. It is believed that the result which is here demonstrated using a one-dimensional topology (linear array of processing units) and a simple two-dimensional input density function, is easily generalizable for two-dimensional topology and arbitrary dimensionality of the input-vector density function.

Assume that the system consists only of *five* units connected as a linear array.

Their input weights (μ_{i1}, μ_{i2}), $i = 1, 2, \ldots, 5$ and the components of the input vectors $x = (\xi_1, \xi_2)$ are represented as an already familiar illustration in Fig. 5.29. The relative variances in ξ_1 versus ξ_2 are now varied as shown by the supports (borderlines) of x in Fig. 5.29. As long as one of the variances is significantly higher, the weight vectors form an almost straight line which is aligned in the direction of the greater variance.

On the other hand, if the variances are almost equal, or if the length of the array is much greater than the range of lateral interaction, the straight form of

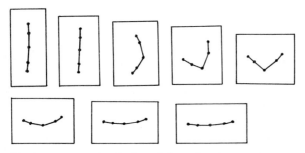

Fig. 5.29. Automatic selection of dimensions for mapping

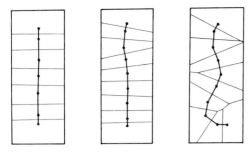

Fig. 5.30. Distribution of weight vectors with different lengths of a linear array

the distribution is switched into a "Peano curve". The transition from straight to curved line is rather sharp, as shown in Fig. 5.30.

Here the variances are fixed but the length of the array is varied; the selective regions have also been drawn to the picture. It seems that the limit of straight form is obtained when the influence regions are approximately square.

The next picture, Fig. 5.31 further illustrates what may happen when the input vectors have a higher dimensionality than the network topology (which in this case was two). As long as variance in the third dimension (ξ_3) is small

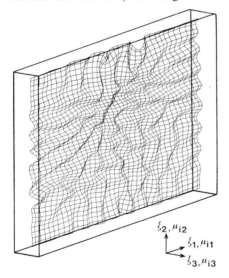

ξ_2, μ_{i2}
ξ_1, μ_{i1}
ξ_3, μ_{i3} **Fig. 5.31.** Formation of "stripes"

enough, the map would remain straight. However, with increasing variance and short lateral interaction range the map tends to become corrugated, and one should pay attention to the "zebra stripes" the kind of which have been found in the brain maps experimentally. Here the "stripes" have a very simple and natural explanation, namely, they occur whenever a two-dimensional map tries to approximate a higher-dimensional signal distribution which has significant variance in more than two dimensions.

6. Optimal Associative Mappings

It was pointed out in Chap. 1 that the most elementary form of associative recall is signal transfer operation in a physical network, whereby a spatial input pattern, the key, is directly *transformed* into a corresponding output pattern, the recollection. This operation resembles filtering; more accurately the system acts as a "diffusor"which supplements the input key excitation with associated information stored in the system (i.e., in its transfer function).

It should be distinguished between two types of transformation operations, the *autoassociative recall,* whereby an incomplete key pattern is replenished into a complete (stored) version, and the *heteroassociative recall* which selectively produces an output pattern y_k in response to the input pattern x_k; in the latter case the paired associates x_k and y_k can be selected freely, independently of each other. This operation is a generalization of the simple stimulus-response (S-R) process.

All results derived in this chapter are independent of particular physical implementation; they might, if the conditions were favourable, be realized in electrical networks, optical filters, neural networks, etc. They are also implementable as computer algorithms. The main purpose of this formalism is to prove that there exist transformations between spatial patterns or equivalent vectorial representations which can be designed *optimally*, i.e. which, with relation to a wanted input-output transfer relation between patterns, minimize the effect of noise or other imperfections present in the key inputs.

The mathematical results have a fundamental bearing on estimation theory and regression analysis. It will be shown that optimal estimation and optimal associative recall may be unified in the same formalism, as two different cases of it.

One particular remark ought to be made: although results of this chapter will be elucidated using *optical images* in the first place, the purpose is by no means to claim that these operations are suitable as such for practical image processing, except in special applications (cf. the novelty filter in Sect. 4.4.2). Neither are these mappings intended for models of biological visual systems.

They may be useful as paradigms in both areas but only in combination with other processing operations. One further interesting property of the optimal associative mappings is that in the first place they always describe the operation of *distributed memories*.

6.1 Transfer Function of an Associative Network

Consider the system of Fig. 6.1 which is a linear physical system that transfers parallel signal patterns. The linear system is the simplest representative of a class of analog physical systems. A method for the analysis of nonlinear systems will be given in Sect. 6.5.2.

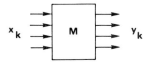

Fig. 6.1. System model for an associative memory

Let us describe the input signals by pattern vectors x_k in a representation space R^n, and let the output signals y_k be vectors in R^p. The patterns are assumed to be transformed linearly by a transfer relation

$$y_k = Mx_k , \qquad (6.1)$$

where M is a $p \times n$ matrix. We are concerned with the existence of solutions to this *paired-associate problem*: does there exist an M such that for a finite set of arbitrarily selected pairs $\{(x_k, y_k)\}$, $k = 1, 2, \ldots, m$, we can always have (6.1) satisfied? This problem will be discussed in Sect. 6.5.1. Let us tentatively assume that it has been solved. We may then regard y_k as the memorized *data*, and x_k as the *search argument* (also called *key*) by which y_k is encoded and retrieved. The excitation of the system by x_k and the subsequent observation of y_k is comparable to table lookup in computational operations.

Another question is what happens if such a system is excited by an erroneous or incomplete search argument. It shall further be shown in Sect. 6.5.1 that there exist solutions to the paired-associate problem which are *optimal* in the sense of least squares; if, in such a system, the input excitation resembles any of the stored patterns, then the output is a corrected approximation of the associated pair.

It may also be asked whether both autoassociative and heteroassociative memory (Sect. 1.3.1) can be described by the optimal mappings. Let us recall that in autoassociative memory, an item is retrieved by its fraction, that is, the recollection comprises a set of data elements of which a fraction is used as the key. In heteroassociative memory, arbitrary keys can be paired with arbitrary responses. Both of these schemes will be discussed below.

Finally it may be remarked that systems of the above kind can be characterized as *memories* if and only if the value of the transfer operator M is formed in an *adaptive process*, by the influence of the occurring signals. Possibilities for the adaptive formation of associative memory were discussed in Sects. 4.4.1, 2. It has been found that the asymptotic transfer properties of such adaptive systems are very often equivalent to *orthogonal projection operators*. On the other hand, it has been intriguing to find that optimal autoassociative recall can be implemented by the orthogonal projection operators, too. Therefore, in the hope that this would constitute a new formalism in the context of associative memory, the next sections are first devoted to associative mappings that are implemented by the orthogonal projection operators.

6.2 Autoassociative Recall as an Orthogonal Projection

6.2.1 Orthogonal Projections

Let there be m distinct Euclidean vectors denoted by $x_1, x_2, \ldots, x_m \in R^n$ which span a subspace $\mathscr{L} \subset R^n$. As mentioned in Sect. 2.2.1, it can be shown that an arbitrary vector $x \in R^n$ is uniquely expressible as the sum of two vectors $\hat{x}$ and $\tilde{x}$ of which $\hat{x}$ is a linear combination of the x_k; in particular, $\hat{x}$ is the orthogonal projection of x on the space $\mathscr{L}$, while $\tilde{x}$ is the remaining contribution in x which is orthogonal to $\mathscr{L}$. So $\hat{x}$ is the best linear combination of the x_k that approximates x in the sense of least squares. Let us denote

$$\hat{x} = \sum_{k=1}^{m} \gamma_k x_k \tag{6.2}$$

with γ_k being scalar factors; they represent the linear regression of the x_k on x.

Hereupon the vectors x_k are understood as the representations of m distinct *memorized items,* also named *reference patterns,* and x is the (possibly incomplete) *key pattern* by which information is associatively searched from the memory. If the key x bears a close correlation with one of the stored items, say x_r, then it is expected that the term $\gamma_r x_r$ of $\hat{x}$ will predominate. If this is the case, it can be said that x_r is *associatively recalled* by x. Notice further that x_r is one of the stored patterns in a perfect form. On the other hand, the other terms in the linear mixture $\hat{x}$ represent a residual which is the noise contribution, with no content other than crosstalk arising from the other stored patterns.

The classical computational method for the evaluation of orthogonal projections is the Gram-Schmidt process; for the subspace $\mathscr{L}$ spanned by the x_k, a new orthogonal vector basis is defined by the recursion

$$
\begin{aligned}
&\tilde{x}_1 = x_1, \\
&\tilde{x}_k = x_k - \sum_{i=1}^{k-1} \frac{(x_k, \tilde{x}_i)}{\|\tilde{x}_i\|^2} \tilde{x}_i \quad (k = 2, 3, \ldots, m),
\end{aligned}
\tag{6.3}
$$

where $(x_k, \tilde{x}_i)$ is the inner product of x_k and $\tilde{x}_i$, and the sum must be taken only over such terms for which $\tilde{x}_i \neq 0$. The decomposition of the key vector x into the projections $\hat{x}$ and $\tilde{x}$ is obtained by continuation of the above recursion one step further, whereby $\tilde{x} = \tilde{x}_{m+1}$, $\hat{x} = x - \tilde{x}_{m+1}$.

6.2.2 Error-Correcting Properties of Projections

The purpose of the following discussion is to show that orthogonal projection operations have the property of correcting and standardizing incomplete key patterns towards "memorized" reference patterns. This fact may result in practical applications as such, for instance, in the correction of broken fonts in character reading, in the filtering of noisy messages, and so on. If the key x is a noisy version of one of the reference patterns x_r,

$$
x = x_r + v,
\tag{6.4}
$$

where v is a stochastic error, then in general, $\hat{x}$ is an improved approximation of x_r. This can be demonstrated analytically in a simple case in which v has a constant length $\|v\| = v_0$ and a direction that is uniformly distributed in R^n. It is a straightforward matter to generalize the result for the case in which v has an arbitrary radial distribution in R^n, for instance a symmetrical multivariate Gaussian one. Notice, first, that the orthogonal projection of x_r on $\mathscr{L}$ is equal to x_r. On the other hand, it has been shown in Sect. 2.1.1 that the projection $\hat{v}$ of v on $\mathscr{L}$ has a distribution with a variance that is m/n times the square of the norm of v, where m is the number of patterns, and n their dimensionality. In other words, the noise occurring in the key pattern is attenuated in the orthogonal projection operation if $m < n$: its standard deviation is

$$
\mathrm{var}^{1/2}(\|\hat{x} - x_r\|) = \sqrt{\frac{m}{n}} \, \|x - x_r\|.
\tag{6.5}
$$

Recall of Missing Fragments. By definition of associative recall, elements lacking from a data set that is otherwise complete ought to be recalled by the rest. If now a defective version of one of the reference patterns, say x_r, is used as the key x, then $x_r - x$ can be regarded as stochastic noise. Its statistics, however, depend upon pattern x_r, and as a result are difficult to define. If it is tentatively assumed, again, that the noise attenuation factor is <1, then $\hat{x}$ is an improved approximation of x_r, and it is said that autoassociative recall of the missing portion has taken place.

Example. A straightforward demonstration of the error-correcting properties of optimal associative mappings can be performed by computer simulation using real patterns. A computer system, described in [6.1], was applied in the following experiment. An optical test pattern, consisting of a few thousand picture elements, here discretized to eight gray levels, could be prepared in digital form and transferred to the computer files automatically by a special scanner. For this study, a rectangular display of 54 by 56 picture elements was chosen. The pictures were treated as 3024-component real pattern vectors. A phototype-setting machine was used for the preparation of reproductions of the eight-shade pictures, using oval dots with corresponding intensities. Figure 6.2 summarizes the results of the demonstrations of noise suppression and autoassociative recall. In the first pair of images, Fig. 6.2a, the key was one of the original patterns, with white noise superimposed on all picture elements. The norm of the noise vector was 1.6 times that of the pattern, and the noise was derived from a uniform distribution. (Actually, such a noise has not a spherical but a cubic distribution.) There is illustrated the corresponding recollection from a "memory" in which 100 reference patterns were stored, giving a conception of the noise suppression ability of this mapping.

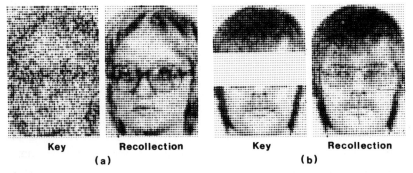

Key   Recollection   Key   Recollection

(a)   (b)

Fig. 6.2a–b. Demonstration of noise suppression and autoassociative recall in the orthogonal projection operation

Another experiment in which the key was derived from another pattern, by masking 25% of it, is shown by the pair of images in Fig. 6.2b.

6.3 The Novelty Filter

The component $\tilde{x}$ of vector x which is orthogonal to subspace $\mathscr{L}$ can be understood as the result of a particular information processing operation resulting in very interesting properties. If it is recalled that $\tilde{x}$ is the residual that is left when the best linear combination of the "old" patterns is fitted to the input data x, it is possible to think that $\tilde{x}$ is the amount that is "maximally new" in x. It may be justified to call this component the "novelty", and the name *novelty filter* is hereupon used for a system which extracts $\tilde{x}$ from input data x and displays it at the output without the $\hat{x}$ component. In Chap. 4, an adaptive scheme was discussed, the asymptotic properties of which reflect the features of the novelty filter.

6.3.1 Two Examples of Novelty Filter

Applications of the novelty filter are demonstrated in the following by two examples. It should be noticed that the filter is opaque to familiar input patterns. In the first case, there were *defects* in some input patterns. Accordingly, the filtered outputs displayed these defects as their negatives. For the clarity of representation, the outputs were made binary by discriminating them properly. In the second example, the anomalies in the patterns were positive, and accordingly, only they were displayed as positive signals at the output.

Figure 6.3 illustrates 10 two-dimensional patterns comprised of 35 dots in which the blank areas have a value of 0, and the black dots attain a value of 1. These patterns are now regarded as 35-component representation vectors x_k (Sect. 2.1.1). The orthogonal projection operator is computed with the x_k used as "old" patterns. A number of old and novel input patterns x are then applied at the input, and multiplied by the projection operator to yield the outputs $\tilde{x}$. For graphic display, the outputs $\tilde{x}$ have been represented as their negatives, and made binary by their being discriminated at a level 0.4. In general, the true outputs are not binary. The input patterns, and the respective output patterns which represent novelty in the input patterns, are indicated on the two lower rows of Fig. 6.3.

Another demonstration introduces a new method for the processing of radiographic images that were obtained by a special device called gamma camera. Figure 6.4 is a map of radioactive accumulation in patients who have taken Tc-99m isotope. The upper row of illustrations shows lateral images of

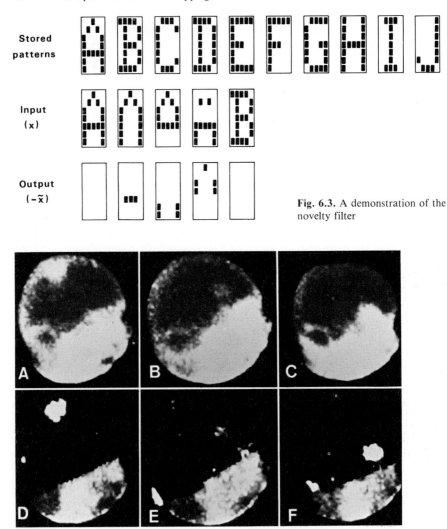

Stored patterns

Input (x)

Output ($-\tilde{x}$)

Fig. 6.3. A demonstration of the novelty filter

Fig. 6.4. Enhancement of abnormalities in autoradiographic brain images

the brain; the corresponding data were available in numerical form, too. A region of interest, a half-elliptical area about the cerebrum, was bordered and the various images were first standardized so that this area was transformed to the same shape and size. A number of numerical samples, 1300 points from this area, were selected as the components of a pattern vector to represent it. In the first phase of experiment, 30 images (not shown in Fig. 6.4) from normal cases were collected; although these too looked rather different mutually, they were classified as normal cases by a clinical diagnosis. The normal patterns were then used as the "old" or reference patterns x_k for which a novelty filter mapping was computed. (In numerical analysis, it is advisable to use the Gram-Schmidt orthogonalization process.) In the second phase of experiment, the new images to be analyzed were used as the input patterns x using similar standardization for them. The output patterns $\tilde{x}$ yielded by the novelty filter were then transformed to their original shape and size and displayed on a cathode-ray tube screen; for visual inspection, discontinuities due to the discretization of the signal values were smoothed out. The lower row of illustrations of Fig. 6.4 shows the outcomes of three abnormal cases. The intensity in the region around the bordered area was left unaltered, let alone some differences due to rescaling, whereas within this area, only the novelty component is visible. Picture A represents an image of an arteriovenous malformation; picture B shows a vascular glioma, and picture C the meningioma of olfactorius. Pictures D, E, and F are the filtered counterparts of images A, B, and C, respectively [6.2].

6.3.2 Novelty Filter as an Autoassociative Memory

It is discernible, e.g., from the demonstration of Fig. 6.3 that missing parts in patterns that were used as the input to the novelty filter are recalled associatively; the main difference of the orthogonal projection $\tilde{x}$ with respect to $\hat{x}$ is that the missing parts are reproduced as negatives, and the portion used as the key is depressed.

6.4 Autoassociative Encoding

As the patterns were defined as a collection of component data, this definition is general enough to allow special meaning to be given for the various components of the patterns. The pattern vector may be formed as a combination of vectors of a smaller dimension, each one representing a subpattern. In particular, one subpattern can be a symbolic representation, a *code* or a *tag* of the rest.

Let us first consider a case where pictorial patterns x_k and symbolic patterns y_k are combined into vectors $x'_k = [x_k^{\mathrm{T}}, y_k^{\mathrm{T}}]^{\mathrm{T}}$ in which all elements are treated equally irrespective of their meaning. If this model has to bear any connection with biological memory, then a similar effect would be the merging of different sensory signals in the same neural area. Now the orthogonalization process is carried out on the x'_k to yield the new basis vectors $\tilde{x}'_k$. If, during recall, a pictorial pattern x is used as the key, the key vector attains the form $x' = [x^T, 0^T]^T$. The orthogonal projection $\hat{x}'$ of x' is then expected to contain the missing code: if x was an approximation of, say, x_r, then the recollection in the code part $\hat{y}$ is expected to be an approximation of that code vector y_r which was associated with x_r.

6.4.1 An Example of Autoassociative Encoding

Unit vectors, i.e., orthonormal coordinate vectors which have one element equal to 1 and all the other elements equal to 0, are the simplest code vectors to be used as the tags y_k. Let us denote a unit vector corresponding to the kth pattern vector by u_k. A computer simulation was carried out in which an extra

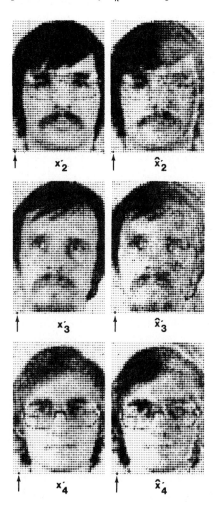

Fig. 6.5. Pairs of stored images and their recollections. There were 100 images stored in this memory, and the left half of the images was used as the key. Notice the tags on the bottom row. (The quality of the recollections is worse than, e.g., in Fig. 1.4 since no preprocessing was used)

tag field corresponding to the u_k was attached to the patterns which attained the form $x'_k = [x^T_k, u^T_k]^T$. As the patterns x_k, digitized optical images consisting of 53 by 56 picture elements were used. The values of the pattern elements were indicated by the dot size; the display was made in an eight-shade scale. (The value of 0 was indicated by the smallest dot size.) In the display, the extra horizontal row of points at the bottom shows the 56 first elements of the unit vector; the rest were not shown in the pictures. There was a dot corresponding to a numerical value of 1 in the dot position that corresponded to the identification number of the picture. When a picture was recalled, the code vector in the key pattern was set equal to 0; after formation of the orthogonal projection of the augmented pattern x', a recollection of the code part was obtained, too. For a successful identification of the pictures it was expected that the correct element in the tag field of the recollection would have a significantly higher intensity than the others. In the demonstration, some results of which are shown in Fig. 6.5, the left half of the patterns was used as the key and identification of one of 100 patterns was successfully demonstrated: an arrow shows the position in the tag field where a large element is found.

The reliability of this associative identification method was checked numerically, too. The values given in Table 6.1 tell the quality of recall when the key was 50% and 10% of the picture area, and the number of images to be identified was 10 and 100, respectively. The recognition was made by comparing the relative values of the elements of the recalled unit vector $\hat{u}$, and the average ratio of its two largest elements here indicates the "safety margin". In all cases studied, identification was correct.

Table 6.1. Average ratio of the two largest elements in $\hat{u}$ in a recall experiment

10 reference patterns		100 reference patterns	
Key 50%	Key 10%	Key 50%	Key 10%
7.68	2.16	4.96	1.88

6.5 Optimal Associative Mappings

Associative recall may in general be defined as a mapping in which a finite number of input vectors is transformed into given output vectors. If the recall must be error-tolerant, all vectors which lie in the neighbourhood of the input vectors in the sense of some metric are mapped into the neighbourhood of the corresponding output vectors. In Sect. 6.2.2, when dealing with orthogonal projection operations, it was shown that random deviations from the reference patterns were optimally corrected in the recall operation; it is now expected that the general linear associative mappings have this same property, too.

6.5.1 The Optimal Linear Associative Mapping

The basic linear recall problem was formulated in Sect. 6.1 as follows: What is the matrix operator M by which a pattern $y_k \in R^p$, for every $k = 1, 2, \ldots, m$ is obtained from the pattern $x_k \in R^n$ as

$$y_k = Mx_k \quad \forall k \in \{1, 2, \ldots, m\}? \tag{6.6}$$

By the introduction of the rectangular matrices Y and X with the y_k and x_k as their columns, respectively,

$$X = [x_1, x_2, \ldots, x_m], \ Y = [y_1, y_2, \ldots, y_m], \tag{6.7}$$

(6.6) can be put in the matrix form [6.3 – 4]

$$MX = Y. \tag{6.8}$$

A formal solution for the unknown M, with X and Y known matrices, is obtained by the Penrose method (Sect. 2.1.4) whereby the least-square approximate solution reads

$$\hat{M} = YX^+. \tag{6.9}$$

With arbitrary Y, a sufficient condition for an exact matrix solution to exist is that

$$X^+ X = I, \tag{6.10}$$

which means that the x_k are linearly independent.

Various procedures for the computation of YX^+ will be derived in Sect. 6.7.

The error-correcting properties of the linear associative mapping can be seen from the following analysis. Assume that the x_k are linearly independent whereby YX^+ is the exact solution denoted by M. If x is a pattern vector which is an approximation of x_r, $r \in \{1, 2, \ldots, m\}$, then $\hat{y} = Mx$ is expected to be an approximation of y_r. Now $\hat{y}$ is derived into a form which enables direct discernment of the quality of the recollection. If it is recalled that $X^+ = X^+XX^+$, then $\hat{y} = YX^+x = YX^+(XX^+x)$. But $XX^+x = \hat{x}$, since XX^+ is the orthogonal projection operator on space $\mathcal{L}$. Then, from (6.9), (6.2), and (6.6) it follows that

$$\hat{y} = M\hat{x} = \sum_{k=1}^{m} \gamma_k(Mx_k) = \sum_{k=1}^{m} \gamma_k y_k, \tag{6.11}$$

so that the relative magnitudes of the terms in mixture $\hat{y}$ directly correspond to the relative magnitudes of the corresponding terms in mixture $\hat{x}$. The statistical analysis which was carried out in Sect. 6.2.2 to find the variance of the projection of a spherically distributed random vector on subspace $\mathcal{L}$ is now transferable to the space in which the y_k are defined. Because the coefficients γ_k in the recollections $\hat{x}$ and $\hat{y}$ are identical, it can be deduced that if one of the terms $\gamma_r y_r$ represents the correct recollection and the other terms $\gamma_k y_k$ together are regarded as noise, the $(m/n)^{1/2}$-law for noise attenuation applies with minor modifications to the output vectors, too.

Optimal Linear Identification. If the purpose of associative recall is only that of identification of a stored item without a need to reconstruct the "stored" image, the linear associative mapping can directly be applied to the generation of identification tags for each pattern, in the same ways as in the autoassociative encoding. The simplest identification tags are unit vectors. Denoting $u_1 = [1, 0, \ldots, 0]^T$, $u_2 = [0, 1, 0, \ldots, 0]^T$, etc., and introducing the matrix $U = [u_1, u_2, \ldots, u_m]$, the problem in optimal identification of patterns is to find a solution to the equations

$$u_k = Mx_k \quad \text{for all} \quad k, \tag{6.12}$$

or, alternatively, a solution to the matrix equation

$$U = MX. \tag{6.13}$$

The least-square solution for M is

$$\hat{M} = UX^+. \tag{6.14}$$

Again, if the x_k are linearly independent, and an unknown vector x is to be identified, it is operated by UX^+, whereby according to (6.11),

$$\hat{u} = \sum_{k=1}^{m} \gamma_k u_k = [\gamma_1, \gamma_2, \ldots, \gamma_m]^T. \tag{6.15}$$

The values γ_k in the recollection correspond to the relative intensities of the patterns x_k in the vector $\hat{x}$ which is the orthogonal projection of the key x on the space spanned by the x_k.

Improvement of Identifiability by Spatial Differentiation. It ought to be noticed that the above identification methods characterized as optimal were optimal only with respect to random errors that occur in the key patterns. However, a characteristic situation in associative recall is one in which a pattern has to be identified from a *fragment*, whereby random noise can yet be superimposed on it.

In general, it has become evident that the selectivity of the associative mappings is better with reference patterns which are mutually more orthogonal. This may give an idea that the quality of associative recall in general is good if arbitrary fragments of the reference patterns are as orthogonal as possible with respect to the corresponding fragments in all the other patterns. Chances of this occurring are higher if only high spatial frequencies occur in the patterns. In order to achieve this property, the reference patterns, as well as the key, can be *preprocessed* before application of the mappings. Functional operators which enhance high frequencies and thus increase the orthogonality are derivatives or difference operators of various orders.

In the following demonstration we are dealing with optical patterns. Three different preprocessing methods to improve the orthogonality were tried: (i) Subtraction of the mean from the elements of the reference patterns x_k and the key x. (ii) Formation of the absolute value of the two-dimensional gradient of the patterns. (iii) Operation of the patterns by the two-dimensional Laplace operator ("Laplacian") $\partial^2/\partial\zeta_h^2 + \partial^2/\partial\zeta_v^2$, where ζ_h and ζ_v are the horizontal and vertical coordinates in the image plane, respectively.

Since the images were defined at discrete lattice points, the derivative operators had to be replaced by their difference approximations. Assuming that the lattice had a unity spacing in the horizontal and vertical direction (this assumption was not quite exact, but does not significantly affect the results), the *gradient* can be computed, for instance by the following formula. Denoting the primary picture elements in the grid by $\xi_{i,j}$, where i is the horizontal and j the vertical index, respectively, and the corresponding picture elements of the transformed picture by $\eta_{i,j}$, respectively, the first differences yield

$$\eta_{i,j} = \sqrt[+]{C^2 + D^2}, \tag{6.16}$$

where

$$C = \tfrac{1}{2}(\xi_{i+1,j} - \xi_{i-1,j}) \quad \text{and} \quad D = \tfrac{1}{2}(\xi_{i,j+1} - \xi_{i,j-1}).$$

Diagonal differences, or differences averaged over a larger portion of the grid, might also be used.

The *Laplacian* is obtained by the second differences, whereby

$$\eta_{i,j} = -4\xi_{i,j} + \xi_{i,j+1} + \xi_{i,j-1} + \xi_{i+1,j} + \xi_{i-1,j}. \tag{6.17}$$

Another means of description of the Laplacian is by regarding it as the two-dimensional convolution of the primary picture with the 5-point kernel defined in Fig. 6.6. A good indication of the orthogonality of preprocessed patterns can be obtained in the Gram-Schmidt orthogonalization process: when the relative norms of the "novelty components" $\tilde{x}_k$ are plotted versus the ordinal

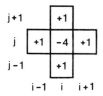

Fig. 6.6. Convolution kernel

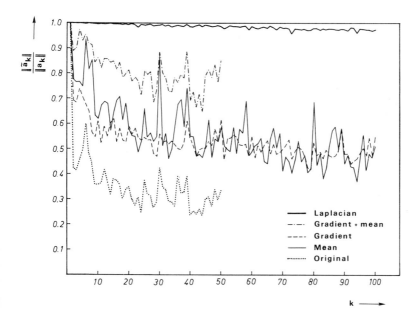

Fig. 6.7. Norms of successive basis vectors obtained in the Gram-Schmidt orthogonalization of photographic images. (*Original*) images were orthogonalized as such. (*Mean*) the mean of the picture elements was subtracted before orthogonalization. (*Gradient*) the absolute value of the gradient was taken. (*Gradient + mean*) after taking the gradient, the mean of it was subtracted. (*Laplacian*) the images were preprocessed by the Laplacian before orthogonalization

number of the patterns k, the value of this entity decreases the slower with k the more orthogonal the patterns are inherently. An experiment with 100 optical images, each one consisting of 3024 elements, shows the effect of different preprocessing methods. It is discernible that the Laplacian is superior to the other methods studied (Fig. 6.7).

Results obtained from experiments in which images were recognized from their fragments are listed in Table 6.2. As the preprocessing method, the *Laplacian* was used. The recognition was based upon comparison of the coefficients γ_k in (6.15). As a criterion for correct recognition, the ratio of γ_r, corresponding to the correct image, to the next largest γ_k was used (compare with Table 6.1).

Table 6.2. Average ratio of the largest element γ_r in the recollection to the next largest γ_k. Preprocessing operator: Laplacian

10 reference patterns		100 reference patterns	
Key 50%	Key 10%	Key 50%	Key 10%
34.86	13.45	17.08	5.65

6.5.2 Optimal Nonlinear Associative Mappings

Linear associative mappings may be regarded as the lowest-order approach to the problem of associative transformations, in an attempt to find a mathematical operator by which arbitrary output patterns can be obtained from arbitrary input patterns. In view of the results of Sect. 2.1.4 it may be clear that the question about the existence of such a transformation is equivalent to the problem concerning the existence of a solution to the corresponding matrix equation. If the output responses are arbitrary, a necessary condition for an exact solution to exist is the linear independence of the columns of X, or of the patterns x_k. At least when the number of patterns is greater than their dimensionality, the vectors must be linearly dependent and no exact solution exists. For this reason there arises a need to generalize the class of associative mappings. Using nonlinear transformations it is possible to implement selective associative mappings for patterns which on account of their linear dependence would not be distinguishable in a linear transformation. The problem again can be formulated as follows: Between a set of column vectors $\{x_k\}$ which represents a set of input patterns, and another set of column vectors $\{y_k\}$ which corresponds to the set of output patterns associated with the x_k by pairs, there is to be found a transformation T by which every y_k is obtained from the corresponding x_k, either exactly, or approximately in the sense of least squares, as $y_k = T(x_k)$. It should be noted that in a special case, the y_k can be identified with the unit vectors.

Because there are infinitely many classes of nonlinear mappings, it may not be proper to speak of nonlinear transformations which are optimal in an absolute sense. The expression "optimal nonlinear associative mapping" used here only refers to a case in which a certain nonlinear functional form is assumed for the relation between the input and output vectors, and there is a finite number of parameters in this form which have to be optimized. Consider, for instance, polynomial transforms [6.3]

$$P_r(X) = L_0 + L_1(X) + L_2(X, X) + \ldots + L_r(X, \ldots, X), \qquad (6.18)$$

in which X is a matrix with the x_j as its columns, and L_q, $q = 0 \ldots r$ is a product form of degree q. The expression $P_r(X)$ is written explicitly as

$$(P_r(X))_{ik} = (L_0)_{ik} + \sum_{\alpha_1} (L_1)_{i\alpha_1} \xi_{\alpha_1 k} + \ldots + \sum_{\alpha_1 \ldots \alpha_r} (L_r)_{i,\alpha_1 \ldots \alpha_r} \xi_{\alpha_1 k} \cdots \xi_{\alpha_r k},$$
$$\qquad (6.19)$$
where

$$x_k = [\xi_{1k}, \xi_{2k}, \ldots, \xi_{nk}]^T.$$

Denoting by Y a matrix with the y_k as its columns, the scalar coefficients

$$(L_j)_{i,\alpha_1 \ldots \alpha_j}$$

are to be determined in such a way that $P_r(X)$ approximates Y in the sense of least squares.

The above case belongs to a class of regression problems which are linear in the parameters although nonlinear with respect to the input vectors. It is demonstrable that the polynomial case can be discussed in a more general setting. Assume an arbitrary preprocessing transformation for the primary input patterns x_k, such that every $x_k \in R^n$ is transformed into a new column vector $f_k \in R^q$. A matrix F is now defined which has the f_k as its columns. In the above example,

$$f_k = [1, \xi_{1k}, \xi_{2k}, \ldots, \xi_{nk}, \xi_{1k}^2, \xi_{2k}^2, \ldots, \xi_{nk}^2, \xi_{1k}\xi_{2k}, \ldots]^T. \qquad (6.20)$$

The problem is to find a linear form LF which approximates the matrix Y of the output vectors y_k in the sense of least squares, or possibly equals it. Here L is a matrix for which the least-square solution by the previous formalism reads as $\hat{L} = YF^+$. The most important result achievable by the nonlinear preprocessing transformation is that the dimensionality of the vector $f_k \in R^q$ is increased; the probability for the transformed vectors becoming linearly independent thereby respectively increases.

A Numerical Example. The nonlinear preprocessing mapping is particularly effective if the primary pattern vector is of low dimensionality. In the following example, the primary patterns consisted of acoustic spectra taken with a commercial spectrum analyzer; the frequency scale was divided into 100 channels between 0 and 2 kHz, and the intensities of the channel outputs, integrated in each channel with a certain time constant, were chosen as the pattern elements. Figure 6.8 shows one typical example of the spectra studied in the experiment [6.4].

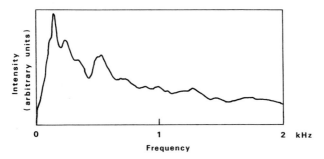

Fig. 6.8. A sample of acoustic spectra used in the identification experiment

If the preprocessing function is a homogeneous polynomial of the ξ_{ik}, then it is easy to see that multiplication of the original vector by a scalar results in a new f_k which is multiplied by another scalar; in other words, the relative magnitudes of the elements of f_k are not changed. This is an advantageous property in identification. In this particular example, the following form for the preprocessing function was selected:

$$f_k = [\xi_{1k}\xi_{2k}, \; \xi_{1k}\xi_{3k}, \; \ldots, \; \xi_{n-1,k}\xi_{n,k}]^{\mathrm{T}}. \qquad (6.21)$$

This vector had $n(n-1)/2 = 4950$ elements, a dimensionality that is quite manageable by the above optimal mappings.

The primary purpose of this example was to demonstrate the following effect. It was pointed out in Sects. 6.2 and 6.5.1 that random noise is attenuated in an associative mapping by a factor $\sqrt{m/n}$, where m is the number of reference patterns and n their dimensionality. If n could artificially be enlarged, for instance, by the above nonlinear mapping where it was increased from 100 to 4950, one might expect that the noise-attenuation factor would be improved correspondingly. The theoretical analysis of Sect. 6.2 is not directly transferable to the present case since the elements of f_k depend on each other; nonetheless, numerical experiments have shown that the basic idea was valid. Figure 6.9 shows results from an identification experiment with original and preprocessed vectors.

There were 45 spectra used as reference patterns, and the key patterns were formed by superimposing artificial white noise with different intensities on the original spectra. The reliability of the recognition was measured in terms of the relative magnitudes of elements in the output vector $\hat{u}$. As the ratio of the two largest elements is roughly inversely proportional to noise intensity, its inverse value was shown as the ordinate in the diagram.

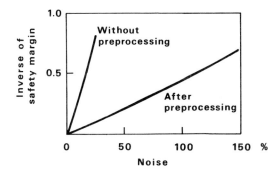

Fig. 6.9. Demonstration of improved class-separation when nonlinear preprocessing was used

The above results show that the reliability of identification of a noisy spectrum was improved by a factor of 6.2 to 6.9. Although this number theoretically is not quite the same as the inverse of the noise-attenuation factor, it may be interesting to compare that these two numbers were demonstrated to be close to each other: $\sqrt{4950/100} \approx 7$.

6.6 Relationship Between Associative Mapping, Linear Regression, and Linear Estimation

6.6.1 Relationship of the Associative Mapping to Linear Regression

Consider again the linear mapping $y_k = Mx_k$, $k = 1, 2, \ldots, m$, where $x_k \in R^n$, $y_k \in R^p$. The case in which m was smaller than n was discussed above in detail.

The associative mapping has a superficial resemblance to certain statistical regression problems in which a linear dependence between stochastic vectorial variables x and y is assumed. Notice carefully, however, that a linear statistical model *a priori* assumes y *dependent* on x, for instance, by $y = \Omega x$, where Ω is a matrix that may describe a physical, economical, or other process. Any deviations from this dependence are solely assumed to be due to stochastic errors or noise, and if (x_k, y_k) is a pair of realizations of x and y, respectively, then $y_k = \Omega x_k + v_k$, where v_k is the residual which has a certain statistical distribution. Hence x_k and y_k cannot be selected independently. The mathematical regression problem is to find the best value of Ω for which the average of v_k over a large number of observed realizations x_k and y_k is minimized in the sense of some statistical measure; in the simplest case, the sum of the $\|v_k\|^2$ is used. The number of pairs (x_k, y_k) may now be much greater than the dimensionality of x_k. Formally, however, the problem can be set as before: denoting

$$X = [x_1, x_2, \ldots, x_m], \quad Y = [y_1, y_2, \ldots, y_m] \tag{6.22}$$

the problem is to minimize the norm of the matrix expression $Y - \Omega X$.

Because the Penrose formalism was applicable to matrix equations of any dimensionality, the best approximate solution to the above problem can formally be written

$$\hat{\Omega} = YX^+. \tag{6.23}$$

Notice, however, that the columns of X are now linearly dependent. If the x_k are stochastic variables with, say, a normal distribution, the *rows* of X, however, can then be assumed linearly independent. For this reason, the regression solution for the matrix $\hat{\Omega}$ reads

$$\hat{\Omega} = YX^T(XX^T)^{-1}. \tag{6.24}$$

For comparison, let us recall that a matrix of the form BA^+, with the *columns* of A linearly independent, can be written $B(A^TA)^{-1}A^T$.

The difference between these two cases shall yet be subjected to closer inspection in Sect. 6.7, where recursive computational solutions to matrix equations are derived.

6.6.2 Relationship of the Regression Solution to the Linear Estimator

The least-squares optimal solution to the matrix equation $Y = \Omega X$ has a close relationship to the so-called best linear unbiased estimator (BLUE). If, namely, a linear statistical dependence between the stochastic vectors x and y is assumed, and x is regarded as a measurement from which y is to be estimated, the problem is to construct an operator Ω (called estimator) by which the best approximation $\hat{y}$ of y in the sense of least squares is obtained as $\hat{y} = \Omega x$. In estimation problems, the a priori statistical information about the vectorial variables x and y may be expressed in terms of the theoretical correlation matrices

$$E(xx^T) = C_{xx} \quad \text{and} \quad E(yx^T) = C_{yx}, \tag{6.25}$$

which are assumed to be known. The BLUE of y, given an observation x, is then [6.5]

$$\hat{y} = C_{yx}C_{xx}^{-1}x = \Omega x. \tag{6.26}$$

It is assumed that the inverse of C_{xx} exists, which holds true if x is a stochastic variable for which the rank of C_{xx} is full.

On the other hand, the regression solution for $\hat{\Omega}$ from (6.24) can be written, after expanding by m^{-1},

$$\hat{\Omega} = YX^T(XX^T)^{-1} = \left(\frac{1}{m} \sum_{k=1}^{m} y_k x_k^T \right) \left(\frac{1}{m} \sum_{k=1}^{m} x_k x_k^T \right)^{-1} = \hat{C}_{yx}\hat{C}_{xx}^{-1}. \tag{6.27}$$

It is now directly discernible that $\hat{\Omega}$ corresponds to the operator $\Omega = C_{yx}C_{xx}^{-1}$, with the only difference that the theoretical correlation matrices C_{xx} and C_{yx} have been replaced by their approximations $\hat{C}_{xx}$ and $\hat{C}_{yx}$, respectively, computed from a finite series of observations; thus there is a simple correspondence between regression and the BLUE.

6.7 Recursive Computation of the Optimal Associative Mapping

The purpose of this section is to point out what the theoretically fastest adaptive processes are by which a new value for the operator describing the optimal associative mapping can be determined. This kind of computation is based on a mapping which is optimal with respect to a set of pairs of earlier input-output vectors (x_i, y_i), and on a new pair of input-output vectors that shall be taken into account, too. As this is a mathematical problem, it is not stipulated in the first place that it must have a physically realizable implementation. The mathematical discussion yields an upper limit for the system performance against which various physical realizations can be compared. The recursive formulas that result may as such be useful as computational algorithms when the associative mappings are implemented in digital computers.

6.7.1 Linear Corrective Algorithms

Consider the optimal linear associative memory that transforms input patterns x_k into output patterns y_k by a linear operation $y_k = Mx_k$. The best value of M was determined by the matrix equation method in Sect. 6.5.1. A new problem that is central to the present section is the following: if it is assumed that the transfer matrix M is optimal for a series of observations ending up with the pair (x_{k-1}, y_{k-1}), then what is the *correction* to M if its new value shall be optimal with respect to all of the previous patterns and the new pair (x_k, y_k), too? This is a so-called *recursive* problem. The new optimal value M_k is a function of the previous optimal value M_{k-1} and of the new observations x_k and y_k. All the cases of recursive processes discussed in this context obey the following difference equation

$$M_k = M_{k-1} + (y_k - M_{k-1}x_k)c_k^T, \tag{6.28}$$

where c_k^T is a *gain vector* that defines the correction. It may be noted that $M_{k-1}x_k$ is a *prediction* of y_k, denoted by $\hat{y}_k$; the correction is always directly proportional to the prediction error $y_k - \hat{y}_k$. Expressions for the gain vector for various choices of data shall be derived. It will be interesting to notice that simpler adaptive systems too are governed by adaption equations which very much resemble (6.28), with the principal difference that another value for the gain vector is used. Accordingly, the correction is then not optimal but suboptimal; the optimal value of M can be achieved only if the presentation of the pairs (x_k, y_k) is repeated iteratively.

The General Setting for the Computation of $M = YX^+$. If exact solutions to the matrix equation $Y = MX$ exist, $M = YX^+$ is that particular solution which yields the associative mapping with the best error-tolerance. If exact solutions do not exist, $M = YX^+$ is the best approximative solution in the sense of least squares. Hereupon YX^+ is called the "best" solution. Evaluation of YX^+ follows the same lines as the computation of the pseudoinverse X^+ for an arbitrary matrix X. For this purpose, consider matrix X which has the input vectors $x_1, x_2, \ldots, x_k$ as its columns. This matrix is partitioned as $[X_{k-1} \,\vert\, x_k]$ and, with k columns, denoted by X_k. Similarly matrix Y formed of $y_1, y_2, \ldots, y_k$ is also partitioned and, with k columns, denoted as $Y_k = [Y_{k-1} \,\vert\, y_k]$. If matrix M, when computed from X_k and Y_k, is denoted by $M_k = Y_k X_k^+$, it obtains the recursive form (Sect. 2.1.4)

$$
\begin{aligned}
M_k = Y_k X_k^+ &= [Y_{k-1} \,\vert\, y_k] \left[\frac{X_{k-1}^+(I - x_k p_k^T)}{p_k^T} \right] \\
&= Y_{k-1}X_{k-1}^+ + (y_k - Y_{k-1}X_{k-1}^+ x_k)p_k^T \\
&= M_{k-1} + (y_k - M_{k-1}x_k)p_k^T, \tag{6.29}
\end{aligned}
$$

where the "gain vector" p_k^T has the value given in (2.45). It should be noticed that M_k is always immediately the "best" solution when a pair of new observations (x_k, y_k) has been taken into account; the recursion is started with $M_0 = 0$.

6.7.2 Best Exact Solution (Gradient Projection)

The expression p_k of (2.45) is simpler if exact solutions to $Y = MX$ exist. This is the case which normally occurs in the design of optimal associative mappings. If x_k is now linearly independent of the previous columns, then $(I - X_{k-1}X_{k-1}^+)x_k$ is a nonzero vector and the upper expression for p_k in (2.45) is applied. In the case that x_k is a linear combination of the previous columns, the lower expression of p_k yields

$$M_k = M_{k-1} + (y_k - M_{k-1}x_k)x_k^T(X_{k-1}^+)^T X_{k-1}^+(1 + \|X_{k-1}^+x_k\|^2)^{-1}. \qquad (6.30)$$

Multiplication of both sides by x_k and rearrangement results in

$$y_k = M_kx_k = M_{k-1}x_k + (y_k - M_{k-1}x_k)\|X_{k-1}^+x_k\|^2(1 + \|X_{k-1}^+x_k\|^2)^{-1}. \qquad (6.31)$$

Since $\|X_{k-1}^+x_k\|^2 \geqslant 0$, the above equation cannot be satisfied unless $y_k - M_{k-1}x_k = 0$. Substitution of this result into (6.29) then yields $M_k = M_{k-1}$. If it is now denoted

$$(I - X_{k-1}X_{k-1}^+)x_k = \phi_{k-1}x_k = \tilde{x}_k, \qquad (6.32)$$

and it is realized that the condition $\tilde{x}_k = 0$ is equivalent to the linear dependence of the columns $x_1, x_2, \ldots, x_k$, then the expression for M_k can be put into the form

$$M_k = \begin{cases} M_{k-1} + (y_k - M_{k-1}x_k)\dfrac{\tilde{x}_k^T}{\|\tilde{x}_k\|^2} & \text{for } \tilde{x}_k \neq 0, \\ M_{k-1} & \text{otherwise}, \end{cases}$$

$$\tilde{x}_k = \phi_{k-1}x_k, \qquad (6.33)$$

$$\phi_k = \phi_{k-1} - \frac{\tilde{x}_k\tilde{x}_k^T}{\|\tilde{x}_k\|^2}, \quad \text{with} \quad \phi_0 = I, \tilde{x}_1 = x_1.$$

Instead of using the last two equations, a computationally easier method is to determine the $\tilde{x}_i$, $i = 1, 2, \ldots, k$ using the Gram-Schmidt orthogonalization process:

$$\tilde{x}_i = x_i - \sum_{j=1}^{i-1} \frac{(x_i, \tilde{x}_j)\tilde{x}_j}{\|\tilde{x}_j\|^2} , \tag{6.34}$$

where the summation over j must be taken for nonzero $\tilde{x}_j$ only.

The derivation of (6.33) also follows directly from a method for the solution of vector equations of the type $Ax = b$, as discussed by *Pyle* [6.6]. Accordingly, the name *gradient projection method* is used for the above method, generalized for matrix equations.

A Computational Scheme. If the objective is to find out the optimal output $\hat{y}$ in response to a key pattern x, computation of matrix operator M may not be necessary. If the estimate of y_i at the ith step is denoted $\hat{y}_i = M_{i-1}x_i$, and its error is $\tilde{y}_i = y_i - \hat{y}_i$, multiplication of M_k of (6.33) by x_k, change of index, and exchange of terms yields [6.4]

$$\tilde{y}_i = y_i - \sum_{j=1}^{i-1} \frac{(x_i, \tilde{x}_j)}{\|\tilde{x}_j\|^2} \tilde{y}_j , \tag{6.35}$$

where use is made of the existence of exact solutions, whence there must hold $M_i x_i = y_i$, $M_{i-1}x_i = \hat{y}_i$. In the computational scheme, recursive evaluation of the $\tilde{y}_i$ proceeds in parallel with the Gram-Schmidt process used for the calculation of the $\tilde{x}_i$, and only the $\tilde{y}_i$, $i = 1, 2, \ldots, k$ are stored. Application of (6.35) one step further yields

$$\hat{y} = \sum_{i=1}^{k} \frac{(x, \tilde{x}_i)}{\|\tilde{x}_i\|^2} \tilde{y}_i . \tag{6.36}$$

6.7.3 Best Approximate Solution (Regression)

If the number of columns in X and Y is greater than the dimension of the x_k, the latter are then linearly dependent. This is the case in which the best approximate solution in the sense of least squares to $Y = MX$ is called *linear regression*. The recursive expressions derived from the algorithm of Greville can now be applied, when for the "gain vectors" p_k the lower alternatives from (2.45) are selected. It should be carefully noticed that the recursive expressions do not yield correct solutions unless they are correctly initiated, and in order to be sure that the lower alternative for p_k from (2.45) is always applicable, the new column x_k must be a linear combination of the columns of X_{k-1}. Obviously a sufficient condition for this occurrence is that there are n linearly independent columns among the $x_1, \ldots, x_{k-1}$. If the x_k are stochastic variables and $k-1 \geqslant n$, it is known from elementary statistics that this is normally the case. In order to guarantee numerical stability in practical computations, it is advantageous to have in X_{k-1} columns in excess to n. Now the recursion can be initiated by computing X_{k-1}^{+} as

$$X_{k-1}^{+} = X_{k-1}^{T}(X_{k-1}X_{k-1}^{T})^{-1}. \tag{6.37}$$

For the matrix inversion, for instance, a method derived from the familiar Gauss-Jordan elimination procedure can be used; the inverse of a square matrix C of full rank can be computed by solving the matrix equation $CX = I$, partitioned as $C \cdot [x_1, x_2, \ldots, x_n] = [u_1, u_2, \ldots, u_n]$, with u_i, $i = 1, 2, \ldots, n$ the unit vectors. The vector equations $Cx_i = u_i$ are then solved independently by the Gauss-Jordan algorithm, whereby $X = C^{-1}$ is obtained. Another possibility, although a little heavier computationally, is to apply the gradient projection method until n linearly independent vectors x_k are found, and then to switch over to the present method.

Under the assumption that $(X_{k-1}X_{k-1}^{T})^{-1}$ exists, $(X_kX_k^{T})^{-1}$ can be derived from the matrix inversion lemma (Sect. 2.1.4). Denoting

$$\psi_k = (X_kX_k^{T})^{-1} = (X_{k-1}X_{k-1}^{T}+x_kx_k^{T})^{-1}, \tag{6.38}$$

there follows

$$\psi_k = \psi_{k-1} - \frac{\psi_{k-1}x_kx_k^{T}\psi_{k-1}}{1+x_k^{T}\psi_{k-1}x_k}. \tag{6.39}$$

This recursion for the square matrix ψ_k, with its initial condition computed, for instance, by the matrix inversion method, is applied together with the formula for M_k obtained as follows. Based on the general properties of pseudoinverses, p_k^{T} is written

$$p_k^{T} = \frac{x_k^{T}(X_{k-1}X_{k-1}^{T})^{+}}{1+x_k^{T}(X_{k-1}X_{k-1}^{T})^{+}x_k} = \frac{x_k^{T}\psi_{k-1}}{1+x_k^{T}\psi_{k-1}x_k}, \tag{6.40}$$

where use is made of the fact that $(X_{k-1}X_{k-1}^{T})^{+} = (X_{k-1}X_{k-1}^{T})^{-1}$ if the inverse exists. Then, according to (6.29),

$$M_k = M_{k-1}+(y_k-M_{k-1}x_k)\frac{x_k^{T}\psi_{k-1}}{1+x_k^{T}\psi_{k-1}x_k}. \tag{6.41}$$

6.7.4 Recursive Solution in the General Case

It shall now be demonstrated that the recursive solutions for the general equation $Y = MX$ can be unified. The following formulas [6.7] are presented here without derivation (their proof is in fact computational and follows from the algorithm of Greville and general properties of the pseudoinverse matrices). Two sequences of square matrices $\{\phi_k\}$ and $\{\psi_k\}$ are defined by

$$\phi_k = I - X_k X_k^+, \; \psi_k = (X_k X_k^T)^+ = (X_k^+)^T X_k^+, \tag{6.42}$$

their initial conditions being $\phi_0 = I$ and $\psi_0 = 0$. Two sequences of vectors h_k and g_k are defined by

$$h_k = \phi_{k-1} x_k, \; g_k = \psi_{k-1} x_k. \tag{6.43}$$

If now $h_k = 0$, then the following formulas are applied:

$$p_k = g_k (1 + g_k^T x_k)^{-1},$$
$$\phi_k = \phi_{k-1}, \tag{6.44}$$
$$\psi_k = \psi_{k-1} - g_k p_k^T.$$

If, on the other hand, $h_k \neq 0$, then

$$p_k = h_k (h_k^T h_k)^{-1},$$
$$\phi_k = \phi_{k-1} - h_k p_k^T, \tag{6.45}$$
$$\psi_k = \psi_{k-1} + (1 + x_k^T g_k) p_k p_k^T - g_k p_k^T - p_k g_k^T.$$

With the sequence $\{p_k\}$ so defined,

$$M_k = M_{k-1} + (y_k - M_{k-1} x_k) p_k^T, \quad \text{with} \quad M_0 = 0. \tag{6.46}$$

The main significance of these equations may not lie on the computational side, because the practical applications are normally either of the type of associative mapping or of linear regression; it may also be difficult to decide in computation, whether $h_k = 0$ or $h_k \neq 0$, due to numerical instabilities. Nonetheless, these expressions make it possible to obtain an answer to the theoretical question what happens if there are terms in the sequence $\{x_k\}$ which are irregularly either linearly dependent or independent with respect to the previous terms.

6.8 Special Cases

6.8.1 The Correlation Matrix Memory

Especially in the modelling of adaptive associative networks, the correlation matrix formalism (Sects. 3.3 and 4.4.1) is often obtained as a solution to system equations. As matrix product it reads

$$M = \sum_{k=1}^{m} y_k x_k^{\mathrm{T}} = YX^{\mathrm{T}} \tag{6.47}$$

with X and Y two rectangular matrices having the key vectors x_k, and some associated data y_k as their columns, respectively. The recollection y is the product of M with a key pattern x, i.e.,

$$y = Mx = \sum_{k=1}^{m} (x, x_k) y_k, \tag{6.48}$$

so that y is a linear mixture of the patterns y_k, with relative intensities proportional to the *inner products* (x, x_k).

It may be stated that the correlation matrix is equivalent to the optimal linear associative operator if the stored vectors x_k are *orthonormal*; in this case, the correlation matrix mapping has the same error-correcting properties as the optimal operators. The optimality condition can be shown, for instance, by the following direct derivation: since the x_k are orthonormal, there follows that $X^{\mathrm{T}}X = I$. The optimal solution for M is then

$$YX^+ = Y(X^{\mathrm{T}}X)^{-1}X^{\mathrm{T}} = YX^{\mathrm{T}}. \tag{6.49}$$

As it may be difficult to realize an adaptive physical system that directly implements the optimal associative mapping for arbitrary x_k, the above result now gives us an idea how the same result could be achieved easier. The x_k can be orthogonalized, at least approximately, by proper *preprocessing*. It has been shown earlier in Sect. 6.5.1 that differentiation of the primary patterns, especially formation of the second spatial differences (Laplacian) is a very effective orthogonalization method. Incidentally, a simple pattern processing function named *lateral inhibition* (Sect. 5.2) which occurs in neural systems has an approximately equivalent effect.

Von Neumann Expansion. It may also be interesting to note that the correlation matrix is obtained as the lowest-order term in a certain serial expansion of the optimal operator. According to a result derived by *von Neumann* [6.8], matrix M can be put into the form

$$M = \alpha Y \sum_{k=0}^{\infty} (I - \alpha X^\mathsf{T} X)^k X^\mathsf{T},$$
(6.50)

where $0 < \alpha < 2/c$, and c is the largest eigenvalue of $X^\mathsf{T} X$. The first term in the series is $M_0 = \alpha Y X^\mathsf{T}$; the first two terms together make

$$M_1 = M_0 + M_0(I - \alpha X X^\mathsf{T}).$$
(6.51)

6.8.2 Relationship Between Conditional Averages and Optimal Estimator

In some learning processes (Sects. 3.3 and 3.4.2) the adaptive circuits imple-mented "conditioned reflexes". In this case the input stimuli could better be regarded as binary, say, $\xi_j \in \{0, A\}$, where A is some positive value corre-sponding to an active signal. The expectation values of responses conditioned by the stimulus signals are then

$$\mu_{ij} = E\{\eta_i | \xi_j = A\}.$$
(6.52)

This result is now derivable from the optimal estimator as a special case. Ac-cording to (6.24) the best linear estimate of the output vector, for input x, is

$$\hat{y} = \hat{E}(yx^\mathsf{T})[\hat{E}(xx^\mathsf{T})]^{-1}x,$$
(6.53)

where $\hat{E}\{\cdot\}$ means the expectation value computed from the observed time series of $\eta_i^{(k)}$ and $\xi_j^{(k)}$. The special case is obtained if $\hat{E}(xx^\mathsf{T})$ is *diagonal*, i.e. the components of x are uncorrelated. Then (6.53) is reduced into the form

$$\hat{\eta}_i = \sum_{j=1}^{n} \frac{\sum_{k=1}^{N} \eta_i^{(k)} \xi_j^{(k)}}{\sum_{k=1}^{N} (\xi_j^{(k)})^2} \xi_j = \sum_{j=1}^{n} \mu_{ij} \xi_j,$$
(6.54)

where, since the $\xi_j^{(k)}$ were assumed binary, only those terms in the sums over k need be considered for which $\xi_j^{(k)} \neq 0$. Then it directly follows (with $A = 1$)

$$\mu_{ij} = \hat{E}\{\eta_i | \xi_j = A\}.$$
(6.55)

7. Pattern Recognition

Pattern recognition (PR) may be regarded as a special case of associative mappings, namely, as a process in which classes of patterns are directly mapped on a set of discrete elements. Many pattern recognition methods are related to learning schemes; however, the problem is then largely that of mathematical statistics and does not necessarily presuppose physical realizability. On the other hand, as most of the applications of pattern recognition have quickly been pushed to serve practical purposes such as remote sensing or biomedical imaging, the theoretical foundations have remained rather heterogeneous. It is possible to find many excellent textbooks in specialized areas such as image analysis and even statistical methods of pattern recognition, whereas good reviews of the complete field are scarce. An introduction to the general problematics may be obtained from, e.g., the book of *Young* and *Calvert* [7.1], and contemporary structural methods of pattern analysis are well presented by *Pavlidis* [7.2]. On the other hand, to concentrate on one of the special problems, it is advisable to pick up, e.g., one of the books of which a listing is given in the Bibliography.

This chapter contains only a few aspects of pattern recognition which are believed to be most relevant to the discussion of self-organization and associative memory.

7.1 Discriminant Functions

Let us consider patterns which are represented as vectors in the multidimensional Euclidean space R^n. One of the most fundamental approaches in pattern recognition is the classification of patterns by means of *discriminant functions*. Assume that the representation vectors (or their end points in R^n) are grouped into a finite number of clusters, each of them corresponding to a particular class. The problem is then to mathematically define the equations of those hypersurfaces which optimally separate all clusters from each other. To the first, it should be noticed that there are infinitely many alternatives for mathematical forms; one possibility is to try the simplest ones. The lowest-degree surface is linear (hyperplane); if the clusters are not linearly separable, it is then possible to take polynomial forms of successively higher degree. Of course, expansions in other elementary or special functions can be tried for the separating surfaces if there are good reasons to assume that the data are distributed accordingly. But it ought to be noticed, too, that the separation of points can be optimal only with respect to some criterion which, for instance, takes into account the distances of all points from the separating surfaces. One frequently used criterion is the sum of squares of the Euclidean distances.

The separating surface between two classes can be defined in terms of *discriminant functions* $\delta_k(x)$, $k = 1, 2, \ldots, m$ which are continuous, scalar-valued functions of the pattern vector x. The separating surface between classes S_i and S_j is then defined by the equation

$$\delta_i(x) - \delta_j(x) = 0 . \tag{7.1}$$

If $x \in S_i$, then for all $j \neq i$ there must hold $\delta_i(x) > \delta_j(x)$,   or

$$\delta_i(x) = \max_k \{\delta_k(x)\} . \tag{7.2}$$

The Linear Classifier. As an example of the application of discriminant functions, the linear classifier may be mentioned. The discriminant functions take the form

$$\delta_k(x) = w_k^T x + \kappa_k, \tag{7.3}$$

where w_k is the kth *weight vector,* and κ_k is a scalar. A hyperplane which separates the classes S_i and S_j has the equation

$$w'^T x = \kappa' ,$$

where

$$w' = w_i - w_j \quad \text{and} \quad \kappa' = \kappa_j - \kappa_i . \tag{7.4}$$

If κ' can be set equal to zero, in other words, if only the relative magnitudes of the pattern elements are considered to be significant, or if the mean of the elements is always subtracted from all patterns, then the discriminant functions of the linear classifier have a relationship to the optimal linear associative mapping. In that formulation, the problem is to find a matrix M by which pattern x is to be multiplied to obtain a set of linear discriminant functions,

$$Mx = [\delta_1(x), \delta_2(x), \ldots, \delta_m(x)]^T \qquad (7.5)$$

the latter performing the separation of the given patterns in the sense of least squares. This problem is solved by assuming that for all *reference patterns* belonging to the kth class, the $\delta_j(x)$ must be of the form δ_{jk} (the Kronecker delta, cf. p. 37). Equation (7.5) is obviously equivalent to the matrix equation

$$MX = U, \quad \text{with} \quad X = [x_1, x_2, \ldots, x_m]^T, \ U = [u_1, u_2, \ldots, u_m]^T, \qquad (7.6)$$

the u_j being unit vectors having a 1 at their kth position if x_j belongs to class S_k. The familiar solution reads

$$M = UX^+. \qquad (7.7)$$

Let us tentatively check, what happens if M is replaced by the suboptimal approximation $\hat{M} = UX^T$ as done in some very simple (biologically motivated) recognition schemes. The discriminant functions are now proportional to inner products of x with the x_k:

$$\hat{u} = Mx = \sum_{k=1}^{m} (x, x_k) u_k. \qquad (7.8)$$

Notice that if the x_k were orthogonal, we had a classifier completely equivalent to (7.6, 7). Inherent orthogonality of patterns, of course, cannot be presupposed, but it is often possible to improve orthogonality by preprocessing. With pictures, such an effective and simple preprocessing method is spatial differentation, already mentioned in Sect. 6.5.1. Operation of the patterns by higher-order spatial differential operators, e.g., by the two-dimensional Laplacian $\partial^2/\partial\zeta_h^2 + \partial^2/\partial\zeta_v^2$, or perhaps by $\partial^2/\partial\zeta_h\partial\zeta_v$, where ζ_h and ζ_v are the horizontal and vertical coordinates in the image plane, respectively, has often been successful. The effect of differential operators is to suppress lower spatial frequencies with the result that the orthogonality of any arbitrarily selected portion of a pattern with respect to the same portion in all other patterns is increased.

7.2 Statistical Formulation of Pattern Classification

In (7.5 − 8), the discriminant functions were completely defined by the reference data. The efficiency of classification might significantly be improved, however, if all available a priori knowledge is utilized. In many cases there are good reasons to assume on the basis of physical or other properties of observations that their distribution has some familiar theoretical form; it is then possible to derive mathematical forms for the discriminating surfaces which are optimal from the statistical point of view.

Pattern classification is a process that is related to decision making, detection theory, etc., and may be discussed in these settings. The only motive for the following discussion is to point out that certain forms of separating surfaces, for instance, the linear and quadratic ones, may have a statistical justification.

A Note on Probabilistic Notations. If a process is assumed in which only a finite number of distinct events X_1, X_2, ..., X_s may occur, the relative frequencies of their occurrences are denoted by $P(X_k)$, $k = 1, 2, ..., s$, where $P(\cdot)$ may be identified with the usual *probability* function. On the other hand, if x is a continuous-valued stochastic variable with a *distribution* $p(x)$, then $p(\cdot)$ has the property of a density function and is often called *probability density*. If the domain of x, being a subset of Euclidean space R^n, is divided into contiguous volume differentials dV_x, then, obviously, $p(x)dV_x$ is the probability for the occurrence of a value x within this differential volume. In the following, probabilities for discrete events are denoted by capital letter $P(\cdot)$, and the probability for X on the condition that Y occurs is $P(X|Y)$. The probability densities are denoted by lower-case letters $p(\cdot)$, and the probability density of variable x on the condition that Y occurs is $p(x|Y)$. It should be noted that quite consistently in this convention $P(Y|x)$ is the probability for Y on the condition that the continuous variable x attains a certain value.

Statistical Definition of the Discriminant Functions. When the prototype data are replaced by conditional distributions of the patterns, the a priori probability density for the occurrence of an observation of a continuous-valued vector x is denoted by $p(x)$. The probability for any observed pattern really belonging to class S_k is abbreviated $P(S_k)$. The distribution of those pattern vectors which belong to class S_k is $p(x|S_k)$. This expression is the usual conditional probability of x, or its a priori probability on a condition abbreviated as S_k. In many cases, the theoretical form of $p(x|S_k)$ can be assumed, or can be approximately found out from samples in preliminary studies.

The theories of decision processes are centrally based on the concept of a *loss function* (cost function) the value of which depends on external factors, for instance, the importance of detection of a particular occurrence, or of a miss to detect it. Let $C(S_i, S_k)$ be the unit cost of one decision which indicates the reward or punishment of classification of a pattern to S_i when it was actually from S_k. If all patterns were considered equally important and the cost of a correct classification were denoted by 0, then all false classifications may cause a unit cost. (In classification, only relative costs are significant.) Therefore, one simple case of unit cost function might be $C(S_i, S_k) = 1 - \delta_{ik}$. Now the *conditional average loss,* or the cost of classifying patterns into class S_k their actually being statistically distributed into classes S_i, $i = 1, 2, \ldots, m$ is

$$L(x, S_k) = \sum_{i=1}^{m} P(S_i|x) C(S_k, S_i), \tag{7.9}$$

where $P(S_i|x)$ is the probability of pattern with value x belonging to class S_i. This conditional probability is related to $p(x|S_i)$, and it may be thought to result from the fact that the distributions $p(x|S_i)$ may overlap in R^n, whereby there is a definite probability for x belonging to any class. There is a fundamental identity in the theory of probability which states that if $P(X, Y)$ is the joint probability for the events X and Y to occur, then

$$P(X, Y) = P(X|Y)P(Y) = P(Y|X)P(X). \tag{7.10}$$

This is the foundation of the so-called Bayesian philosophy of probability which deals with probabilities that are dependent on new observations. When applied to the present case, the above formula yields

$$L(x, S_k) = \sum_{i=1}^{m} p(x|S_i) P(S_i) C(S_k, S_i). \tag{7.11}$$

It will now be seen that the negative of the loss function satisfies the requirements set on the discriminant functions: since the cost of classifying x into S_i any other than S_k is higher, $-L(x, S_k) = \max_i \{-L(x, S_i)\}$. On the other hand, when considering candidates for discriminant functions, any factors or additive terms in this expression which are common to all classes can be dropped. It may now be a good strategy to select the discriminant functions as

$$\delta_k(x) = - \sum_{i=1}^{m} p(x|S_i) P(S_i) C(S_k, S_i). \tag{7.12}$$

One basic case of discriminant functions is obtained by taking $C(S_k, S_i) = 1 - \delta_{ki}$, whereby

$$\delta_k(x) = - \sum_{i=1}^{m} p(x|S_i) P(S_i) + p(x|S_k) P(S_k). \tag{7.13}$$

Since now all possible classes occur among the S_i, $i = 1, 2, \ldots, m$, then an identity holds that

$$\sum_{i=1}^{m} p(x|S_i) P(S_i) = p(x) \tag{7.14}$$

and being constant with k, this term can be dropped. For a new discriminant function it is possible to redefine

$$\delta_k(x) = p(x|S_k)P(S_k) . \tag{7.15}$$

It should be realized that according to the definition of discriminant functions, the form of the separating surface is not changed if any monotonically increasing function of $p(x|S_k)P(S_k)$ is selected for $\delta_k(x)$.

An Example of Parametric Classification. Assume that the patterns of every class have normal distributions with different statistics:

$$p(x|S_k) = \lambda_k \exp\left[-\tfrac{1}{2}(x-\mu_k)^T C_k^{-1}(x-\mu_k)\right] , \tag{7.16}$$

where λ_k is a normalizing constant that depends on C_k. For the discriminant function, $\log\{p(x|S_k)P(S_k)\}$ is selected:

$$\delta_k(x) = \log \lambda_k - \tfrac{1}{2}(x-\mu_k)^T C_k^{-1}(x-\mu_k) + \log P(S_k), \tag{7.17}$$

which is a quadratic function of x. Consequently, the separating surfaces are *second-degree surfaces*.

As a special case, distributions which have equal covariance matrices $C_k = C$ may be studied, whereby $\lambda_k = \lambda$. This may be the case, e.g., with patterns derived from univariate time series. All terms independent of k are now dropped. Moreover, the symmetry of covariance matrices is utilized for simplification, whereby

$$\delta_k(x) = \mu_k^T C^{-1} x - \tfrac{1}{2}\mu_k^T C^{-1}\mu_k + \log P(S_k) . \tag{7.18}$$

Surprisingly, this is *linear* in x even for arbitrary a priori probabilities of the classes, and with arbitrary class means.

7.3 Comparison Methods

The most trivial of all classification methods is to compare the unknown pattern with all known reference patterns on the basis of some criterion for degree of similarity, in order to decide to which class the pattern belongs. The opposite of similarity between two patterns x and x_k is their mutual distance $d(x, x_k)$ in some metric. For instance, Euclidean metric is often quite useful. It is obvious that for the final resolution plenty of computations are needed, unless a small representative set of reference patterns from each class can be used for comparison. In the *Nearest-Neighbour* (NN) *method,* $d(x, x_k)$ is computed for all reference patterns and pattern x is classified according to the smallest value. In order to increase reliability, a majority decision over a number of nearest neighbours is sometimes taken for the basis of classification. The nearest-neighbour methods usually yield separating surfaces which are piecewise linear, i.e., they consist of segments of hyperplanes.

In the most practical applications, especially if the pattern elements represent values in arbitrary parameter spaces, one cannot assume that the pattern elements are statistically independent nor have identical weight. A more natural similarity measure is then the *weighted Euclidean distance* (2.85), whereby the covariance matrix of the pattern vectors again ought to be known.

If the statistics of the patterns is not describable by multivariate Gaussian density functions, or if the patterns may undergo various scale transformations in their representation space, then a suitable similarity or distance criterion, e.g., one of those reviewed in Sect. 2.2 ought to be applied.

Just in order to point out that in practical problems a proper choice for the criterion may be a very simple one, the following case may be mentioned separately. It further has a connection with the more effective methods to be discussed in Sect. 7.4.

Identification of Patterns by the Angles. If the structures in patterns are definable by the *relative* intensities of pattern elements, e.g., in the comparison of pictures or spectra before any preprocessing analysis is performed on them, one might best use the directions of pattern vectors as a basis of similarity. Because the patterned representations may have different norms, and the norm of a key pattern too depends on the number of data elements employed in it, it is therefore reasonable to define as the degree of similarity of the key with stored patterns the *angle* between these vectors: in the n-dimensional space, the angle between vectors x and x_k was defined as

$$\theta_k = \arccos \frac{(x, x_k)}{\|x\| \|x_k\|} . \tag{7.19}$$

7.4 The Subspace Methods of Classification

The classification strategy described in this section has a bearing on statistical methods named *regression analysis*. This method has been selected for detailed representation here, since it also has a close relationship to the adaptive processes and associative mappings discussed in this book. Moreover, when compared with many other pattern recognition algorithms, the subspace methods may have the closest relation to possible implementations by adaptive networks.

7.4.1 The Basic Subspace Method

There exist many practical applications in which classes of patterns are reasonably well definable as linear manifolds or *subspaces*, spanned by a set of prototype vectors. Examples of this are encountered in the classification of various *spectra*. Consider, for instance, a source of acoustic signals; in most cases the signals are produced by various modes of mechanical vibration. The resonant frequencies are fixed but the intensities of the vibratory modes depend on exciting conditions which vary more or less stochastically. A direct comparison of spectra based on some of the previous similarity measures (e.g., Euclidean distance, direction cosines, or correlation) may not be expected to produce good results. On the other hand, if we would describe each class by at least as many linearly independent prototype vectors (spectra) as there are vibratory modes, then it is expected that if a *regression* of the prototypes on the unknown vector is made for each class separately, and the residual with respect to a particular class is smaller than for other classes, then the vector can be assumed to belong to that class. In other words, the distance of a vector from a class is measured by the best (least-square) fit to the set of prototypes, whereas no single prototype need be similar. The regression analysis can now be formulated very simply in terms of vector space concepts as shown below.

Let $\mathscr{L}_i$ be the subspace spanned by the prototypes of class S_i; then the distance of vector x from $\mathscr{L}_i$ is obtained if x is first decomposed as

$$x = \hat{x}_i + \tilde{x}_i, \tag{7.20}$$

where $\hat{x}_i$ is the linear regression, or the best linear combination of the prototypes that approximates x in the sense of least squares. The norm of the residual $\|\tilde{x}_i\|$ is the Euclidean distance of x from $\mathscr{L}_i$, and classification is performed by finding the nearest subspace of x. As described in Sect. 2.1.5, the $\hat{x}_i$ (or $\tilde{x}_i$) are easily calculated by the Gram-Schmidt orthogonalization process. The class-affiliation of x is then decided by

$$x \in S_k, \quad \text{if} \quad \|\hat{x}_k\| = \max_i \{\|\hat{x}_i\|\} . \tag{7.21}$$

(In case there are several maxima, some additional tie-breaking rule must be applied.)

Notice now that in the subspace method one may define the discriminant function as

$$\delta_i(x) = \|\hat{x}_i\|^2 = \|x\|^2 - \|\tilde{x}_i\|^2 . \tag{7.22}$$

7.4.2 The Learning Subspace Method (LSM)

In the basic subspace method of classification, a simple least-square error criterion was used which is strictly justified only if the noise is Gaussian and has zero mean value. In most practical applications these assumptions are not valid; at least the effect of a bias, or unsymmetry in the noise distribution should then be taken into account. Without loading the analysis too heavily with statistical considerations, it can now be shown that the basic subspace method which is computationally very light can easily be modified to compensate for non-Gaussian noise properties, at least to remove the worst bottlenecks. This modification is named *Learning Subspace Method* (LSM), and it has yielded very good results in the first stages of speech recognition systems [7.3, 4].

The LSM is a *supervised classification method*; it is in fact a *parametric* method (Sect. 7.2) since the forms of the discrimination functions are derived from the basic subspace method whereas their parameters are modified in a training procedure, using training vectors with known class-affiliation. The aim of training is to make the classification of at least all training vectors correct. Nevertheless, the modifications applied in the LSM have a deeper-going statistical meaning than just heuristically defined correction; the central idea is to replace the set of true prototypes of each class by another set of basis vectors which would compensate for the non-Gaussian properties of noise. This compensation then tends to be *optimal with respect to best classification results*. As an example of improved performance it may be mentioned that the accuracy of classification of *phonemes* could be raised from about 65 to 80% by the learning procedure. Some details of the LSM are now described below.

Dimensionalities of the Subspaces. The discriminant functions defined by (7.22) are *quadratic*; accordingly, the decision surfaces in the general case are quadratic, too. Only in the case that two classes have the same dimensionality, i.e., they are spanned by an equal number of linearly independent prototypes, the decision surface between these classes is a hyperplane. It will be clear that the form of the decision surface should comply with the statistical properties of the neighbouring classes; accordingly, the dimensionalities of the class subspaces should be determined first.

A straightforward learning procedure for the determination of dimensionalities is *decision-controlled choice of the prototypes*; for this, as well as the other learning methods, we have first to define a *training set of vectors* with known class-affiliation. The initial set of prototypes, with one prototype per class, may be selected from the training set at random. After that, new prototypes are accepted only if a training vector is classified incorrectly. The training vector itself is thereby added to the set of basis vectors of the correct subspace. In order to avoid numerical instability in practical calculations, the new prototype is not accepted if it is very close to be linearly dependent on the previous prototypes. The value $\|\tilde{x}_i\|/\|x\|$ can be used as an indicator: for acceptance of a prototype, this value has to exceed, e.g., five to ten per cent. In order to prevent the dimensionality from growing too high, an upper limit, e.g., six to ten, can also be set to the number of prototypes per class.

When a new prototype is added to the correct class, from the subspace into which the training vector is wrongly classified one of its prototypes is at the same time deleted, namely that one which makes the smallest angle with the training vector. This deletion is not performed unless a certain minimum number, e.g., one or two of prototypes, is always left in the class.

After each addition and deletion, a new orthonormal basis for the subspace shall be computed.

It has been suggested [7.5, 6] that the subspaces $\mathscr{L}_i$ might optimally be spanned by the eigenvectors of the covariance matrix of the prototypes, and the dimensionality of $\mathscr{L}_i$ then could be optimally reduced by choosing only a subset of eigenvectors with the largest eigenvalues. A further suggestion is to exclude intersections of the $\mathscr{L}_i$ [7.7]. There are indications that at least for the LSM algorithm, the latter modification does not bring about significant improvement, whereas the eigenvalue method in some cases may be even better than the decision-controlled choice of the prototypes. We have found out, however, that the final results depend only weakly on the absolute dimensionalities of the subspaces; on the other hand, the relative dimensionalities are more decisive, which is understandable as they strongly affect the forms of the decision surfaces [7.8].

Rotation of the Subspaces. If the usual subspace method commits errors, the recognition results can be improved in a straightforward way by modifying the subspaces to change the relative lengths of projections on them. This is done by *rotating* the subspaces. The rotating procedure may be derived, e.g., in the following way. If x is an arbitrary vector of R^n, then $P_0 = (I - xx^T / \|x\|^2)$ is a matrix operator which orthogonally projects any vector of R^n onto the subspace $\mathcal{L}^{\perp}(x)$, i.e., the set of all vectors which are orthogonal to x. Now assume that x is the pattern vector $x(t)$ which was wrongly classified into S_i. Multiplication of all the basis vectors of $\mathcal{L}_i$ by P_0 would result in a new rotated subspace $\mathcal{L}'_i$ in which all vectors are orthogonal to x, i.e., the projection of x on $\mathcal{L}'_i$ would be a zero vector. However, correction of subspace $\mathcal{L}_i$ with respect to only one vector does not guarantee good performance for all vectors. Therefore, corrections must be made iteratively over the whole set of training vectors, and the degree of rotation must be moderated by selecting for the *rotation operation matrix*

$$R_d = I - \alpha xx^T / \|x\|^2, \tag{7.23}$$

where $0 < \alpha < 1$.

Obviously, if α were *negative*, the projection of x would then *increase*. The principle aimed at in training in fact should be such that the projection on the wrong subspace is decreased, and the one on the correct subspace increased.

As with any learning method, the adaptation gain α ought to be some suitable function of the training step to warrant a good compromise between final accuracy and speed of convergence. A possible strategy is to make α at each training step just about sufficient to correct the classification of the last training vector.

Let the relative projection of x on subspace $\mathcal{L}_i$ be defined as

$$\beta_i = \|\hat{x}_i\| / \|x\|. \tag{7.24}$$

Let R_d be a rotation operator which, when applied to all the basis vectors of a given subspace changes the relative projection of x from β_i to β'_i. We shall show below that the following relation holds:

$$\alpha = 1 - \frac{\beta'_i}{\beta_i} \sqrt{\frac{1 - \beta_i^2}{1 - \beta'^2_i}}. \tag{7.25}$$

Let us call that subspace to which the training vector belongs the "own" subspace, and the subspace which the training vector is closest to the "rival" subspace, respectively. Then, in order to determine the value of α which is just sufficient for corrective action, assume that the classification of a training vector was wrong in the sense that its relative projection on the own subspace, denoted by β_0, was smaller than its relative projection β_r on the rival subspace. If a rotating procedure is now applied by which the new projections become

$$\beta_o' = \lambda \beta_o \quad \text{and} \quad \beta_r' = \beta_r/\lambda ,$$

(7.26)

then a correct classification ($\beta_o' > \beta_r'$) is obtained if

$$\lambda = \sqrt{\beta_r/\beta_o} + \Delta ,$$

(7.27)

where Δ is a small positive constant. Notice that β_r and β_o define λ which, by (7.26 and 27), again determines α. A proper choice of Δ in our experiments was 0.005 to 0.02. The correcting procedure has to be iterated over the training set.

Now we shall revert to the derivation of (7.25). It will be useful to show first that the orthogonal projection of x on $\mathscr{L}'$, denoted by $\hat{x}'$, can be computed as a projection on a certain line.

> **Theorem 7.1.** The orthogonal projection of x on $\mathscr{L}'$ is identical to the orthogonal projection of x on a line spanned by the vector
>
> $$z = \hat{x} + \alpha \beta^2 x ,$$
>
> provided that $\hat{x}$ was nonzero and x does not belong to $\mathscr{L}$.

Proof. Let us tentatively denote the latter projection by $\hat{x}_z$ whereby $x = \hat{x}_z + \tilde{x}_z$. The other orthogonal component $\tilde{x}_z$ will first be shown to be orthogonal to $\mathscr{L}'$. To this end it has to be orthogonal to all the new basis vectors

$$a_i' = \left(I + \alpha \frac{xx^{\mathrm{T}}}{\|x\|^2} \right) a_i .$$

The following formulas are fundamental for orthogonal projections:

$$\tilde{x}_z = \left(I - \frac{zz^{\mathrm{T}}}{z^{\mathrm{T}}z} \right) x ,$$

$$\hat{x}^{\mathrm{T}}x = \hat{x}^{\mathrm{T}}\hat{x} = \beta^2 x^{\mathrm{T}}x ,$$

(7.28)

$$\hat{x}^{\mathrm{T}}a_i = x^{\mathrm{T}}a_i .$$

Denote tentatively

$$z = \hat{x} + \xi x .$$

(7.29)

By substitution it is readily obtained

$$\tilde{x}_z^T \left(I + \alpha \frac{xx^T}{\|x\|^2} \right) a_i = \frac{(\xi - \alpha\beta^2)(\beta^2 - 1)}{\beta^2 + 2\xi\beta^2 + \xi^2} x^T a_i . \tag{7.30}$$

If $\xi = \alpha\beta^2$ as assumed then $\forall i$, $\tilde{x}_z^T a_i' = 0$, or $\tilde{x}_z \in \mathcal{L}'$.

Secondly it is shown that z belongs to $\mathcal{L}'$:

$$z = \left(\hat{x} + \alpha \frac{x^T \hat{x}}{x^T x} x \right) = \left(I + \alpha \frac{xx^T}{\|x\|^2} \right) \hat{x} . \tag{7.31}$$

Now, because $\hat{x}$ is a linear combination of the a_i (or belongs to $\mathcal{L}$) and it is rotated by the same operator as the a_i to get z, then it can be seen that z is a linear combination of the a_i', or it belongs to $\mathcal{L}'$.

Since $\hat{x}' \in \mathcal{L}'$, then also $\tilde{x}_z \in \hat{x}'$ holds true, and because $z \in \mathcal{L}'$, then also $\tilde{x}' \in \hat{x}_z$ holds true. It is to be recalled that $x = \hat{x}_z + \tilde{x}_z = \hat{x}' + \tilde{x}'$ (where $\tilde{x}'$ is the orthogonal distance vector to $\mathcal{L}'$). Now

$$(\hat{x}_z - \hat{x}')^T (\hat{x}_z - \hat{x}') = (x - \tilde{x}_z - x + \tilde{x}')^T (\hat{x}_z - \hat{x}')$$
$$= \tilde{x}'^T \hat{x}_z - \tilde{x}'^T \hat{x}' - \tilde{x}_z^T \hat{x}_z + \tilde{x}_z^T \hat{x}' = 0 , \tag{7.32}$$

which cannot hold unless $\hat{x}_z = \hat{x}'$. Q.E.D.

Now

$$\hat{x}' = \frac{x^T z}{z^T z} z , \tag{7.33}$$

and by substitution

$$\beta'^2 = \frac{\hat{x}'^T \hat{x}'}{x^T x} = \frac{\beta^2 (1 + \alpha)^2}{1 + 2\alpha\beta^2 + \alpha^2\beta^2} . \tag{7.34}$$

Solution for α yields

$$\alpha = \pm \frac{\beta'}{\beta} \sqrt{\frac{1 - \beta^2}{1 - \beta'^2}} - 1 , \tag{7.35}$$

where the positive sign for the square root has to be selected.

Another strategy which has produced slightly improved results in the classification of spectra results from the following rather natural conditions. Let $\hat{x}_o$ and $\hat{x}_r$ be the projections of x on the own and rival subspaces before correction, and after that they shall be denoted $\hat{x}_o'$ and $\hat{x}_r'$, respectively. A proper choice for α obviously includes at least the following considerations:

i) $\|\hat{x}'_o\| - \|\hat{x}'_r\| > \|\hat{x}_o\| - \|\hat{x}_r\|.$

ii)   The corrections must form a monotonically converging series.

We have applied the following computationally simple rule for the determination of α at each step; its derivation has been presented elsewhere [7.4]. Let λ be a parameter which controls the amount of correction such that

$$\|\hat{x}'_o\| = \|\hat{x}_o\| + \lambda/2 ,$$

$$\|\hat{x}'_r\| = \|\hat{x}_r\| - \lambda/2; \tag{7.36}$$

$$\lambda = \begin{cases} \|\hat{x}_r\| - \|\hat{x}_o\| + \Delta\|x\|, & \text{if } \|\hat{x}_o\| \leq \|\hat{x}_r\| \\ \|\hat{x}_r\| - \|\hat{x}_o\| + \sqrt{(\|\hat{x}_r\| - \|\hat{x}_o\|)^2 + \Delta^2\|x\|^2}, & \text{if } \|\hat{x}_o\| > \|\hat{x}_r\| \end{cases}$$

with Δ a small numerical constant (e.g., $\Delta = 0.002$). The values of α_o and α_r, referring to the own and rival subspaces, respectively, follow from the projections:

$$\alpha_o = \frac{\|\hat{x}'_o\|}{\|\hat{x}_o\|} \sqrt{\frac{\|x\|^2 - \|\hat{x}_o\|^2}{\|x\|^2 - \|\hat{x}'_o\|^2} - 1} , \tag{7.37}$$

and a similar expression is obtained for α_r, with subscript r replaced for o. (Notice that $\alpha_o > 0$, $\alpha_r < 0$.)

In our experiments, this procedure has always provided fast learning and large separation between subspaces. It has also ensured at least moderate classification accuracy for "rare" classes.

A particular caution, however, is due. Although the subspace methods have shown very effective in particular applications, and they are relatively easy to apply and program, for best results (and fastest convergence) the α-sequence ought to be designed even more carefully than devised above. It is a very interesting academic question and one of particular importance, too, to find out these sequences. Although for reasonably good classification accuracy the subspace methods easily lend themselves to practical application, for ultimate results some expertize in these methods is needed.

Finally we would like to comment on a very important property of the subspace algorithms which is influential from the computational point of view. If all input and prototype vectors are normalized to unit length, then the projection operations produce new vectors *all components of which are in the range* $[-1, +1]$. Accordingly, the fixed-point (or integer) arithmetic operations are then feasible, and due to this property these algorithms are readily programmable for microprocessors, thereby achieving a high speed of computation (usually in real time).

7.5 Feature Extraction

The representations of information discussed in this book are mostly definable as *pattern vectors*. The digital image of an object, some spectrum emitted by it, or a set of characteristic measurements made about it may be considered to constitute a pattern. Mathematically a pattern is then an ordered set of values. In practice, the dimensionality of patterns would often become intolerably large. Therefore it is common to *preprocess* these values, by forming various functionals over selected subsets (or all) of the pattern elements. Such functionals are then named *features*, and in many cases they contain important correlations or other relationships which comprise the intrinsic information. The features may be chosen heuristically, based on an insight into the problem, or some kind of statistical analysis may be performed (e.g., the well-known Karhunen-Loève expansion of statistics [7.8]) to extract a set of characteristic and statistically representative variables or their combinations ("factors"). The resulting set of feature values for a pattern is then defined as the *feature vector*. If there is no danger of confusion, the feature vector may be named the *pattern vector*.

Figure 7.1 illustrates the role of feature extraction (or preprocessing) in a simple pattern-recognition scheme.

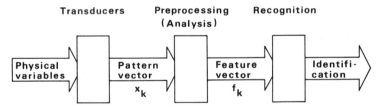

Fig. 7.1. Organization of a pattern recognition system

7.6 Clustering

Another approach for the reduction of data to be stored in a recognition or memory scheme is to perform a classification of primary data (e.g., pattern vectors) into representative subsets; it is then often possible to relate these subsets structurally, whereby in these structures no attention is paid to the individual data points.

In the scientific tradition, there has always existed an endeavour to organize all available knowledge into the framework of various systematics. The most characteristic examples of this are met in natural sciences, especially in genetics where *taxonomic classifications* are used. The basic task is thereby to construct a system of relations between a set of distinct items based on the degree of their mutual *similarity*. The comparison of items, and the resulting classification, has often been based on subjective evaluation of similarity; the use of quantitative measures, especially those amenable to computerized analysis, is rather new. The items, called *operational taxonomic units* (OTU's) or *taxons*, are then described by an ordered set of numbers, the characteristics (or attributes). An extra problem which is typical to genetics is that not all items belonging to the systematics are observable or have been found; there obviously exist samples which are more similar to the observed OTU's than these latter are mutually. It might be more precise to talk of *numerical taxonomy* [7.10], if classification is based on measurable characteristics solely. This method then also applies to the classification of more abstract concepts (e.g., in documentation).

The above kind of classification can be formalized as a mathematical problem, and the standard methods for its handling are the *clustering methods* discussed in this section. Some of them are able to discover generic or hierarchical relationships between the items which is a prerequisite for the representation of so-called *knowledge structures*. It seems, however, that the capabilities of conventional automatic methods in converting primary data into knowledge structures are still rather limited; in most operating knowledge-base systems, definition of the relations must be based on human evaluation.

It may not be necessary to aim at a complete survey of clustering methods here: let it suffice to mention some of the most central references [7.11 – 20].

7.6.1 Simple Clustering (Optimization Approach)

The clustering problem may be set up, e.g., in the following way: assume that $A = \{a_i; i = 1, 2, \ldots, n\}$ is a finite set of representations of items. This set has to be partitioned into disjoint subsets A_j, $j = 1, 2, \ldots, k$, such that with respect to this division, some functional describing the "distance" between items attains an extremum value. This functional ought to describe the quality of groupings in the sense that the mutual distances between all a_i belonging to the same A_j are as small as possible while the distances between different A_j are large.

In the simplest case, for the distance between two vectorial items, the (weighted) Euclidean distance measure may be chosen; more general Minkowski metrics are frequently used, too. The functional describing the grouping may contain, e.g., sums of some powers of the distances. Determination of the subsets A_j is a global optimization problem, whereby a set of simultaneous algebraic equations describing the optimality criterion is solved by direct or iterative methods.

7.6.2 Hierarchical Clustering (Taxonomy Approach)

A significant reduction in computational load is achieved if the subsets A_j are determined in several sequential steps; then, however, the optimality criterion can be applied only at each individual step whereby the final grouping usually remains suboptimal. This kind of *hierarchical clustering*, on the other hand, is able to find generic relationships which exist between the resulting clusters; in classification, encoding, and retrieval of empirical data this advantage is often of great importance. There is one major application area in which hierarchical clustering is a standard method, namely, *numerical taxonomy*.

The main types of hierarchical clustering are the *splitting* (divisive, partitioning) methods, and the *merging* (agglomerative, coalescence) methods.

Splitting Methods. These are straightforward methods which are related to the optimization approach. The set A is first partitioned into disjoint subsets A_1 and A_2, whereby some *interclass distance* $d = d(A_1, A_2)$ is maximized. There are many choices for d. One of the simplest is that using Euclidean metrics in the representation space,

$$d = \sum_{j=1}^{k} n_j \|\bar{x}_j - \bar{x}\|^2, \tag{7.38}$$

where n_j is the number of representations in A_j, $\bar{x}_j$ is the mean of A_j, and $\bar{x}$ is the mean of A, respectively; usually $k = 2$. The dichotomy is continued for A_1 and A_2 to produce the subsets A_{11}, A_{12}, A_{21}, and A_{22}, and so on. A stopping rule (e.g., if d falls below a given limit) may be applied to automatically prevent a further division of a subset. This method then directly produces a *binary tree structure*.

Instead of applying distance measures of the *representation space* directly, one might first construct a tree structure, the so-called *minimal spanning tree* (which links all representation "points" by the shortest path; cf. the next paragraph). This structure, by means of its topology, then defines the mutual distance of any two points in it. Using an arc-cutting algorithm [7.21] the tree can then be partitioned optimally.

Merging Methods. In these which are more common than the splitting methods, one starts with single-element subsets $A_i^{(0)} = \{a_i\}$. At every successive step (s), k most similar subsets $A_{j1}^{(s-1)}$, $A_{j2}^{(s-1)}$, ..., $A_{jk}^{(s-1)}$ are merged into a larger subset $A_j^{(s)}$. Usually $k = 2$. It is to be noted that the following cases may occur: the closest subsets consist of (a) single elements, (b) one single element and another set of cardinality >1, (c) two sets of cardinality >1. In the merging method, the distance between two disjoint subsets A_i and A_j can conveniently be defined, e.g., as the minimum of $d(a_k, a_l)$, where $a_k \in A_i$ and $a_l \in A_j$ (so-called *single linkage*). In fact, this measure also directly defines the minimal spanning tree, if a link (arc) between the nearest a_k and a_l is set at the same time when they are merged into a new subset.

Figure 7.2 illustrates division of a set of points into two subsets, and their representation by the minimal spanning tree, respectively.

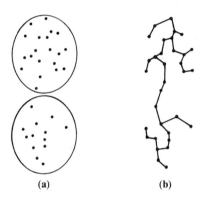

(a)   (b)

Fig. 7.2a, b. Examples of clustering. (a) Division into subsets. (b) Minimal spanning tree

7.7 Structural Pattern Recognition Methods

As remarked, it is not the objective of this chapter nor of this book to expound the whole field of pattern recognition (PR) research; one reason is that the PR methods are often heuristical, aiming at technological applications rather than basic information processes. The reader is advised to consult some of the many excellent textbooks published on PR and image analysis (e.g., see Bibliography). However, if one's aim is to find the basic paradigms of information processing, especially those which we are looking for in the biological brain, we should *not* follow the developments in artificial PR since they are dictated by the resources of existing computers.

The following brief review is only intended to show what other kinds of computational methods have been used in practical applications, especially image analysis which is nowadays a major subfield of PR. Most of the technological PR methods can roughly be divided into two categories: the *statistical* and the *structural* ones. The statistical methods, some of which were already discussed above, come from the statistical decision theory. The structural ones, on the other hand, stem from linguistics and especially from the theory of formal languages.

In classical decision theory, the variables were always assumed to be described by low-order statistics, i.e., their structural relationships were neglected. Decision-theoretical methods may work well in PR, if statistical noise is the worst problem, and the patterns are structurally very simple. This is the case, e.g., in the classification of most *spectra*, which are composed of more or less independent modes. So, for instance, in the recognition of phonemes from continuous speech, and classification of multispectral picture elements in remote sensing, statistical methods may be very useful. On the other hand, if the intrinsic information about an object is in its structure, or in the structure of its representation, then description of a class (or zone in the pattern space) can be made more uniquely and economically by the description of the *topological properties,* irrespective of accurate metric properties of the representation.

The only practicable computerized methods for the description of structures in *pictures* have so far been restricted to the analysis of *line drawings.* Notice that the primary information in a digitized image is usually represented by values of intensity (shades) of picture points, or in multispectral or multilayered images, as a set of vectors, each describing the spectral decomposition of a picture point. Conversion of shaded images into line figures may begin with *edge enhancement.* The two-dimensional field of values representing the image may be operated by a differential operator like gradient (and taking its magnitude), Laplacian, or some other directional derivative operator which is more optimal for discrete-point pictures. Sometimes borderlines can be found quite accurately with the aid of *grey-level histograms,* by labelling those picture points which correspond to intensity values at relative minima of the histogram. Edge enhancement methods produce more or less thin zones of points which must still be converted into line drawings, e.g., by fitting of line segments. Before fitting, some kind of thinning algorithms ("erosion") can be used to reduce the widths of the zones.

After a shaded and usually noisy image has been converted into a line drawing by segmentation, edge enhancement and line fitting, or by using other methods, it is necessary to describe the lines so obtained. A line drawing in general consists of several separate lines or curves. A concise description of the *form* of a line or a curve can be made by *chain codes* [7.22], or more generally, recording the changes in line orientation as a function of arc length. A chain code is a string of symbols, each one describing a discrete step in a particular quantized direction.

Structural analysis of line drawings can be based on two fundamentally different approaches: the *topological* and the *syntactic* method.

It should be noted that a chain code tends to describe the absolute form of a line, or shape of an area. In many cases, however, the intrinsic information is mainly contained in the *topological* relations of curves. Fortunately it is fairly simple to extract the most important topological descriptive features from chain codes [7.23] and to use these for the identification of objects. In addition, chain codes contain metric information which can be used to increase resolution between objects. It is also possible to apply string matching algorithms directly to the chain codes; this is then reduced to classification by the nearest-neighbour method using some distance measure for the dissimilarity of strings.

The *syntactic* methods begin with the extraction of *primitives* from the patterns. With regard to line drawings, the primitives can be line segments defined, e.g., by regions of certain curvature, or segments between distinct points such as intersections or branchings. Angles, arcs, and forks which indicate corners have been used as primitives. In principle, any subpattern in the original image, when suitably segmented and labelled, could also be defined as a primitive. It would, of course, be desirable for the primitives to have some correspondence to parts in real objects such as arms in a chromosome, or nose or wings in an aeroplane. The next task is then to set up a *picture grammar* based on the primitives and their possible occurrences together. It then becomes possible to derive a *syntactic description* using *parsing* methods similar to those used in linguistics. The linguistic method is applicable only if the primitives can be found reliably. In both topological and linguistic descriptions, the result is usually a *string of symbols*; identification of a pattern is reduced to the comparison of its string with reference strings of various classes.

A characteristic drawback of structural methods is the arbitrariness in the selection of primitives; accordingly, e.g., there exist an indefinite number of ways for the construction of grammars for pictures (or other patterns to which syntactic methods are applied).

Instead of using the syntactic parsing method, one may directly develop an automatic method for the description of *relations* and *relational structures* that define the contents of a picture.

Simpler Structural Methods. For the identification of objects, in particular, the forms of which are rigid and unique but which may appear in arbitrary positions and orientations, it has been customary to select as features some invariant measures of their projection images such as area, length of perimeter, geometric moments, etc. This is the situation usually encountered in industrial robotics. Since the identification of features can then be done almost uniquely, classification may be performed in several steps described by a *decision tree*, defining successive dichotomies over the set of possible classes, and usually referring to one feature at a time. This kind of decision-tree method is normally applied to the identification of machine parts in automatic production. The decision-tree analysis is a special case of *sequential methods* in which classification in general is carried out in several steps; previous results thereby control the classification in later steps.

8. More About Biological Memory

8.1 Physiological Foundations of Memory

Apparently the memory functions of biological organisms have been implemented in the neural realms; but in spite of extensive experimental research pursued on biological memory, it seems that many central questions concerning its functional and organizational principles have remained unanswered. In view of the theoretical knowledge recently acquired about the information processing principles of adaptive networks, it seems that the experimental results need a new theory to which they can be related.

8.1.1 On the Mechanisms of Memory in Biological Systems

An intriguing experimental fact about biological memory is that it does not seem to apply principles known from computers. First of all, there is plenty of experimental evidence, starting with the classical results of *Lashley* [8.1], that information is stored in the brain tissue as some sort of collective effect. When lesions were made in various parts of the cortex, the level of performance sustained in various behavioral tasks in the first place seemed to depend on the amount of damage and to much lesser extent on the exact location of the lesion. Thus every fragment of the tissue seemed to carry information relating to similar learned behaviour. Although the original experimental techniques have been criticized, subsequent research (of which a review can be found in [8.2]) has validated the essential ideas. It can be stated that the memory in the cortex is of the distributed and not of the local type.

A particular notice about the biological memory is due. The role of the complex and apparently specific anatomical organization of the central nervous system should not be ignored. As the biological organisms have been formed in a very long course of phylogenesis, adaptation that has occurred in the evolution means that complex structural forms, the purposes of which are not completely clear to us, have been produced. In the macroscopic scale, different neural areas have been specialized for signals of different sensory modalities, for information processing operations at different levels, as well as for the animal and vegetative functions of the organism. Consequently, memory traces from different kinds and levels of experience may be left in different areas, although they were locally distributed.

On the Chemical and Neural Theories of Memory. In brain research there are two opposed faculties which hold different views of the embodiment of memory. The largest discrepancy in opinions concerns the principle of encoding of "memories". In the neurochemical branch of research it is thought that the stored information is represented as permutations of molecular components, perhaps mononucleotides, which form long chain-like macromolecules in a similar way as the genetic information is expressed in the DNA and messenger RNA molecules. The "memory molecules" in this theory are assumed to reside in the intracellular cytoplasm of the neural cells [8.3, 4].

The second faculty of research identifies the memory traces with functional and partly structural changes of the neural networks; the collective transmission properties of the network are changed by the signals. The neural network is thereby regarded as an adaptive filter. Reading of information is equivalent to an action in which new features are added to the primary input (key) signals when they are transmitted through the network. The adaptive associative memory networks discussed in the previous chapters may thereby constitute one paradigm.

Since it is self-evident that macromolecule reactions may play a role with any complex activity in living organisms, and the experimentally observed changes in intracellular macromolecule concentrations during specific learning tasks are therefore easily explained by the fact that strong specific neural activity has been present, the problem that is left concerns the question, whether the neural signals are directly translated into molecular codes, or the representation of information is more indirect, expressed in the micro-anatomical and microphysiological features of the neural network. In the latter case, the molecular changes may be thought to belong as an integral part to the complex process in which the neural tissue is modified. In the present work the latter view is preferred, especially since it becomes possible to demonstrate that adaptive networks can have a sufficiently high memory capacity. For samples of proposed memory mechanisms, see [8.2, 5 – 10].

One of the most severe objections to the code theory concerns the representation of associations. If, as it is apparent, information is not stored as isolated items but the encoding of every item by the other items is necessary for their later retrieval, then the storage of a large number of signals must be made in parallel, at the same time preserving their interrelations. This is not possible unless the cells are able to interact, for instance, through neural communication. A view about direct translation of cell activity into a code which then would be stored in it does not take into account this requirement. Accordingly, reconstruction of a simultaneous, highly coherent, patterned activity in thousands of cells during recall is not possible if the only storage of information were intracellular, i.e., isolated from the other cells.

It should also be noticed that our experiences are seldom quite unique and distinct, and if direct coding were used, there would be a different specific code for each experience. How can then, for instance, stereotypic representations be formed of many almost similar but incomplete versions? Even if it were supposed that information could be averaged by some sort of collation mechanisms, a particular difficulty arises when trying to explain the reading of information: as the code on a macromolecule is a linear array, it must be scanned (by ribosomes) since no address decoder mechanism is known to exist. But where should the reading be started and where to be stopped? Assume that this problem were solved in some way. The ribosome, however, only produces another protein, and this should be translated into neural signals. Although the neurochemists might claim that this still can be rendered possible, in view of the degree and number of assumptions involved, the code theory does not quite comply with Newton's Rule: "We are to admit no more causes of natural things, than such as are both true and sufficient to explain their appearances".

Suppose now that the neural memory can be regarded as a filter function. There yet remain different opinions about the type of adaptive processes involved.

Holographic versus Nonholographic Neural Memory. It has been suggested, although never demonstrated by any simulation, that distributed memory in the neural systems might be based on holography [8.11 – 17]. However, there seem to arise plenty of difficulties in the application of this principle to the neural realms; for instance, there would be a need of optic-quality media, coherent wave fronts, and reference waves by which the stored information should be encoded. It seems that the hypothesis about holography as the principle of biological memory was originally introduced in lack of knowledge about the existence of other principles which also allow spatial distributedness of information; for instance, the adaptive network model is an alternative principle which has a high selectivity in the associative recall of information from it. The holographic explanations of biological memory have one particular advantage, namely, it is possible to recall information from them although the key pattern were translated from its due position. The responses and perceptions of human beings and animals are similarly known to have a limited invariance with respect to size, rotation, and form of the stimulus patterns. But it should be realized that only translational invariance is taken into account by the holographic mapping. The linear filter models used in this book to exemplify selective recall from simple physical systems, on the other hand, also have a limited ability to interpolate and extrapolate patterns that have been shown in a few reference versions; this ability is not restricted to translation but other types of variation, too (Sect. 1.4.2).

A further possibility for the achievement of stimulus-equivalence ought to be mentioned. Since all sensory information that enters the memory is preprocessed by peripheral systems, a significant degree of standardization of the patterns can be performed before memorization. Examples of effective and simple standardizing devices are the oculomotor systems of biological organisms which by regulatory control keep the optic images fixed on the retina for short intervals of time. The saccadic movements of the eyes tend to direct the gaze at important details of the patterns, irrespective of their mutual distances.

If it is supposed that the adaptive associative network models may serve as a basic paradigm of biological memory functions, one can proceed to the details of neural systems that may implement it.

8.1.2 Structural Features of Some Neural Networks

Laminar Structures in Neural Networks. There are many types of neural cells and structures in the nervous system. A high degree of specialization is found in the sensory organs and in the older parts of the brain, whereas within the cerebral cortex which incorporates the newest and highest functions, the variety of cells does not greatly differ between the various areas. If consideration is restricted to the highest levels of the central nervous system where memory and higher information processing operations probably are located, the neurons are found to form laminated structures (the various types of cortices, the grey substance).

The main body of the neural cell, called *soma*, contains those intracellular components that are common to most cells: the nucleus and different kinds of particles necessary for the metabolism and protein synthesis. The intracellular liquid, the cytoplasm, together with some particles fills all parts of the cell.

As it is necessary for a neuron to make signal contacts with many other neurons, the outer cell membrane is usually shaped into many extensive branches called *dendrites*. There are cells in which the dendrites almost form a star. A very important cell type is the pyramidal cell (Fig. 8.1), in which there

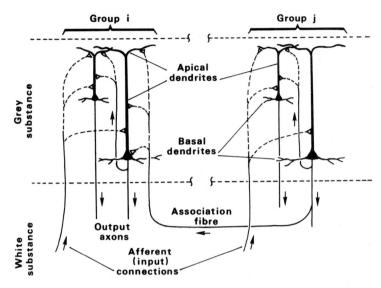

Fig. 8.1. Simplified diagram of the cerebral neocortex showing tightly interconnected "groups" of neurons, and distant connections between the "groups" via the white substance. The "groups", however, need not have any sharp borders and they may even overlap (Sect. 8.1.5 and [8.18]). Only pyramidal cells are shown since there are many types of intervening connections at short distance. These are often made through interneurons, roughly corresponding to the dashed portions of the lines

are two sets of dendrites; those which are most distant from the soma are the apical dendrites, and they are connected to the soma through a shaft-like formation of the membrane. At the base of the pyramidal soma, there is another set of branches called the basal dendrites.

In Fig. 8.1, a section of the cerebral neocortex that forms the main part of the brain in man is shown. The majority of the cells are of the pyramidal cell type which transmit neural signals mainly in the top-down direction. A neuron sends signals to other neurons through its output fibre, the *axon*. The external signal input to the cortex comes through the output axons of the other cells which ascend the cortex either directly or through small intervening cells, the interneurons. Details of these connections are temporarily left unspecified and denoted by dashed lines in Fig. 8.1. The pyramidal cells, again, make connections with other neurons through their axons, and part of these cells are output cells which send signals to the muscles, glands, etc. The pyramidal cells are interconnected in the lateral direction in different ways. Within the cortex, this occurs through the so-called collateral branches of their output axons, either direct, or through interneurons. In man, these intracortical connections have a maximum range of 2 to 3 mm. Some recent studies strongly stress the possibility that short-range interactions may spread directly between the dendrites, too (Sect. 8.1.5). At longer distances, reaching over centimeters, the mutual interconnections are exclusively made by the output axons of the pyramidal cells which then form the well-known white substance. These connections are called subcortical. Very roughly speaking it is possible to distinguish in the cortex between the top-down parallel lines, and the transversal connections.

The Columnar Organization of the Neocortex. In recent years, plenty of evidence has been collected which indicates that at least in the cerebral neocortex, the smallest operational unit is not a single neuron but the cell mass is organized into much larger units which act collectively [8.19]. In the neocortex there is a typical vertical dispersion in cell activity; all cells which lie along a line perpendicular to the cortex respond in an approximately similar way. This effect is most marked in the primary visual cortex, where the signals from the eyes terminate: this area is known to be organized in "columns" of the order of 100 µm wide, the cells in one column responding, for instance, to line segments of a certain orientation in the visual field [8.20 – 22]. It is a common view that a similar columnar organization may be found anywhere in the cortex. The following facts support the assumption that the cortical neurons operate as large groups:

i) Anatomical studies have indicated that the pyramidal cells send their axon collaterals in definite directions. This structure is known up to a distance of 2 to 3 mm in man; the same types of connections seem to be found everywhere in the cortex. *Szentágothai* [8.18] has recently found in anatomical studies that the axon collaterals of the cortical pyramidal cells form circuits which make at least 30 neurons to operate as a tightly controlled group; the intracortical collaterals from one cell may actually contact as many as 700 cells.

ii) In a cell mass with dimensions of about one column, all the different cell types that occur in a particular area are present.

iii) The ascending (afferent) axons hit the cortex with an accuracy of the order of 1 mm, and their terminal arborization has a diameter of about 100 to 400 µm.

iv) Electrophysiological recordings show that cells in the same column respond similarly. They have the same receptive fields, i.e., sensory regions where they originate.

v) Some newer findings show that neural signals are spread at short distance via interactions of different kinds, for instance, from one dendrite to another [8.10].

Coupling of Signals Between Neurons. It seems safe to state that one of the main purposes of a neural cell is to function as a signal-amplifying element, in the similar way as amplification is implemented by transistors in electronic circuits. But, in addition, a neuron performs information processing in it. Usually, there is a very great number of input signals converging upon a neuron, for instance, some thousands in pyramidal cells, but as many as 10^5 in Purkinje cells. There also exist small neurons with only a few hundred inputs. Each cell has one output which, however, may branch to many places by the collateral branches mentioned above. It is not quite clear, however, whether a neural cell with many inputs and one output from a system-theoretical point of view should be regarded as a logic gate, as sometimes believed, or whether it is more like an analog computing device. The view held in this work is biased in the latter direction.

The neural signals are transmitted as series or volleys of electrical impulses that travel along the output fibres, the axons, as propagatory waveforms. It is not possible to discuss in detail within this context how this phenomenon is generated; let it be mentioned that the cell membrane is biophysically active. By selective ionic diffusion, an electrical resting potential of about 70 mV is built up between the outside and the inside of the tubular membrane. It is possible to increase the permeability of the membrane to ions by the application of certain chemicals, or by electric excitation. An increased diffusion of ions depolarizes the membrane. This again increases the permeability. Thus there is a positive (regenerative) biophysical feedback action on account of which the membrane potential and the diffusion of sodium, potassium, and chlorine ions through the membrane undergo a dynamic triggering cycle which generates the neural impulses about 100 mV high and 0.5 to 2 ms wide. The triggering of the impulses is initiated at the junction of the axon and the cell body, called the axon hillock. The travelling speed of the impulses down the axon varies from 0.5 m/s to about 100 m/s, depending on the diameter of the axon, and the tissue covering it.

The signals are connected from the axons of the neurons to the dendrites or to the soma of other neurons via special formations called *synapses* (Fig. 8.2). Every axon has a synaptic ending or terminal which is able to release chemicals called transmitters. There are many different types of them, but one neuron usually has only one type of transmitter. A small amount of transmitter is released from the terminal at every neural impulse, and after passing a narrow cleft, it arrives at the membrane of the receiving (postsynaptic) cell. The transmitter substances are as such able to excite the membrane, but the coupling is made far more efficient by special proteins called chemical receptors, or briefly, receptors, located at the postsynaptic membrane. By a combined action of transmitters and receptors, hereupon called transmission, the electrical potential over the postsynaptic membrane is changed by a small amount at every input impulse. As there is a large number of inputs, the

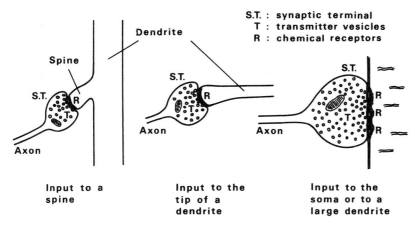

Fig. 8.2. Various types of synaptic connections, briefly named synapses

potential of the membrane is gradually changed until its value (at the axon hillock) reaches a threshold; an output pulse is thereby initiated. If the input transmission is continuous and high enough, the neuron generates a continuous series of output impulses which, again, are able to excite other neurons.

Signal transmission and amplification are thus electrochemical and partly more complicated biophysical processes. There are some additional details associated with the synapses and the transmission which cannot be discussed here. From a functional point of view it would be most important to know what the mathematical law is that describes the dependence of the output impulses on the input transmission. Two facts can be mentioned: with reasonable accuracy, the effects of the different synapses on the membrane potential are summed up linearly. This is called spatial summation. Individual synapses, however, may have different weights or efficacies in signal coupling which depend on their sizes and perhaps even more on the amount of their receptors. Two main types of synapses are now distinguished: the *excitatory* ones which increase the postsynaptic depolarization, or bring the neuron closer to triggering, and the *inhibitory* ones which work in the opposite direction. Both types are necessary in order to achieve a stable operation, as will be seen below. The type of the synapse is determined by the chemical receptors.

In time, the cell integrates the small changes in the membrane potential caused by the inputs, but this does not occur linearly with the time integral of transmission; the potential tends to level off. If transmission is constant, the levelling occurs approximately according to an exponential law, as will be shown in connection with Fig. 8.4. This effect is named temporal summation.

Actually even the exponential law is not quite accurate; in reality, the levelling occurs a bit more quickly.

8.1.3 Functional Features of Neurons

On the Analytical Modelling of the Transfer Function. In spite of the indisputable fact that rather little of information has been gathered about the exact functional laws of signal transmission in different neural cells, with the exception of the motoneuron (the output neuron in the spinal cord which relays signals from the brain to the muscles) that has been studied extensively, certain simplified models for general neurons are continuously circulated in cybernetic literature and rather far-reaching conclusions are made concerning the possible organizations and computational algorithms of the neural units. One frequently referred model for a neural cell is the so-called *formal neuron* as suggested by *McCulloch* and *Pitts* [8.23]; there a neuron is imagined as a triggering device which has a threshold. When the sum of the input signals exceeds this threshold, an output with a value, say, "1" is obtained. Otherwise the output is "0". In this way it is possible to identify a formal neuron with a logic gate which may implement arbitrary Boolean functions depending on the input weights and the threshold. Because a computer of any complexity can be built of such logic gates, it has thereby frequently been concluded that the brain is a computer, perhaps not quite numerically-oriented, but anyway using functional principles as they occur in digital computer technology. It now becomes necessary to have a deeper look at the neuron models in light of the present knowledge.

Let us start with the basic assumptions of the formal neurons [8.23]:

"i) The activity of the neuron is an 'all-or-none' process.

ii) A certain fixed number of synapses must be excited within the period of latent addition in order to excite a neuron at any time, and this number is independent of previous activity and position of the neuron.

iii) The only significant delay within the nervous system is synaptic delay.

iv) The activity of any inhibitory synapse absolutely prevents excitation of the neuron at that time.

v) The structure of the net does not change with time."

The most fatal misinterpretation of these assumptions now concerns the "all-or-none"-principle. It ought to be generally known that, on the highest levels of the central nervous system at least, neurons are firing continuously and their firing rate can be raised by excitatory inputs and lowered by the inhibitory ones. It cannot be said that an inhibitory input always absolutely blocks the activity, but the efficacy of an inhibitory synapse is normally much higher than that of the excitatory one. There is another generally accepted principle that the signal intensities, at least in the peripheral nerves, are coded by their impulse frequency, i.e., in a continuous scale of values. Why should the flow of information in higher-level neurons be interrupted, when the first output impulse is triggered? The transfer function of a neuron is more akin to that of a *pulse-frequency modulator*. Referring to Fig. 8.3 and (8.1 – 3), the operation of a neuron is first illustrated by a coarse but clearly comprehensible electrical model, consisting of passive electrical components and an active triggering device. If all input to a neuron resulting from excitatory and inhibitory presynaptic transmitter actions is simply represented by a generator of electrical current $I(t)$, the transmission has an electrical analogy in which the generator charges up a capacitor C, representing the membrane capacitance, shunted by a leakage resistance R. When the voltage of the capacitance exceeds a critical value, the triggering threshold T, an output impulse with high energy is obtained and the capacitance is simultaneously discharged to a value L. In real neurons the triggering threshold is time-variable after the firing [8.24], and the discharge might not be as ideal as assumed here; these refinements, however, do not change the qualitative fact accentuated here, namely, that in a continuous operation the *rate* of the output impulses continuously follows the input transmission, as soon as this is sufficiently high.

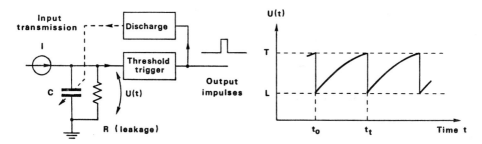

Fig. 8.3. Pulse-frequency modulator model of a neuron

In the simplified electrical model of temporal summation shown in Fig. 8.3, the charging and discharging phenomena of the membrane capacitance, here represented by C, are isolated from the generation of the output impulses. Accordingly, the voltage waveform $U(t)$ which is built up at the capacitance is not quite the same as that recorded from a real cell, mainly because the triggering of the neuron is not superimposed on it.

Suppose now that the input transmission is a constant I, and after discharge, the voltage $U(t)$ begins to rise from a level L at time t_0. A simple dynamical analysis shows that the voltage is the following function of time (before the next triggering):

$$U(t) = RI + \left(\frac{L}{RC} - \frac{I}{C} \right) \exp\left(- \frac{t-t_0}{RC} \right). \tag{8.1}$$

The instant at which $U(t)$ reaches the threshold value T is denoted by t_t, whereby, after normalization of the time constant RC as unity,

$$t_t - t_0 = \ln(I - L/R) - \ln(I - T/R). \tag{8.2}$$

After discharge, the same waveform is repeated. The triggering rate, denoted by f, is

$$f = \frac{1}{t_t - t_0}. \tag{8.3}$$

A graph describing function $f(I)$ in relative coordinates is shown in Fig. 8.4. It is found that there exists a "threshold" for the input transmission, not the same as T, before the system becomes active. Notice, however, that if the state of normal operation is biased at a higher value by superimposing a constant background transmission on the input, the operation of the element becomes continuous and linear: variations in I are then reflected in directly proportional variations in f. This is the so-called *linearization assumption* which is very central to the present theory.

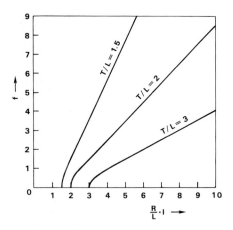

Fig. 8.4. Output frequency versus input current of the model of Fig. 8.3

Simulations of the transfer function of a real neuron (the second-order neuron from the dorsal spino-cerebellar tract) have been carried out by *Walløe* et al. [8.24], using more realistic models of the cell membrane, as well as of the statistical distribution of the neural impulses. The simulation results, shown in Fig. 8.5 were also compared with physiological recordings. It ought to be noticed that a normalized background activity is implicit in the curves, whereby at zero input there is assumed a spontaneous-like output activity, 20 impulses/s. Deviations from linearity are not great, whereby the linearization assumption may be regarded valid in the continuation, in the first approximation at least.

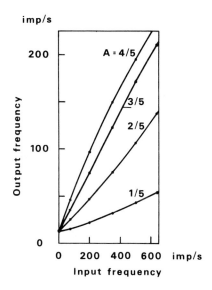

Fig. 8.5. Output frequency versus input frequency in a simulation with a Poisson-distributed input impulse train. The value of A corresponds to the size of the so-called excitatory postsynaptic potentials (EPSP's), i.e., jumps in the membrane potential after each input pulse [8.24]

Summation of the Inputs. The total time-averaged input transmission I of the simplified model can now be expressed as a weighted sum of the impulse frequencies of the individual inputs, converging upon the neuron. If the output frequency is denoted by η, the background activity by η_b, and the presynaptic input frequencies by ξ_i, $i = 1, 2, \ldots, n$, respectively, then a linearized frequency-to-frequency transfer function reads

$$\eta = \eta_b + \sum_{i=1}^{n} \mu_i \xi_i, \tag{8.4}$$

with parameters μ_i that describe the efficacies of the synapses. In Fig. 8.6, a neuron is represented by a circular symbol, and the signal values together with the input weights are shown.

If a synapse is excitatory, the μ-coefficient is positive. For an inhibitory synapse, this coefficient is negative. It is assumed that the range of the linear operation is not exceeded, in other words, (8.4) is valid only within the so-called dynamic range of the neuron. Notice that there are no restrictions for η be-

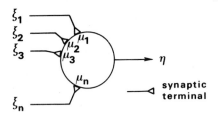

synaptic
terminal

Fig. 8.6. Symbolic notation for a neuron

coming *less* than the background activity, too. This is one feature owing to which the linearized model deviates from many other neuron models, for instance, the formal neurons.

8.1.4 Modelling of the Synaptic Plasticity

The signal transfer properties of a neural network may be changed in many different ways, and two categories of changes can be distinguished: *structural changes*, for instance, the sprouting of new axon collaterals, and *functional changes* in the already existing connections, first of all, changes in the efficacies of the synapses. The latter can be changed by growth or regression of the terminals, or by alteration in the synaptic transmission which again may be due to transmitters or postsynaptic receptors. It seems that structural changes mostly occur at an early age [8.5, 25], whereas chemical changes may be predominant in adults. Sprouting of new axon collaterals, following lesions made at the presynaptic terminals, have been observed in adults, though [Ref. 8.2, pp. 488 – 489]. Primarily we hold the view that the most important memory effects in adults under normal conditions are due to changes in the number of active chemical receptors at the postsynaptic membrane [8.26, 27], followed perhaps by structural changes of the membrane. It is also possible that these phenomena are escorted by other effects of different nature, which makes accurate modelling rather difficult. Fortunately, it has turned out that many functional hypotheses yield almost similar results in simulations, so that an accurate description may not be crucial.

Conjunction and Correlation Models for Synapses. A functional dependence which, in one form or another, is common to most modelling approaches of neural memory is the so-called *conjunction theory* of learning, independently introduced by several authors [8.6, 28]. In order to make the changes in the neural elements specific enough, and in order to be able to encode any information in memory by other information, it must be supposed that changes in a memory element are not possible, unless there is a simultaneous presence of several factors that depend on different signals. There are again several possibilities for such a synergism between various factors. If two signals converge on the membrane of a third neuron at a sufficiently close distance from each other, they may permanently facilitate each other through conformational changes of the membrane proteins, i.e., the sensitivity of the membrane is increased. Another possibility is that two signals make so-called presynaptic couplings (one terminal touching the other), and the strength of this coupling is proportional to both signals.

One of the most influential and frequently cited assumptions of synaptic modifiability, originally introduced by *Hebb* [8.28], is that the efficacy of a particular synapse changes if and only if there is a high triggering activity of the neuron in synchronism with a high input transmission at the synapse in question. The name "conjunction theory" used, e.g., by *Marr* and *Eccles* [8.6] refers to a logic conjunction of "all-or-none" events of which one corresponds to the output activity, the other to the activity at a particular input terminal.

The presynaptic and postsynaptic activities, however, ought to be regarded as stochastic processes. Assume that an output activity exceeding a certain intensity level is a stochastic event Y with the probability of occurrence $P(Y)$, and a high activity at one input, exceeding a certain level, is another stochastic event X_i, with the probability of occurrence $P(X_i)$. The joint probability for the occurrence of both input and output events is $P(X_i, Y)$. Since the output Y depends upon many input events (there may be thousands of synapses at one neuron), it is reasonable to approximate the situation by regarding X_i and Y as being statistically independent, whereby $P(X_i, Y) = P(X_i)P(Y)$.

The conjunction hypothesis can now be formulated in statistical terms by assuming that the average or expectation value of the synaptic efficacy μ_i, denoted by $E(\mu_i)$, changes in time in proportion to $P(X_i, Y)$, and to a free parameter α_i' :

$$\frac{dE(\mu_i)}{dt} = \alpha_i' P(X_i) P(Y) . \tag{8.5}$$

Below, a simplified notation is employed. The input activity is denoted by ξ_i and the output activity by η, and μ_i is written for $E(\mu_i)$. In analogy with (8.5) we then have

$$d\mu_i/dt = \alpha_i \xi_i \eta , \tag{8.6}$$

where α_i is named the plasticity coefficient of this synapse. It can be briefly stated that a synapse in this theory is assumed to change in proportion to the *correlation* of the input and output signals.

A Physiological Theory of Synaptic Modification. The hypothesis of *Hebb* [8.28] was originally introduced, without specification of its physiological mechanisms, in order to explain the formation of specific connections in neural networks; after 30 years its experimental verification has finally succeeded [8.29 – 32]. In view of the memory principle maintained in this book, experimental validation of the law according to which specific changes in synapses occur is very difficult, since the effects are distributed over a great number of cells, and the individual changes may be extremely small. As it is necessary, however, to have some model of synaptic modification in order to explain any memory effects in neural realms at all, the physiological foundations of this theory must be subjected to closer inspection.

There is one feature in the simple conjunction hypothesis which does not quite comply with general biological principles. If the synapses changed in one direction only, i.e., either growing or regressing monotonically in time, resources of the modifiable elements would soon be exhausted. In most biological processes, however, there occur reversible changes in state variables. If the synaptic efficacies ensued from the postsynaptic receptor molecules, reversibility would mean that their number can be increased or decreased. If, as it seems, the receptor molecules are complex proteins, it is plausible that the total number of receptors within a cell cannot be changed promptly; the proteins must be synthetized in slower reactions. Therefore, the possibility sounds more reasonable that during a shorter span, the most important dynamic process is the *redistribution* of the receptors between the synapses of the same cell according to demand; quick relative changes in the synaptic efficacies can thereby be effected.

Differences Between Synapses. Even though the general mechanism of plasticity were universal for all types of synapses, there can exist qualitative and quantitative differences of the following types between different synaptic systems:

- structural (sprouting of new synapses, morphological changes) and/or functional (conductance) effects
- short/long term effects
- growth/regression with use/disuse
- proportional to pre/postsynaptic activity or their *conjunction*
- individual/cooperative changes

For instance, the organization of the neuronal system of invertebrates is practically deterministic, and there exists a high degree of coding of information in the specific location of individual neurons in such a system. Learning in this case may be very simple, proportional to presynaptic activity. On the other hand, for *associative learning* which is most clearly implemented in the mammalian neocortex it is theoretically possible to achieve the necessary selectivity of specific responses to specific input patterns only by some sort of conjunction learning, which facilitates feedback of information from the output.

One further remark is due. The decay of synaptic efficacy in time (= passive forgetting) is not included in the following discussion; it seems that the most significant changes in synapses are of the *active* type, i.e., proportional to the cell activity as discussed in Chap. 4. This will further be elucidated below.

Physiological Possibilities for Plasticity. The main sources of synaptic plasticity can be of the following types. If the changes are *presynaptic* (i.e., they occur on the side of the terminal), one of the following effects might account for it: (1) Changes in the amount of free transmitter at the terminal. (2) Amount of some ions like Ca^{2+} which affect transmission. (3) Morphological changes in the presynaptic terminal.

If, on the other hand, the changes are *postsynaptic* (occurring on the cell side), one of the following factors may be responsible for them: (1) Changes in the number of active subsynaptic receptor molecules. (2) Changes in the shape and size of spines. (3) Conformative changes in the membrane proteins. (4) Changes in ionic conductivity.

The role of DNA and RNA including activation and repression mechanisms may be seen as maintaining the structural changes that have been caused. We argue that the most plausible long-term effects are caused by changes in the postsynaptic receptors, probably followed by morphological changes in the terminals or spines. To be more specific, there are some alternatives left which would lead to slightly different forms of system equations. These alternatives are the following.

For presynaptic control, the following alternatives are possible: (1) Clamping of the subsynaptic membrane potential by chemical transmission, which induces an increased ionic conductivity. (2) Effect on postsynaptic receptors by some amount of transmitter substance leaking into the postsynaptic cell. (3) For the activation of the postsynaptic receptor complex, part of it may come from the transmitter molecules.

For postsynaptic changes, the two following processes seem to be most significant: (1) *De novo* synthesis or release of receptor molecules from postsynaptic polysomes due to increased Ca^{2+} and cAMP concentration, the latter being result from and proportional to postsynaptic triggering rate ([8.26] and Fig. 8.7); (2) Migration or field-dependent transport of receptor molecules or their parts along the membrane by polarity reversal, an effect which is propor-

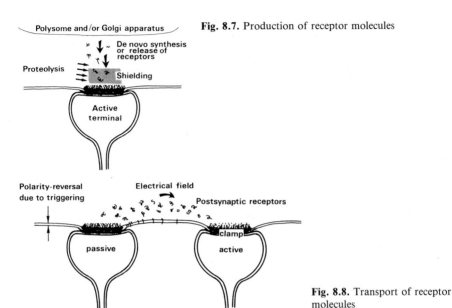

Polysome and/or Golgi apparatus

De novo synthesis or release of receptors

Proteolysis

Shielding

Active terminal

Fig. 8.7. Production of receptor molecules

Polarity-reversal due to triggering

Electrical field

Postsynaptic receptors

clamp

passive   active

Fig. 8.8. Transport of receptor molecules

tional to triggering rate, whereby presynaptic transmission can control this locally by clamping the membrane potential ([8.27] and Fig. 8.8).

There are thus many alternatives for possible biochemical phenomena at the synapses, some of which may not have been mentioned above. What is most important is that they all seem to induce changes in the synaptic efficacy according to similar functional laws. Thus, without having to commit oneself to a particular hypothesis, it seems possible to derive the *kinetic equations* of synaptic efficacy in a general form, assuming some hypothetical *synaptic resources* the amount of which within the cell, during a short period of time, must be approximately constant.

Let us first discuss *two symmetrical adjacent synapses*. The rate of redistribution of the resources may then be assumed proportional to the difference of presynaptic signals $(\xi_1 - \xi_2)$; further it seems possible to assume that the changes are proportional to the cell activity (η). Thus the plasticity equations would read

$$d\mu_1/dt = \alpha(\xi_1 - \xi_2)\eta,$$
$$d\mu_2/dt = \alpha(\xi_2 - \xi_1)\eta.$$

(8.7)

If then one synapse is assumed to interact with many surrounding synapses, the average activity of the latter could be represented by an effective background value (ξ_b), and we then have

$$d\mu_i/dt = \alpha(\xi_i - \xi_b)\eta .\tag{8.8}$$

Here $\xi_i - \xi_b$ is the effective input signal which can be positive or negative; (8.8) is of the form that is needed in the correlation matrix models of memory, and some other adaptive functions, too.

A Comment on the State of the Receptors. As it might seem that the distribution of the postsynaptic receptors is not stable enough in order to serve as a basis of memory, two facts ought to be realized. One is that the memory traces in a linearly superpositive distributed memory, as discussed in Sect. 8.2 will change whenever new information is accumulated, and therefore there is no need for the distribution to be stationary. The second fact is that in general, receptor molecules seem to be fixated onto the membrane before they can be regarded as completely activated for chemical transmission. The rate of this kind of "consolidation" can now be assumed directly proportional to the number of free receptors attached to the membrane by electrical fields, whereby the distribution of the free receptors corresponds to a medium-term memory, and the fixated receptors to a long-term memory. This consolidation may be followed by a growth process in which the thickness of the membrane, or the shape of the spine is permanently altered [Ref. 8.10, pp. 326–327].

8.1.5 Can the Memory Capacity Ensue from Synaptic Changes?

There exist several parts in the nervous systems which exhibit memory effects. Consideration is here mainly restricted to the cerebral neocortex. It may be reasoned that, since this part is very pronounced in man who among all beings also has the greatest capability to memorize, the most important memory capacity, especially for the associations, is provided by the cerebral cortex. (Although some clinical studies have shown that the ability to memorize is very sensitive to lesions made in deeperlying parts of the brain, this effect can be explained by the fact that these parts have general importance in the control of attention.) The cerebral cortex is a pleated sheet about 2 to 3 mm thick and about two times 1000 cm^2 wide in man. There are a little more than 10^{10} neural cells in this tissue; the number of synapses, however, is a few thousands for every neuron on the average. If the neural memory capacity would ensue from the changes in the synapses, then there might be some 10^{13} to 10^{14} memory elements available in the cortex alone.

In all probability, the physiological memory relies on a large number of variable elements and a mechanism by which they can be made to change specifically in a great number of variations. If those elements are synapses, it then becomes possible to try to estimate the memory capacity thereby achievable.

Information Capacity of a Distributed Memory. The capacities of memories are often expressed in information-theoretical units of elementary choices, i.e., in bits. As a view is held throughout this work that the practical limit for stored information in adaptive distributed networks is set by the *selectivity* achieved in associative mappings, the conventional information-theoretical estimates of the memory capacity of the brain are considered neither pertinent nor reliable. Furthermore it is not believed that the memory elements, for instance the synapses, take on binary values but they represent more or less continuous-valued couplings, at least statistically. A more reliable estimate for the practicable capacity of memory then depends on the number of independent patterns that can be stored in it without crosstalk in recall.

The central question is whether it is possible to modify the synapses individually, or only in groups or pools. Even if the latter would be the case, it is plausible that the activated pools are different from one case to another, whereby the synaptic efficacies may be determined to a great extent individually.

In Chap. 4, models of neural networks were set up which in effect are distributed, linear adaptive systems. From the previous discussions it may be obvious that the memory capacity of a linear system must be estimated in terms of the number of linearly independent patterns that can be represented in it. It is now crucial, how the pattern elements are defined. Let us assume that a "column" about 100 μm wide is regarded as one pattern element, whereby it contains about 500 neurons. If it is now assumed that each neuron has on the average some 5000 (modifiable) synaptic inputs, there would be more than 10^6 inputs to such a "group", by which it can be encoded. This is then the parameter which roughly describes the number of linearly independent patterns, by which the "group" can selectively be controlled. In other words, in a piece of network which consists of "groups" of this kind, it is possible to superimpose over 10^6 patterns in distributed form.

How Much Memory Does a Human Being Need? The following analysis is based on an assumption that information is transferred into memory only under attentive concentration which accordingly fluctuates in time. At a high degree of attention, a great number of simultaneous or almost simultaneous signals, roughly corresponding to a pattern or a superpattern, are transferred into memory. If it were assumed that one sensory experience or other occurrence were stored every ten seconds on the average, a number which is apparently overestimated, there still would be no more than about 10^8 occurrences (or patterns) in the waking-state life of a human being to be stored.

The second important fact to notice is that signals of different sensory modalities (origin) use different cortical areas; if patterns caused by different experiences in general do not overlap very much, this means that one piece of the neural network needs a memory capacity which can be orders of magnitude smaller than the capacity of 10^8 patterns mentioned above. It will be pointed out below that there are yet other possibilities to lighten the burden of the neural memory.

Possibilities for Effective Utilization of the Memory Capacity. For explanation of the real capacity of biological memory, in particular the human memory, it seems necessary to incorporate further features in this model. If memory traces were collected from all the ongoing signals, a great deal of redundant information would be stored. The temporal differentiation of signals exerts an effect of improvement, since the most relevant information is usually associated with changes of state. It is known that neural systems enhance signal transients (phasic information); an equivalent effect is habituation, which in central systems may be of more complex nature than just a fatigue effect. An extremely selective type of habituation is exhibited by the novelty filter-type system which may be embodied in neural realms in the form discussed in Sect. 4.4.2.

The experimentally demonstrated fact that memory traces are fixed only under attentive concentration implies that the modifiability of the network depends upon its macrostate; this state, or the modifiability of the synapses, might correspond to the chemical state of the network or of the cells, controlled by activation systems. The gating of the neural signals or their memory effects can also be implemented by a known type of connections named presynaptic couplings where one synapse directly contacts another one. It seems possible that such a control, whatever its mechanism may be, can be exerted by the so-called arising reticular activation system existing in the brain stem [8.33]; [Ref. 8.2, pp. 436–448]. This control ensures that only those signals which are of importance to the organism are stored in this way.

One advantage of the linear memory is that, in a general way, it responds to certain classes of patterns. Linear combinations of the old input patterns need not be stored, since the memory has already learned them and the activation control system recognizes them as familiar. This ability to generalize may apply to many classes of stored patterns, with the result that a great deal of memory space is saved by this means.

Finally, emphasis is due that very probably primary signal patterns are not stored as such. A great deal of experimental evidence exists that cells or cell units have a fine structure which is specialized in the detection of various features. In the primary sensory areas, these may be very simple; rather complex triggering conditions, however, may be due in the associative areas. Some discrepancy exists in regard to the origin of these feature detectors; some researchers have claimed that they are formed genetically [8.33, 34], whereas other results relate to their post-natal formation in slow adaptive processes [8.20 – 22]. Whatever the truth may be, such detectors have a high selectivity to patterns, and thus effectively reduce the amount of nonspecific signal activity. It is quite possible that such detectors are modifiable, and that memory traces are predominantly left at the higher processing steps.

8.2 The Unified Cortical Memory Model

The previous parts of this book contained descriptions of many important separate functions. How do they all work together? How are structures of knowledge represented in the neural realms, and how does thinking utilize them? How are the recollections interpreted?

We are now trying to make a further attack to these problems. It has to be emphasized that most of the results presented before, e.g., the mathematical formalisms comprise irrefutable facts; contrasted with them, a unified explanation of the complete system behaviour of memory must be based on a view which is still somewhat subjective. It is quite possible that the organizational view of the brain could be outlined in alternative ways, using different kinds of building blocks and their formalized operations. Nonetheless, there are no details in the organizational model to be presented below which would be in contradiction with the present knowledge; the most that might be said is that some detailed structures may have been omitted from it.

8.2.1 The Laminar Network Organization

Histological analysis of the brain lends support to the idea that neurons are organized into horizontal sheets. This *laminar organization* is found in neocortex, allocortex, cerebellum, nuclei, and ganglia. (For an extensive collection of empirical results on different laminated structures, see [8.35].) Recent findings on these histological structures seem to point to a type of functional organization, whose overall behaviour might be approximately described by the mathematical apparatus reviewed earlier. The structure of neocortex is used in the following description as a prototype of all cortical laminated structures.

Although it is morphologically possible to distinguish several layers in the cortical lamina, physiological studies on the mammalian cortex have revealed, as stated above, that the responses are similar in all cells that are confined within vertical columnlike aggregates of cells extending over the depth of the

cortex [8.19]. It is generally accepted that such columns (or slabs) are organized around *specific afferent axons*, the input of which they seem to analyze.

Consider the two types of afferent input to the cortex, as illustrated in Fig.
8.9. The specific input is usually mediated through *stellate neurons*, which
then usually perform some feature-extraction operation. The different cortical areas, on the other hand, are densely interconnected internally as well as
mutually through the *association fibres* and *nonspecific axons* of the
pyramidal cells, which, after passing the white matter, ascend vertically making a very great number (hundreds, possibly thousands) of connections in its
target area upon passing the branches of apical dendrites [8.36]. The great
number of synaptic inputs to the cells may be explained by this fact. As the
structures of pyramidal cells are to a great extent intermingled, it further
seems that the ascending axons predominantly make connections with different cells.

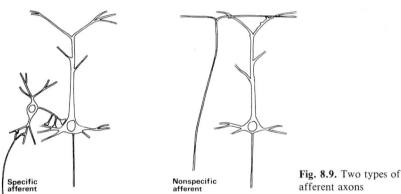

Specific afferent   **Nonspecific afferent**   **Fig. 8.9.** Two types of afferent axons

As every pyramidal cell has further axon collaterals that branch within the
cortex, one may distinguish between the following three types of horizontal
connectivity: 1) intracortical excitatory connections spreading to a distance up
to 100 µm; 2) intracortical inhibitory connections, usually mediated through
interneurons, which extend to a distance of 500 µm, and depend strongly on
distance; and 3) cortico-cortical excitatory connections that may extend over
any distance within the cortex. If the latter connections are made within the
same area, then connectivity is independent of distance.

It is now assumed that the connections of Type 3 carry out the interaction
between columns which is necessary for the implementation of the *autoassociative memory function*. This is assumed to operate within such an interconnected area, and probably also between cells belonging to different areas.
The integrated memory effects are mediated by the excitatory synapses at the

apical dendrites. The spatial spread of the apical dendrites and the axons terminating at top layers of the cortex ensures a high degree of connectivity.

On the other hand, connections of Types 1 and 2 seem to serve a different purpose. First of all, they are necessary for the implementation of the columnar organization. As already stated in Sect. 5.2, the "clustering" of activity, which is needed for self-organization of the neural representations, also ensues from these connections. It is not quite clear whether in most areas of the brain one should at all make a distinction between columns and "clusters". Let us briefly state that the short-range connections in some way or another implement the organization of neural representations.

8.2.2 On the Roles of Interneurons

Throughout the history of neuroanatomy and neurophysiology, there has been much speculation about the purpose of the polysynaptic circuits made by various *interneurons* in the central-nervous-system structures. Some investigators seem to be looking for complex computational operations while others see in them the basic implementation of feature detectors for sensory signals.

Lateral inhibition, due to the short-axon inhibitory (stellate) interneurons surrounding the pyramidal cells, seems to significantly enhance contrast in afferent signal patterns, as well as to increase mutual orthogonality between subsequent, statistically independent signal representations; this property warrants an improved selectivity in pattern recognition and memory operations (Sect. 6.5.1). There are, however, quite special circuits made by some curious cells, like the bipolar and chandelier cells in the cortex, for which a more detailed explanation would be desired.

The roles of the above-mentioned cells, as well as the characteristic ramification of axon collaterals of all cortical cell types would become quite obvious, if the purpose was to implement a neural network with a predominantly two-dimensional organization. The bipolar cells, the recurrent axon collaterals of various cells, and the general vertical texture of the cortex warrant a high degree of conductance and spreading of signal activity in any *vertical* penetration. On the other hand, if it were necessary to implement the "Mexican-hat function" type of lateral interaction (Sect. 5.2), then the short-axon excitatory and inhibitory interneurons, the intracortical axon collaterals of the pyramidal cells, and all the dendritic processes would account for such a lateral coupling. It seems probable that such lateral couplings then greatly contribute to *self-organization*.

Every type of interneuron has a characteristic interaction width; it might even be stated that *the fraction of a certain cell type in the composition of all neurons is a tuning parameter by which an optimal form of local interaction can be defined.* The specific structures in the branchings of a particular cell type may roughly serve a similar purpose as what the different basis functions have in mathematical functional expansions. This view would also explain why all cell types are not present in different species, or even in different parts of the brain: for some purpose it may be sufficient to "tune" a certain form of interaction with fewer types of cell (basis functions), while for more exacting tasks a richer variety of cells would be needed. Such a recruitment of new forms is in complete agreement with the general principles of evolution.

Although all that was said above fits well with a two-dimensional view of the brain structures, stratification of cells in various lamina in the vertical direction may have a further purpose not much different from what was said above; a certain degree of vertical ordering of the cells could correspond to an elementary self-organization in the third dimension, i.e., along with the depth coordinate.

8.2.3 Representation of Knowledge Over Memory Fields

For each area of the brain that contains memory we shall now use an idealized description that we henceforth call a *memory field*. In its simplest form a memory field corresponds to a layer of functional units (cells or tightly connected agglomerates of cells such as columns) that have a great number of mutual connections, assumed to be distributed uniformly over the field. The memory field is in the following represented by its *top view*.

There is sensory or other primary input to every element in this field. Each specific afferent axon brings to the memory fields, to volumes roughly corresponding to that of a column, a signal activity which represents a particular feature or other value that has resulted in the place where this axon came from. However, there also exists ample evidence for a conception that many areas of the brain are in themselves able to process information, thereby producing *feature maps* of the type described in Chap. 5. In order to make this possible, it is only necessary to assume that the inputs to the cortex are made through adaptive connections which are varied in a self-organizing process as described earlier. Such input connections need not be made with a similar spatial accuracy as that of the specific axons; on the contrary, it would be even more favourable if these inputs were scattered diffusely over the memory field. In fact, the nonspecific afferent axons are known to exist in abundance; the projections from other cortical areas (i.e., the cortico-cortical connections that are made directly) reaching from a few millimeters to centimeters, constitute them. Also the contralateral projections that come from the opposite hemisphere of the brain through the thick tract called *corpus callosum* are of this type.

There is, in principle, neither very much difference between the roles of the nonspecific connections assumed to organize the feature maps, and the association fibres which are thought to be responsible for distributed autoassociative memory. One might say that there are plastic changes in the cortex with different time constants, and the feature maps are probably formed in slower processes which last over weeks or even years; on the other hand, the autoassociatively encoded memory traces have to be formed promptly, eventually in a single exposure to the exciting pattern. It is thereby necessary that the degree of plasticity of the neural connections can temporarily be made very high, modulated, e.g., by a high level of noradrenergic (NE) neural input (Sect. 8.2.4; "now print!").

Representation of Relations. In the unified view, it is thus possible to assume that within a memory field certain local areas, which we schematically distinguish by circular regions in Fig. 8.10, have a well-defined modality and meaning. *A region with a dimension of a few millimeters is now identified with an attribute, and the spatial cluster of activity within the region represents the value of that attribute.*

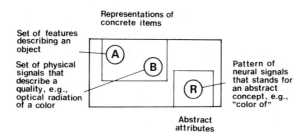

Fig. 8.10. Representation of relations over the memory field

There are good experimentally verified reasons to assume that for a particular sensory experience or other occurrence the pattern of activity over the complete memory field consists of only a few activated local areas (attributes) whereas the rest of the elements in the field are silent, having signal value corresponding to background activity (or rather, being regarded as signalless). This theory of representation now makes it possible to compare the memory field model directly with an abstract *relational representation.*

A *relation* has earlier been defined as an ordered set of concomitant attribute values. There are no restrictions for an arbitrary number of attributes making a sensory experience; the attentive control, however, seems to restrict the conscious part of observation to a few distinct items at a time. The *rela-*

tional triples (Sect. 1.4.5) represent the simplest sets of items from which structures of knowledge can be constructed. Such representations have originally been introduced for *artificial data bases,* especially for the implementation of *query languages* which form only a very restricted part of all information processing. It is possible to question the generality of this formalism in the description of brain functioning. We feel that linguistic expressions in general have an extremely high degree of coding based on conventions and implicit assumptions, like the meaning associated with syntactic rules; in natural languages, this is accentuated by assignment of a particular meaning to prefixing, suffixing, and other formats. Expressions like *(R, A, B)* only *look* simple; in fact treatment of their deep semantic meaning in the brain might need complicated processing, probably augmenting the representation of the arguments by contextual information that indicates their role. However, since there are researchers who think that the formal types of relational structures should be representable even by the simplest biological memory models, we shall now try to demonstrate, how this could be possible. Thereby it must be clearly understood that this case is meant for illustrative purposes only, and probably does not occur as such in the brains.

Assume for simplicity that there are only three active local areas as in Fig. 8.10, labeled *A, R,* and *B.* The signals at *A* and *B* may stand for features that make up the representations of two items, for example, one being the representation of an object and the other some concrete physical observation, whereas the region for *R* might contain neural signals that respond to some *class* of representations; accordingly, these signals then stand for, e.g., an abstract, relational attribute. Notice that the memory field model would allow an arbitrary number of such attributes to be present on one occurrence. If *A, B,* and *R* are regarded as symbolic (distinct) *items,* then *(R, A, B)* is a *relational triple:* For example, *R* = colour of; *A* = an apple; *B* = is red; *(R, A, B)* = colour of an apple is red. Assume that an arbitrary number of such triples have been stored in the laminar memory network, as representations over the memory field, whereby the memory traces have been left in the lateral connections.

It is frequently stipulated that genuine models of memory should be able to automatically generate answers to complex queries, or to perform searches for pieces of memorized information that are only implicitly defined by their relational structure. Because the associative mappings have the ability of representing and retrieving patterned information that may also be clustered in "attribute maps", it would be interesting to develop these models in a direction in which they too could be made to search for implicitly defined memorized information on the basis of separately given cues. Contrary to what is generally believed, such processes are implementable by rather simple mechanisms. It is even possible to demonstrate some elementary forms of thinking and problem-solving processes, although we are still a long way from implementing real thought processes.

It is relatively easy to understand how missing parts (items) in relations are recalled. If, for instance, the incident activation of the memory field would correspond to a pattern of the type $(R, A, \emptyset)$, where $\emptyset$ stands for initially passive signals, then this incomplete pattern acts as a key for an autoassociative memory, and the latter reconstructs the missing portion B.

It seems that a search task in which the target item is specified only implicitly must be performed by *multiple queries* that are *separated in time*. Thus, although the memory network from which associative recall is possible is distributed, and the operations in it are fully parallel, nonetheless there must exist a phase in the operation in which intermediate results are temporarily stored, e.g., as subliminal activity (which does not exceed the triggering threshold). Such retention of signals with a duration of, say, several seconds is easily implemented by any kind of local aftereffects (short-term memory, STM) in the network. For the outputs to become active, it will then be necessary to activate the network by several key patterns in close succession, the effects of which are *temporally integrated* as illustrated by the following simple example.

An Example of a Searching Process. Consider the data structure shown in Fig. 8.11, which results when a number of relational triples (A, P, B), (A, Q, C), etc., have been stored. The middle elements always comprise the link labels, and the two others the associated items. Notice that the structure is completely implicit. Assume that item C had to be retrieved on the basis of two incomplete search patterns (A, Q, X) and (E, R, X), with X unknown. The normal search procedure by computer programs would first determine the set of solutions for X for each search pattern separately, and then find the value $X = C$ as the intersection of these two sets.

Let us now study how the same task would be solved by distributed memory. Assume that the triples have been stored as patterns of activity as shown

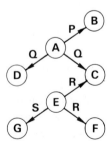

Fig. 8.11. Data structure for the search example

in Fig. 8.12a. Assume that two cues, two incomplete key patterns, are given as shown in Fig. 8.12b and c. If either of these were separately applied as inputs to an autoassociative memory network, the responses from the latter would remain subliminal (Fig. 8.12d, e). If, on the other hand, the two key patterns were applied one after the other with a delay that is less than the integrating time constant of the STM, then the component pattern *C* would be recalled with approximately double the intensity of the other components, and it would therefore be able to exceed the threshold. Figure 8.12f displays only the above-threshold signals that now constitute the solution of the search task.

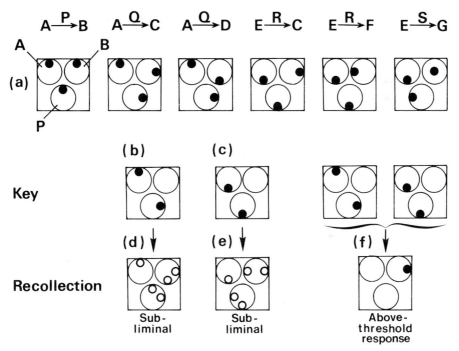

Fig. 8.12a – f. Search example. **(a)** Six stored triples, represented as patterns over the memory field. **(b, c)** Key patterns. **(d – f)** Recollections (see text)

8.2.4 Self-Controlled Operation of Memory

It was proposed in the laminar memory model that information is processed in interconnected cortical areas. This type of organization emphasizes the fact that each area may have inputs from different processing levels or from different auxiliary areas. Although it is possible to have a hierarchy of processing levels between certain parts of the brain, the areas may as well have a more parallel organization in which the various subareas are laterally interconnected like the tree-formed maps of Sect. 5.6, resulting from self-organization.

The digital computing devices are built of chips containing only logic gates. Similarly we can imagine an *associative processor*, consisting of many distributed memory units interconnected by bundles of signal lines over which they pass key patterns and recollections to each other. If the system had closed signal circuits, this passing and transformation of information would proceed recurrently or iteratively, whereby the operation of the *total* system resembles that of automata.

Unlike digital computers, distributed memory systems do not need a highly sophisticated control that opens and closes every signal path in a programmed sequence. If any gating of signal paths exists, it can be of a more general nature. Such a control, corresponding to the state of arousal or attention, is exerted by the ARAS, or ascending reticular activation system, located in the brain stem. It has been empirically shown [8.37] that the consolidation of memory traces is affected by the activity of ARAS. It thus has the effect of increasing the selectivity and optimizing the resources of the information-processing units by suppressing some activities and enhancing others. This also implies that the plasticity of the network depends on its chemical state or on some other global property.

8.2.5 A Note on the "Connectionistic" View

The semantic network paradigm (cf. Sect. 1.1.3) used for the description of linguistic meaning has sometimes given a reason for a rather primitive view of the brain network. Although hardly anyone nowadays believes in a simple "switchboard" organization of the neural system, the brain network has been thought to contain representations and circuits termed "connectionistic". It is thereby assumed that some cells directly represent items, abstract attributes, etc., and these might be identified with the *nodes* of a semantic networks. "Associations" would in this view correspond to direct links between nodes. Obviously this model represents an extreme case in which every single element of the memory field has a semantic interpretation. This is a standpoint adopted by some earlier psychological models of memory [8.38]. Not only must the signals corresponding to every sensory experience then be guided to the nodes with perfect spatial resolution and selectivity, but one must also assume that the location of such a node was determined from the beginning, independently of any sensory experiences.

We may here refer to *Simon* [8.39]: "Nothing in contemporary information-processing theories of memory requires that memories be specifically localized; and nothing in those theories is incompatible with a distributed or even holographic theory of physiological basis for memory." In fact, in information processing by a laminar network, operations are performed by a "hazy connectionistic network" in which the local areas corresponded to nodes, and their interactions are mediated through the adaptive lateral connections.

The possibility of constructing spatial maps for attributes and features by self-organization further settles the question of *how symbolic representations for concepts could be formed automatically*; most of the models of automatic problem solving and representation of knowledge by connectionistic models have simply skipped this question.

8.3 Collateral Reading

The present section contains some references in addition to those mentioned elsewhere in this book. The list is strictly meant for providing background information to the approaches made above, whereas it is not aimed at a survey of biocybernetical modelling, brain research, or artificial intelligence. For one thing, the field seems too incoherent for any exhaustive review. It may be more expedient to concentrate on some relatively recent lines of research that are comparable with the contents of this book, and which contain different aspects of the same topics.

8.3.1 Physiological Results Relevant to Modelling

A comprehensive introduction to the neurophysiological foundations is given by the book of *Kuffler* and *Nicholls* [8.40]. Various aspects of the cortical architectonics have been presented by *Brazier* and *Petsche* [8.41]. Memory mechanisms have been reviewed by *Brazier* [8.42], as well as *Rosenzweig* and *Bennett* [8.43]. A comprehensive book on neuronal plasticity has been published by *Cotman* [8.44]. The following papers give more information on cortical structures: *Braitenberg* [8.45], *Cowey* [8.46], *Goldman* and *Nauta* [8.47], *Imig* and *Reale* [8.48]. Experiments dealing with synaptic plasticity have been reported by *Bliss* [8.49], *Changeux* and *Danchin* [8.50], *Lømo* [8.51], *Robbins* [8.52], *Ryall* [8.53], *Shagal* [8.54], and *Thesleff* and *Sellin* [8.55]. The September 1979 issue of Scientific American also gives an illustrative view of brain research.

8.3.2 Related Modelling

Models dealing with conjunction learning have been published by *Amari* [8.56], *Anderson* [8.57], *Cooper* [8.58], *Gilbert* [8.59, 60], *Grossberg* [8.61], *Kohonen* et al. [8.62, 67], *Longuet-Higgins* et al. [8.68], *Marr* [8.69], *Nakano* and *Nagumo* [8.70], *Palm* [8.71, 72] as well as *Willshaw* et al. [8.73].

The effect of recurrent feedback connections has been discussed by *Fukushima* [8.74], *Wigström* [8.75, 76], *Willwacher* [8.77], as well as *Barto* et al. [8.78].

Formation of feature-sensitive cells has been analyzed by *Cooper* et al. [8.79], *Fukushima* [8.80], *Grossberg* [8.81], *Malsburg* [8.82] as well as *Nass* and *Cooper* [8.83].

Recent works on self-organization have been reported in the book of *Amari* and *Arbib* [8.84]. Various aspects of associative memory can be found in the book of *Hinton* and *Anderson* [8.85].

Bibliography on Pattern Recognition

Arkadew, A.G., Braverman, E.M.: *Learning in Pattern Classification Machines* (Nauka, Moscow 1971)

Becker, P.W.: *Recognition of Patterns* (Polyteknisk Forlag, Copenhagen 1968)

Becker, P.W.: *An Introduction to the Design of Pattern Recognition Devices* (Springer, Wien, New York 1972)

Bongard, N.: *Pattern Recognition* (Spartan-Macmillan, New York 1970)

Braddick, O.J., Sleigh, A.C. (eds.): *Physical and Biological Processing of Images* (Springer, Berlin, Heidelberg, New York 1983)

Braverman, E.M. (ed.): *Automatic Analysis of Complex Images* (MIR, Moscow 1969)

Chang, S.K., Fu, K.S. (eds.): *Pictorial Information Systems*, Lecture Notes Computer Sci., Vol.80 (Springer, Berlin, Heidelberg, New York 1980)

Chen, C.H.: *Statistical Pattern Recognition* (Hayden, Washington, DC 1973)

Chen, C.H. (ed.): *Pattern Recognition and Artificial Intelligence* (Academic, New York 1976)

Cheng, G.C., Ledley, R.S., Pollock, D.K., Rosenfeld, A.: *Pictorial Pattern Recognition* (Thompson, Washington, DC 1968)

Corcoran, D.W.J.: *Pattern Recognition* (Penguin, Aylesbury, Bucks 1971)

Devijver, P.A., Kittler, J.: *Pattern Recognition: A Statistical Approach* (Prentice-Hall, London 1982)

Duda, R.O., Hart. P.E.: *Pattern Classification and Scene Analysis* (Wiley, New York 1973)

Flanagan, J.L.: *Speech Analysis, Synthesis and Perception* (Springer, Berlin, Heidelberg, New York 1965)

Fu, K.S.: *Sequential Methods in Pattern Recognition and Machine Learning* (Academic, New York 1968)

Fu, K.S.: *Pattern Recognition and Machine Learning* (Plenum, New York 1971)

Fu, K.S.: *Syntactic Methods in Pattern Recognition* (Academic, New York 1974)

Fu, K.S. (ed.): *Digital Pattern Recognition* (Springer, Berlin, Heidelberg, New York 1976)

Fu, K.S. (ed.): *Syntactic Pattern Recognition, Applications* (Springer, Berlin, Heidelberg, New York 1977)

Fu, K.S., Whinston, A.B. (eds.): *Pattern Recognition – Theory and Application* (Noordhoff, Leyden, The Netherlands 1977)

Fu, K.S., Ichikawa, T: *Special Computer Architectures for Pattern Processing* (CRC Press, Boca Raton, FL 1982)

Fu, K.S., Kunii, T.L. (eds.): *Picture Engineering*, Springer Ser. Inform. Sci., Vol.6 (Springer, Berlin, Heidelberg, New York 1982)

Fukunaga, K.: *Introduction to Statistical Pattern Recognition* (Academic, New York 1972)

Grenander, U.: *Pattern Synthesis*, Lectures in Pattern Theory, Vol.1 (Springer, Berlin, Heidelberg, New York 1976)

Grenander, U: *Pattern Analysis*, Lectures in Pattern Theory, Vol.2 (Springer, Berlin, Heidelberg, New York 1978)

Grimson, W.E.L.: *From Images to Surfaces: A Computational Study of the Human Early Visual System* (MIT Press, Cambridge, MA 1981)

Haken, H. (ed.): *Pattern Formation by Dynamic Systems and Pattern Recognition*, Springer Ser. Synergetics, Vol.5 (Springer, Berlin, Heidelberg, New York 1979)

Hall, E.: *Computer Image Processing and Recognition* (Academic, New York 1979)

Hanson, A.R., Riseman, E.M.: *Computer Vision Systems* (Academic, New York 1978)

Huang, T.S. (ed.): *Picture Processing and Digital Filtering*, Topics Appl. Phys., Vol.6 (Springer, Berlin, Heidelberg, New York 1975)

Huang, T.S. (ed.): *Image Sequence Analysis*, Springer Ser. Inform. Sci., Vol.5
    (Springer, Berlin, Heidelberg, New York 1981)
Kanal, L.N. (ed.): *Pattern Recognition* (Thompson, Washington, DC 1968)
Klinger, A., Fu, K.S., Kunii, T.L. (eds.): *Data Structures, Computer Graphics,
    and Pattern Recognition* (Academic, New York 1977)
Kolers, P.A., Eden, M. (eds.): *Recognizing Patterns, Studies in Living and
    Automatic Systems* (MIT Press, Cambridge, MA 1968)
Kovalevsky, V.A.: *Character Readers and Pattern Recognition* (Spartan Books,
    Rochelle Park, NY 1968)
Kovalevsky, V.A.: *Image Pattern Recognition* (Springer, Berlin, Heidelberg, New
    York 1980)
Lipkin, B.S., Rosenfeld, A. (eds.): *Picture Processing and Psychopictorics*
    (Academic, New York 1970)
Marr, D.: *Vision* (Freeman, San Francisco 1982)
Meisel, W.S.: *Computer-Oriented Approaches to Pattern Recognition* (Academic,
    New York 1972)
Mendel, J.M., Fu, K.S.: *Adaptive, Learning, and Pattern Recognition Systems:
    Theory and Applications* (Academic, New York 1970)
Minsky, M., Papert, S.: *Perceptrons* (MIT Press, Cambridge, MA 1969)
Niemann, H.: *Methoden der Mustererkennung* (Akademische Verlagsgesellschaft,
    Frankfurt 1974)
Niemann, H.: *Pattern Analysis*, Springer Ser. Inform. Sci., Vol.4 (Springer,
    Berlin, Heidelberg, New York 1981)
Palgen, J.J.: *International Bibliography of Pictorial Pattern Recognition* (Allied
    Research Ass., Concord, MA 1970)
Patrick, E.A.: *Fundamentals of Pattern Recognition* (Prentice-Hall, Englewood
    Cliffs, NJ 1972)
Pavlidis, T.: *Structural Pattern Recognition*, Springer Ser. Electrophys., Vol.1
    (Springer, Berlin, Heidelberg, New York 1977)
Pratt, W.: *Digital Image Processing* (Wiley, New York 1978)
Rosenfeld, A.: *Picture Processing by Computer* (Academic, New York 1968)
Rosenfeld, A. (ed.): *Digital Picture Analysis*, Topics Appl. Phys., Vol.11
    (Springer, Berlin, Heidelberg, New York 1976)
Rosenfeld, A., Kak, A.C.: *Digital Picture Processing* (Academic, New York 1976)
Sayre, K.M.: *Recognition: A Study in the Philosophy of Artificial Intelligence*
    (University of Notre Dame Press, Notre Dame, IN 1965)
Sebestyen, G.S.: *Decision Making Processes in Pattern Recognition* (Macmillan,
    New York 1962)
Stucki, P. (ed.): *Advances in Digital Image Processing* (Plenum, New York 1979)
Tou, J.T., Gonzalez, R.C.: *Pattern Recognition Principles* (Addison-Wesley,
    Reading, MA 1974)
Turbovich, I.T., Gitis, V.G., Marlov, V.K.: *Pattern Identification* (Nauka,
    Moscow 1971)
Tzemel, G.I.: *Identification of Speech Signals* (Nauka, Moscow 1971)
Uhr, L. (ed.): *Pattern Recognition: Theory, Experiment, Computer Simulations,
    and Dynamic Models of Form Perception and Discovery* (Wiley, New York 1966)
Uhr, L.: *Pattern Recognition, Learning, and Thought* (Prentice-Hall, Englewood
    Cliffs, NJ 1973)
Ullman, J.R.: *Pattern Recognition Techniques* (Butterworth, London 1973)
Ullman, S.: *The Interpretation of Visual Motion* (MIT Press, Cambridge, MA 1979)
Watanabe, S.: *Knowing and Guessing* (Wiley, New York 1969)
Watanabe, S. (ed.): *Methodologies of Pattern Recognition* (Academic, New York
    1969)
Watanabe, S. (ed.): *Frontiers of Pattern Recognition* (Academic, New York 1972)
Wathen-Dunn, W. (ed.): *Models for the Perception of Speech and Visual Forms*
    (MIT Press, Cambridge, MA 1967)
Winston, P.H. (ed.): *The Psychology of Computer Vision* (McGraw-Hill, New York 1975)
Young, T.Y., Calvert, T.W.: *Classification, Estimation, and Pattern Recognition*
    (Elsevier, New York 1974)
Zagoruyko, N.G., Zasgovskaya, T.I.: *Pattern Recognition in Social Studies*
    (Nauka, Novosibirsk 1968)
Zagoruyko, N.G.: *Recognition Methods and Their Application* (Radio Sovetskoe,
    Moscow 1972)

References

Chapter 1

1.1 R. Sorabji: *Aristotle on Memory* (Brown University Press, Providence, RI 1972)
1.2 M.R. Quillian: Semantic Memory, in *Semantic Information Processing*, ed. by M. Minsky (MIT Press, Cambridge, MA 1968)
1.3 T. Kohonen, P. Lehtiö, J. Rovamo, J. Hyvärinen, K. Bry, L. Vainio: Neuroscience **2**, 1065 (1977)
1.4 T. Kohonen: *Content-Addressable Memories*, Springer Ser. Inform. Sci., Vol.1 (Springer, Berlin, Heidelberg, New York 1980)
1.5 M.L. Minsky: *Computation: Finite and Infinite Machines* (Prentice-Hall, Englewood Cliffs, NJ 1967)
1.6 T. Pavlidis: *Structural Pattern Recognition*, Springer Ser. Electrophys., Vol.1 (Springer, Berlin, Heidelberg, New York 1977)
1.7 A. Newell, H.A. Simon: Computers in Psychology, in *Handbook of Mathematical Psychology, Vol.I*, ed. by R.D. Luce, R.R. Bush, E. Galanter (Wiley, New York 1963) p.361
1.8 T. Kohonen: *Introduction of the Principle of Virtual Images in Associative Memories*, Acta Polytech. Scand. Electr. Eng. Ser. El 29 (1971)
1.9 T. Kohonen: Int. J. Neurosci. **5**, 27 (1973)
1.10 H.A. Simon, A. Newell: Information-Processing in Computer and Man, in *Perspectives on the Computer Revolution*, ed. by Z.W. Pylyshyn (Prentice-Hall, Englewood Cliffs, NJ 1970) p.266
1.11 D.A. Savitt, H.H. Love, Jr., R.E. Troop: In *1967 Spring Joint Computer Conf.*, *AFIPS Conf. Proc.* (AFIPS Press, Montvale 1967) p.87
1.12 J.A. Feldman, P.D. Rovner: Commun. ACM **12**, 439 (1969)

Chapter 2

2.1 A. Albert: *Regression and the Moore-Penrose Pseudoinverse* (Academic, New York 1972)
2.2 J.E. Mayer, M. Goeppert-Mayer: *Statistical Mechanics* (Wiley, New York 1940)
2.3 T. Kohonen, E. Reuhkala, K. Mäkisara, L. Vainio: Biol. Cyb. **22**, 159 (1976)
2.4 R. Penrose: Proc. Cambridge Philos. Soc. **51**, 406 (1955)
2.5 R. Penrose: Proc. Cambridge Philos. Soc. **52**, 17 (1956)
2.6 A. Ben-Israel, T.N.E. Greville: *Generalized Inverses: Theory and Applications* (Wiley, New York 1974)
2.7 T.L. Boullion, P.L. Odell: *Generalized Inverse Matrices* (Wiley, New York 1971)
2.8 C.R. Rao, S.K. Mitra: *Generalized Inverse of Matrices and Its Applications* (Wiley, New York 1971)
2.9 T.N.E. Greville: SIAM Rev. **2**, 15 (1960)
2.10 R.E. Cline: SIAM J. Appl. Math. **12**, 588 (1964)
2.11 T. Kohonen: IEEE Trans. C-**23**, 444 (1974)
2.12 D.J. Rogers, T.T. Tanimoto: Science **132** (1960)
2.13 L. Ornstein: J. M. Sinai Hosp. **32**, 437 (1965)
2.14 K. Sparck-Jones: *Automatic Keyword Classification and Information Retrieval* (Butterworth, London 1971)
2.15 J. Minker, E. Peltola, G.A. Wilson: Tech. Report 201, University of Maryland, Computer Science Center (1972)
2.16 J.S. Liénard, M. Mlouka, J.J. Mariani, J. Sapaly: Real-Time Segmentation of Speech, in *Preprints of the Speech Communication Seminar*, Vol.3 (Almqvist & Wiksell, Uppsala 1975) p.183

2.17 T. Tanimoto: *An Elementary Mathematical Theory of Classification and Prediction* (Int. Rpt. of IBM Corp. 1958)
2.18 J. Lukasiewicz: Ruch Filos. **5**, 169 (1920)
2.19 E.L. Post: Am. J. Math. **43**, 163 (1921)
2.20 L.A. Zadeh: IEEE Trans. SMC-**3**, 28 (1973)
2.21 R.W. Hamming: Bell Syst. Tech. J. **29**, 147 (1950)
2.22 V.M. Velichko, N.G. Zagoruyko: Int. J. Man Mach. Stud. **2**, 223 (1970)
2.23 V.I. Levenshtein: Sov. Phys. Dokl. **10**, 707 (1966)
2.24 T. Okuda, E. Tanaka, T. Kasai: IEEE Trans. C-**25**, 172 (1976)

Chapter 3

3.1 R.E. Kalman: *Fundamental Study of Adaptive Control Systems* (ASTIA AD 8 28 73, 1962)
3.2 B. Widrow: Generalization and Information Storage in Networks of Adaline Neurons, in *Self-Organizing Systems 1962*, ed. by M.C. Yovits, G.T. Jacobi, G.D. Goldstein (Spartan Books, Washington, DC 1962) p.435
3.3 A.E. Albert, L.A. Gardner, Jr.: *Stochastic Approximation and Nonlinear Regression* (MIT Press, Cambridge, MA 1967)
3.4 L. Schmetterer: Multidimensional Stochastic Approximation, in *Multivariate Analysis II*, ed. by P.R. Krishnaiah (Academic, New York 1969) p.443
3.5 Ya.Z. Tsypkin: *Adaptation and Learning in Control Systems* (Academic, New York 1971)
3.6 Ya.Z. Tsypkin: *Foundations of the Theory of Learning Systems* (Academic, New York 1973)
3.7 F. Rosenblatt: *Principles of Neurodynamics: Perceptrons and the Theory of Brain Mechanisms* (Spartan Books, Washington, DC 1961)
3.8 N.J. Nilsson: *Learning Machines* (McGraw-Hill, New York 1965)
3.9 K. Steinbuch, U.A.W. Piske: IEEE Trans. EC-**12**, 846 (1963)
3.10 K. Steinbuch: *Automat und Mensch* (Springer, Berlin, Heidelberg, New York 1963)
3.11 D.J. Willshaw, O.P. Buneman, H.C. Longuet-Higgins: Nature **222**, 960 (1969)
3.12 T. Kohonen: IEEE Trans. C-**21**, 353 (1972)
3.13 A.M. Uttley: Conditional Probability Computing in a Nervous System, in *Mechanization of Thought Processes* (H.M. Stationery Office, London 1950)
3.14 E.R. Caianiello: J. Theor. Biol. **2**, 204 (1961)
3.15 H.M. Smith (ed.): *Holographic Recording Materials*, Topics Appl. Phys., Vol.20 (Springer, Berlin, Heidelberg, New York 1977) Chap.1
3.16 G.W. Stroke: *An Introduction to Coherent Optics and Holography* (Academic, New York 1966)
3.17 J.C. Dainty (ed.): *Laser Speckle and Related Phenomena*, Topics Appl. Phys., Vol.9, 2nd ed. (Springer, Berlin, Heidelberg, New York, Tokyo 1984)
3.18 W. Kulcke, K. Kosanke, E. Max, M.A. Habegger, T.J. Harris, H. Fleischer: Proc. IEEE **54**, 1419 (1966)
3.19 H. Kogelnik: Microwaves **6**, 68 (1967)
3.20 D.R. Bosomworth, H.J. Gerritsen: Appl. Opt. **7**, 95 (1968)
3.21 M. Sakaguchi, N. Nishida: U.S. Patent No.3,704.929 (1970, Pat.1972)
3.22 G.R. Knight: Appl. Opt. **13**, 904 (1974)
3.23 P.P. Sorokin: IBM J. Res. Dev. **8**, 182 (1964)
3.24 M. Sakaguchi, N. Nishida, T. Nemoto: IEEE Trans. C-**19**, 1174 (1970)
3.25 G.R. Knight: Appl. Opt. **14**, 1088 (1975)

Chapter 4

4.1 W.E. Reichardt, T. Poggio (eds.): *Theoretical Approaches in Neurobiology* (MIT Press, Cambridge, MA 1981)
4.2 S. Geman: SIAM J. Appl. Math. **36**, 86 (1979)
4.3 E. Oja: J. Math. Biol. **15**, 267 (1982)
4.4 T. Kohonen, E. Oja, M. Ruohonen: *Adaptation of a Linear System to a Finite Set of Patterns Occurring in an Arbitrarily Varying Order*, Acta Polytech. Scand. Math. Computer Sci. Ser. 25 (1974)
4.5 E. Oja: IEEE TC-**27**, 65 (1979)
4.6 T. Kohonen: *A Class of Randomly Organized Associative Memories*, Acta Polytech. Scand. Electr. Eng. Ser. 25 (1971)

4.7   T. Kohonen: IEEE Trans. C-**21**, 353 (1972)
4.8   J.A. Anderson, J.W. Silverstein, S.A. Ritz, R.S. Jones: Psych. Rev. **84**, 413 (1977)
4.9   W.T. Reid: *Riccati Differential Equations* (Academic, New York 1972)
4.10 J.K. Hale: *Ordinary Differential Equations* (Wiley, New York 1969)
4.11 D.K. Faddeev, V.N. Faddeeva: *Computational Methods of Linear Algebra* (Freeman, San Francisco 1963)
4.12 T. Kohonen, E. Oja: Biol. Cyb. **21**, 85 (1976)
4.13 E. Oja: Int. J. Syst. Sci. **8**, 1145 (1977)

Chapter 5

5.1   R.M. Sperry: Proc. Natl. Acad. Sci. USA **50**, 701 (1963)
5.2   R.M. Gaze, M.J. Keating: Nature **237**, 375 (1972)
5.3   R.A. Hope, B.J. Hammond, F.R.S. Gaze: Proc. Roy. Soc. London **194**, 447 (1976)
5.4   D.S. Olton: Scientific American **236**, 82 (1977)
5.5   R.K. Hunt, N. Berman: J. Comp. Neurol. **162**, 43 (1975)
5.6   G.E. Schneider: In *Neurosurgical Treatment in Psychiatry, Pain and Epilepsy*, ed. by W.H. Sweet, S. Abrador, J.G. Martin-Rodriquez (University Park Press, Baltimore 1977)
5.7   S.C. Sharma: Exp. Neurol. **34**, 171 (1972)
5.8   S. Amari: Bull. Math. Biol. **42**, 339 (1980)
5.9   C. v. d. Malsburg, D. Willshaw: Proc. Natl. Acad. Sci. USA **74**, 5176 (1977)
5.10 N.V. Swindale: Proc. Roy. S o. Edinburgh Sect. B**208**, 243 (1980)
5.11 D.J. Willshaw, C. v. d. Malsburg: Philos. Trans. Roy. Soc. London Ser. B**287**, 203 (1979)
5.12 T. Kohonen: In *Proc. 2nd Scand. Conf. on Image Analysis*, ed. by E. Oja, O. Simula (Suomen Hahmontunnistustutkimuksen Seura, Otaniemi, Finland 1981) p.214
5.13 T. Kohonen: In *Proc. Italian IAPR Intern. Workshop on Cybernetic Systems* (Salerno 1981) (in press)
5.14 T. Kohonen: In *Competition and Cooperation in Neural Nets*, ed. by S. Amari, M.A. Arbib, Lecture Notes in Biomath., Vol.45 (Springer, Berlin, Heidelberg, New York 1982)
5.15 T. Kohonen: Biol. Cyb. **43**, 59 (1982)
5.16 T. Kohonen: Biol. Cyb. **44**, 135 (1982)
5.17 T. Kohonen: In *Proc. of the 6th Int. Conf. on Pattern Recognition*, ed. by M. Lang (IEEE Computer Society Press, Silver Spring, MD 1982) p.114
5.18 D.W. DeMott: Med. Res. Eng. **5**, 23 (1966)
5.19 T. Kohonen, H. Riittinen, M. Jalanko, E. Reuhkala, S. Haltsonen: In *Proc. of the 5th Int. Conf. on Pattern Recognition*, ed. by R. Bajcsy (IEEE Computer Society, Los Alamitos, CA 1980) p.158
5.20 U. Grenander: Private communication (1981)
5.21 S. Orey: *Limit Theorems for Markov Chain Transition Probabilities* (Van Nostrand, London 1971)
5.22 A.E. Albert, L.A. Gardner, Jr.: *Stochastic Approximation and Nonlinear Regression* (MIT Press, Cambridge, MA 1967)
5.23 S. Geman: SIAM J. Appl. Math. **36**, 86 (1979)

Chapter 6

6.1   T. Kohonen, E. Reuhkala, K. Mäkisara, L. Vainio: Biol. Cyb. **22**, 159 (1976)
6.2   E. Riihimäki, L.-E. Häll, T. Kohonen, P. Eistola, E. Tähti: Application of Computerized Pattern Recognition Technique to Identification of Abnormal Brain Images, in *IV Intern. Symp. Nuclear Medicine, May 20-23, 1975*, Karlovy Vary, Czechoslovakia
6.3   T. Poggio: Biol. Cyb. **19**, 201 (1975)
6.4   H. Riittinen: M. Sc. Thesis, Helsinki University of Technology (1976)
6.5   T.O. Lewis, P.L. Odell: *Estimation in Linear Models* (Prentice-Hall, Englewood Cliffs, NJ 1971)
6.6   L. Pyle: J. ACM **11**, 422 (1964)
6.7   E. Oja: Lic. Tech. Thesis, Helsinki University of Technology (1975)
6.8   C.R. Rao, S.K. Mitra: *Generalized Inverse of Matrices and Its Applications* (Wiley, New York 1971)

Chapter 7

7.1 T.Y. Young, T.W. Calvert: *Classification, Estimation, and Pattern Recognition* (Elsevier, New York 1974)

7.2 T. Pavlidis: *Structural Pattern Recognition*, Springer Ser. Electrophys., Vol.1 (Springer, Berlin, Heidelberg, New York 1977)

7.3 T. Kohonen, G. Németh, K.-J. Bry, M. Jalanko, H. Riittinen: In *Proc. 1979 IEEE ICASSP*, ed. by R.C. Olson (IEEE, Piscataway, NJ 1979) p.97

7.4 T. Kohonen, H. Riittinen, M. Jalanko, E. Reuhkala, S. Haltsonen: In *Proc. 5th Int. Conf. on Pattern Recognition*, ed. by R. Bajcsy (IEEE Computer Society, Los Alamitos, CA 1980) p.158

7.5 S. Watanabe, P.F. Lambert, C.A. Kulikowski, J.L. Buxton, R. Walker: In *Computer and Information Sciences*, Vol.2, ed. by J. Tou (Academic, New York 1967) p.91

7.6 C.W. Therrien: Tech. Note 1974-41 (Lincoln Lab., MIT, Lexington, MA 1974)

7.7 S. Watanabe, N. Pakvasa: In *Proc. 1st Int. J. Conf. on Pattern Recognition* (Washington, DC 1973) p.25

7.8 E. Oja: *The Subspace Methods of Pattern Recognition* (to be published in Research Studies Press)

7.9 K. Karhunen: Ann. Acad. Sci. Fenn., Ser.A, No.1, Vol.37 (1947)

7.10 P.H. Sneath, R.R. Sokal: *Numerical Taxonomy* (Freeman, San Francisco 1982)

7.11 R.C. Tryon, D.E. Bailey: *Cluster Analysis* (McGraw-Hill, New York 1970)

7.12 M.R. Anderberg: *Cluster Analysis for Applications* (Academic, New York 1973)

7.13 E.J. Bijnen: *Cluster Analysis, Survey and Evaluation of Techniques* (Tilbury University Press, Tilbury 1973)

7.14 H.H. Bock: *Automatische Klassifikation* (Vandenhoeck Ruprecht, Göttingen 1974)

7.15 B.S. Duran, P.L. Odell: *Cluster Analysis, A Survey* (Springer, Berlin, Heidelberg, New York 1974)

7.16 E. Diday, J.C. Simon: In *Digital Pattern Recognition*, ed. by K.S. Fu (Springer, Berlin, Heidelberg, New York 1976)

7.17 J.A. Hartigan: *Clustering Algorithms* (Wiley, New York 1975)

7.18 B. Everitt: *Cluster Analysis* (Heinemann Educational Books, London 1977)

7.19 D. Steinhausen, K. Langer: *Clusteranalyse, Einführung in Methoden und Verfahren der automatischen Klassifikation* (de Gruyter, Berlin 1977)

7.20 H. Späth: *Cluster Analysis Algorithms for Data Reduction and Classification of Objects* (Horwood, West Sussex, England 1980)

7.21 V.N. Yolkina, N.G. Zagoruyko: R.A.I.R.O. Informatique **12**, 37 (1978)

7.22 H. Freeman: IRE Trans. EC-**20**, 260 (1961)

7.23 J.T. Tou: Int. J. Comp. Inf. Sci.**9**, 1 (1980)

Chapter 8

8.1 Y.S. Lashley: In *The Neurophysiology of Lashley; Selected Papers of K.S. Lashley*, ed. by F.A. Beach et al. (McGraw-Hill, New York 1960)

8.2 R.F. Thompson: *Introduction to Physiological Psychology* (Harper & Row, New York 1975)

8.3 H. Hyden, E. Egyhazi: Proc. Nat. Acad. Sci. **48**, 1366 (1962)

8.4 G. Ungar: Int. J. Neurosci. **3**, 193 (1972)

8.5 J.C. Eccles: *The Physiology of Synapses* (Springer, Berlin, Heidelberg, New York 1964)

8.6 D. Marr, J.C. Eccles: In *Brain and Human Behaviour*, ed. by A.G. Karcmar, J.C. Eccles (Springer, Berlin, Heidelberg, New York 1972)

8.7 J.S. Griffith: Nature **211**, 1160 (1966)

8.8 A.L. Leiman, C.N. Christian: Electrophysiological Analysis of Learning and Memory, in *The Physiological Basis of Memory*, ed. by J.A. Deutsch (Academic, New York 1973)

8.9 R. Mark: *Memory and Nerve Cell Connections. Criticisms and Contributions from Developmental Neurophysiology* (Clarendon, Oxford 1974)

8.10 G.M. Shepherd: *The Synaptic Organization of the Brain* (Oxford University Press, New York 1974)

8.11 J.P. Cavanagh: Ph. D. Thesis, Carnegie Mellon University (1972)

8.12 P.T. Chopping: Nature **217**, 781 (1968)

8.13 D. Gabor: IBM J. Res. Dev. **13**, 156 (1969)

8.14 P.J. van Heerden: *The Foundation of Empirical Knowledge with a Theory of Artificial Intelligence* (Wistik, Wassenaar, The Netherlands 1968)
8.15 H.C. Longuet-Higgins: Nature **217**, 104 (1968)
8.16 K. Pribram: *Languages of the Brain* (Prentice-Hall, Englewood Cliffs, NJ 1971)
8.17 P.R. Westlake: Kybernetik **7**, 129 (1970)
8.18 J. Szentágothai: Brain Res. **95**, 475 (1975)
8.19 V.B. Mountcastle: J. Neurophysiol. **20**, 408 (1957)
8.20 D.H. Hubel, T.N. Wiesel: J. Comp. Neurol. **158**, 307 (1974)
8.21 D.H. Hubel, T.N. Wiesel: J. Neurophysiol. **18**, 229 (1965)
8.22 D.H. Hubel, T.N. Wiesel: J. Physiol. **160**, 106 (1962)
8.23 W.S. McCulloch, W.A. Pitts: Bull. Math. Biophysiol. **5**, 115 (1943)
8.24 L. Walløe, J.K.S. Jansen, K. Nygaard: Kybernetik **6**, 130 (1969)
8.25 G. Horn, S.P.R. Rose, P.P.G. Bateson: Science **181**, 506 (1973)
8.26 M.O. Huttunen: Persp. Biol. Med. **17**, 103 (1973)
8.27 G.S. Stent: Proc. Nat. Acad. Sci. USA **70**, 997 (1973)
8.28 D. Hebb: *Organization of Behaviour* (Wiley, New York 1949)
8.29 J.P. Rauschecker: Orientation-Dependent Changes in Response Properties of Neurons in the Kitten's Visual Cortex, in *Developmental Neurobiology of Vision*, ed. by R. Freeman (Plenum, New York 1979) p.121
8.30 J.P. Rauschecker, W. Singer: Nature **280**, 58 (1979)
8.31 W. Singer, J. Rauschecker, R. Werth: Brain Res. **134**, 568 (1977)
8.32 W. Levy: Limiting Characteristics of a Candidate Elementary Memory Unit: LTP Studies of Entorhinal-Dentate Synapses (to appear in a book based on the workshop *Synaptic Modification, Neuron Selectivity, and Nervous System Organization*, Brown University, Rhode Island, Nov.16-19, 1980) (Lawrence Erlbaum Ass., in press)
8.33 H.B. Barlow: Nature **258**, 199 (1975)
8.34 C. Blakemore, E.E. Mitchell: Nature **241**, 467 (1973)
8.35 O. Creutzfeld (ed.): *Afferent and Intrinsic Organization of Laminated Structures in the Brain*, Experimental Brain Research, Supplementum I, xii (1976)
8.36 J. Szentágothai: Specificity Versus (Quasi-)Randomness in Cortical Connectivity, in *Architectonics of the Cerebral Cortex*, ed. by M.A.B. Brazier, H. Petsche (Raven, New York 1978) p.77
8.37 V. Bloch: Brain Activation and Memory Consolidation, in *Neural Mechanisms of Learning and Memory*, ed. by M.R. Rosenzweig, E.L. Bennett (MIT Press, Cambridge, MA 1976) p.583
8.38 D.A. Normann: Psych. Rev. **75**, 522 (1968)
8.39 H.A. Simon: The Information-Storage System Called "Human Memory", in *Neural Mechanisms of Learning and Memory*, ed. by M.R. Rosenzweig, E.L. Bennett (MIT Press, Cambridge, MA 1976)
8.40 S.W. Kuffler, J.G. Nicholls: *From Neuron to Brain: A Cellular Approach to the Function of the Nervous System* (Sinauer Associates, Sunderland, MA 1976)
8.41 M. Brazier, H. Petsche (eds.): *Architectonics of the Cerebral Cortex* (Raven, New York 1978)
8.42 M. Brazier (ed.): *Brain Mechanisms in Memory and Learning: From the Single Neuron to Man* (Raven, New York 1979)
8.43 M.R. Rosenzweig, E.L. Bennett (eds.): *Neural Mechanisms of Learning and Memory* (MIT Press, Cambride, MA 1976)
8.44 C. Cotman (ed.): *Neuronal Plasticity* (Raven, New York 1978)
8.45 V. Braitenberg: A Selection of Facts and Conjectures About the Cerebral Cortex Inspired by the Theory of Cell Assemblies, in *Adv. Physiol. Sci.*, Vol.30, Neural Communication and Control, ed. by Gy. Székely, E. Lábos, S. Damjanovitch (1980) p.287
8.46 A. Cowey: Quart. J. Exp. Psych. **31**, 1 (1979)
8.47 P.S. Goldman, W.J.H. Nauta: Brain Res. **122**, 393 (1977)
8.48 T.J. Imig, R.A. Reale: J. Compar. Neurol. **192**, 293 (1980)
8.49 T.V.P. Bliss: Trends Neurosci. **2**, 42 (1979)
8.50 J.-P. Changeux, A. Danchin: Nature **264**, 705 (1976)
8.51 T. Lømo: Trends Neurosci. **3**, 126 (1980)
8.52 N. Robbins: Trends Neurosci. **3**, 120 (1980)
8.53 R.W. Ryall: Trends Neurosci. **1**, 164 (1978)
8.54 A. Shagal: Trends Neurosci. **3**, 116 (1980)
8.55 S. Thesleff, L.C. Sellin: Trends Neurosci. **3**, 122 (1980)

8.56 S.I. Amari: IEEE Trans. C-**21**, 1197 (1972)
8.57 J.A. Anderson: Math. Biosci. **14**, 197 (1972)
8.58 L.N. Cooper: A Possible Organization of Animal Memory and Learning, in
     Proc. Nobel Symp. Collective Properties of Physical Systems, ed. by
     B. Lundquist, S. Lundquist (Academic, New York 1974) p.252
8.59 P.C. Gilbert: Brain Res. **70**, 1 (1974)
8.60 P. Gilbert: Nature **254**, 688 (1975)
8.61 S. Grossberg: Kybernetik **10**, 49 (1972)
8.62 T. Kohonen: *Correlation Matrix Memories* (Helsinki Univ. of Tech. Report
     TKK-F-A310, 1970)
8.63 T. Kohonen: *A Class of Randomly Organized Associative Memories*, Acta
     Polytech. Scand. Electr. Eng. Ser. El 25 (1971)
8.64 T. Kohonen, P. Lehtiö, J. Rovamo: Ann. Acad. Sci. Fenn. A.V. Med. 167 (1974)
8.65 T. Kohonen: Implementation of Associative Memory in Adaptive Neural Networks,
     in *Biological Aspects of Learning, Memory Formation and Ontogeny of the CNS*,
     Proc. Fifth Intern. Neurobiol. Symp., Magdeburg, DDR, June 6-9, ed. by
     H. Matthies, M. Krug, N. Popov (Academy of Sciences of the GDR, Berlin 1977)
     p.43
8.66 P. Lehtiö, T. Kohonen: Med. Biol. **56**, 110 (1978)
8.67 T. Kohonen, P. Lehtiö, E. Oja: Storage and Processing of Information in
     Distributed Associative Memory Systems, in *Parallel Models of Associative
     Memory*, ed. by G. Hinton, J.A. Anderson (Lawrence Erlbaum Ass., Hillsdale,
     NJ 1981) p.105
8.68 H.C. Longuet-Higgins, D.J. Willshaw, O.P. Buneman: Quart. Rev. Biophys. **3**,
     223 (1970)
8.69 D. Marr: J. Physiol. **202**, 437 (1969)
8.70 K. Nakano, J. Nagumo: In *Advance Papers of the Conference, 2nd Int. Joint
     Conf. Artificial Intelligence* (The British Computer Society, London 1971)
     p.101
8.71 G. Palm: Biol. Cyb. **36**, 19 (1980)
8.72 G. Palm: *Neural Assemblies* (Springer, Berlin, Heidelberg, New York 1982)
8.73 D.J. Willshaw, O.P. Buneman, H.C. Longuet-Higgins: Nature **222**, 960 (1969)
8.74 K. Fukushima: Kybernetik **12**, 58 (1973)
8.75 H. Wigström: Kybernetik **12**, 204 (1973)
8.76 H. Wigström: Kybernetik **16**, 103 (1974)
8.77 G. Willwacher: Biol. Cyb. **24**, 181 (1976)
8.78 A.G. Barto, R.S. Sutton, P.S. Brouwer: Biol. Cyb. **40**, 201 (1981)
8.79 L.N. Cooper, F. Liberman, E. Oja: Biol. Cyb. **33**, 9 (1979)
8.80 K. Fukushima: Biol. Cyb. **36**, 193 (1980)
8.81 S. Grossberg: Biol. Cyb. **21**, 145 (1976)
8.82 C. v. d. Malsburg: Kybernetik **14**, 85 (1973)
8.83 N.M. Nass, L.N. Cooper: Biol. Cyb. **19**, 1 (1975)
8.84 S. Amari, M.A. Arbib (eds.): *Competition and Cooperation in Neural Nets*,
     Lecture Notes Biomath., Vol.45 (Springer, Berlin, Heidelberg, New York 1982)
8.85 G. Hinton, J.A. Anderson (eds.): *Parallel Models of Associative Memory*
     (Lawrence Erlbaum Ass., Hillsdale, NJ 1981)

Subject Index

H. Haken

Synergetics

An Introduction

Nonequilibrium Phase Transitions and Self-Organization in Physics, Chemistry, and Biology

3rd revised and enlarged edition. 1983. 161 figures.
XIV, 371 pages
(Springer Series in Synergetics, Volume 1)
ISBN 3-540-12356-3

Contents: Goal. – Probability. – Information. – Chance. – Necessity. – Chance and Necessity. – Self-Organization. – Physical Systems. – Chemical and Biochemical Systems. – Applications to Biology. – Sociology and Economics. – Chaos. – Some Historical Remarks and Outlook. – References, Further Reading, and Comments. – Subject Index.

Synergetics – An Introduction deals with the recently discovered profound and striking analogies between the self-organized behavior of seemingly quite different systems in physics, chemistry, biology, sociology and other fields. The cooperation of many subsystems such as atoms, molecules, cells, animals, or humans may produce spatial, temporal or functional structures. Their spontaneous formation out of chaos is often strongly reminiscent of phase transitions. This book, written by the founder of synergetics, provides an elementary introduction to the field's basic concepts and mathematical tools. Numerous exercises, figures and simple examples greatly facilitate the understanding,. The basic analogies are demonstrated by various realistic examples from fluid dynamics, lasers, mechanical engineering, chemical and biochemical systems, ecology, sociology, and theories of evolution and morphogenesis are included.
For this third edition the treatment on self-organization in continuously extended media has been extensively revised, and the chapter on Banard instability was rewritten. New sections on phase transitions in economy and on discrete maps leading to period doubling, bifurcations, chaos and intermittency were also added.

Springer-Verlag
Berlin
Heidelberg
New York
Tokyo

J. Schnakenberg

Thermodynamic Network Analysis of Biological Systems

Universitext

2nd corrected and updated edition. 1981.
14 figures. X, 149 pages
ISBN 3-540-10612-X

What fundamental ideas and concepts can physics contribute to the analysis of complex systems such as those in biology and ecology? This book shows that thermodynamics – as used in physical systems analysis – has in the last ten years provided new concepts for the analysis of systems far from thermal equilibrium, and that these concepts can be used for describing and modelling biological systems as well. Although thermodynamics is the physical basis of the book, the language used is that of networks of bond graphs. A variety of examples is presented to demonstrate how this language is applied and how it leads to formulations of models for particular biological phenomena in such a way as to include the basic laws of thermodynamics. This new edition has been expanded by including a section on a network model for photoreception and additional examples of feedback networks for excitable systems.

Springer-Verlag
Berlin
Heidelberg
New York
Tokyo